C000193715

The
# Ludlow Castle
## *Heraldic Roll*

# The
# Ludlow Castle
# *Heraldic Roll*

ROSALIND CAIRD, JOHN CHERRY

PHILIP HUME & HUGH WOOD

LOGASTON PRESS

First published in 2019 by Logaston Press
The Holme, Church Road, Eardisley HR3 6NJ, UK
www.logastonpress.co.uk
An imprint of Fircone Books Ltd.

ISBN 978-1-910839-37-9

Text copyright © Rosalind Caird, John Cherry, Philip Hume & Hugh Wood, 2019
Pigment Analysis text copyright © Lisa Shekede & Stephen Rickerby, 2019
Images copyright © Friends of Ludlow Castle, unless otherwise stated in caption

All rights reserved
The moral right of the authors has been asserted

Without limiting the rights under copyright reserved above, no part of this publication
may be reproduced, stored in or introduced into a retrieval system, or transmitted,
in any form or by any means (electronic, mechanical, photocopying, recording or
otherwise), without prior written permission of the copyright owners and the above
publisher of this book.

Designed and typeset by Richard Wheeler
Cover design by Richard Wheeler

Printed and bound in Poland

Logaston Press is committed to a sustainable future for our business, our readers and
our planet. This book is made from paper certified by the Forest Stewardship Council.

British Library Catalogue in Publishing Data.
A CIP catalogue record for this book is available from the British Library.

# Contents

# The Coats of Arms on the Ludlow Castle Heraldic Roll

*brackets indicate those arms lost from the Roll*

# Preface

15 October 2015 was to prove an important day for everyone interested in the history of Ludlow. Hugh Wood conducted a tour of St Laurence's Church for local residents and, noting his enthusiasm for heraldry, Miles Wynn Cato spoke to him afterwards. Miles is a successful art dealer, with considerable experience of buying and selling heraldic paintings and pedigree rolls. He had moved to Ludlow from London a couple of years earlier. Back in March 2012 he had come across a heraldic roll relating to Ludlow Castle at an antiques market in Portobello Road in London. Having no special connection to Ludlow at the time, Miles forgot about it – until his memory was jogged during the tour of St Laurence's over three years later.

Since Hugh knew that many coats of arms had been displayed in the Council Chamber and Chapel of Ludlow Castle, and had been recorded by antiquaries such as William Mytton and Robert Henry Clive, he immediately recognised the potential importance of this heraldic roll. Learning that Marion Gettleson, of Delehar Antiques, still possessed it, he arranged to visit her shop in Portobello Road. Despite there being only a very brief opportunity to inspect the Roll, it was immediately clear that, if genuine, this document could be a very significant find. The text at the top of the Roll states that it is a copy of coats of arms placed in the chapel in the inner bailey of the castle shortly after 1570 by Sir Henry Sidney, Lord President of the Council in the Marches of Wales. Though it has proved impossible to establish a clear line of previous ownership before Delehar Antiques, the Roll was inspected in 2003 by Thomas Woodcock (subsequently Garter King of Arms), who wrote a letter accepting it as authentic.

Returning to Ludlow, Hugh approached several people who were likely to be interested in the Roll, and an action committee was formed, chaired by John Cherry (formerly Keeper of Medieval and Modern Europe at the British Museum). Other members of the committee included Rosalind

Caird (formerly Archivist at Hereford Cathedral), and Philip Hume and Hugh Wood (both Officers of the Mortimer History Society). Tony Mahalski very kindly agreed to act as Treasurer. Marion Gettleson brought the Roll to Ludlow and left it with us so that we had plenty of time to inspect it. We advertised public displays to assess the level of interest within the town and, encouraged by the response, decided to raise the money to secure the Roll for Ludlow. At this point the committee was taken under the wing of the Friends of Ludlow Museum, and we are very grateful for their support. The asking price for the Roll was modest considering its importance to the town. Rolls in good condition often fetch considerably more, but our Roll was of no real interest to collectors of pedigree rolls, as it did not deal with the genealogy and heraldry of a single family. It had also suffered significant damage in places and been repaired.

The committee had ideas and aspirations beyond the initial purchase of the Roll. We were keen to conserve the original and to find out as much as we could about the painter, the scribe and the pigments used. As well as studying and recording the heraldry, we also wanted to learn as much as possible about the historical context of the Roll and the people whose shields appear on it. We particularly wanted to make the Roll easily accessible to everyone, and to use it as a resource in schools and talks.

Since we first 'discovered' the Roll, most of our objectives have been achieved. We launched an appeal and were delighted by the degree of interest shown, and by the financial support we received both nationally and from local individuals and organisations. We are very grateful to the Friends of the National Libraries for supporting the purchase price, and other bodies such as The Arts Society Teme Valley, The Arts Society West Mercia, Ludlow Historical Research Group, Ludlow Tuesday lectures, Powis Castle Trust, Ludlow Town Council and The Friends of Ludlow Museum, and many individual donors. The Mortimer History Society has given valuable support throughout, and many of its members have also helped fund the project.

Several high quality paper facsimiles have been made for us by the National Library of Wales. One of these is now incorporated into the Mortimer History Society's 'Local History in Schools Programme' as part of the unit on heraldry. As well as inspecting the Roll at close quarters, each young student is presented with an illustrated booklet about the Roll which includes a quiz to test their new-found knowledge of heraldry.

We commissioned a detailed pigment analysis by wall painting conservators, Stephen Rickerby and Lisa Shekede, and the Roll has been carefully conserved at Hereford Archive and Records Centre. We have researched the heraldry and biographies of the people whose arms appear on the Roll, and the results form a substantial part of this book.

We are grateful to Miles Wynn Cato for drawing attention to the Roll, and to Liz Bowerman, conservator at Herefordshire Archives, for her help and advice in the early stages of the project. Dr Margaret Clark and Liz Russell have given valuable assistance in contributing to the biographies of the individuals on the Roll. Dr Robert Colley has been very helpful on aspects of Welsh heraldry and the latest research on the painters, Richard Adams and John Knight. Dr Lindsay Darby, archivist at the College of Arms, provided very helpful guidance to their collections. We are grateful to Viscount De L'Isle for his kind permission to use material from his private collection in the account of Sir Henry Sidney.

The Friends of the National Libraries very kindly gave a grant for the digitisation of the Roll, which has been carried out at Shropshire Archives where the Roll is now housed. This enables the document to be available online to scholars worldwide through the Shropshire Archives website.

The Ludlow Castle Heraldic Roll

# INTRODUCTION

The Ludlow Castle Heraldic Roll is a fascinating artefact from Ludlow, which has survived for nearly 450 years. As such, it raises thought-provoking questions about why the Roll was made and who was it made for? Why was heraldry so important in Tudor England? Who might have painted the coats of arms and written the text? And what materials were used? Who were the people whose coats of arms are featured on the Roll?

This book aims to answer these questions (and more!) The first section of the book explores how the Roll was produced, the materials used, and the use of heraldry in the sixteenth century. It focuses on the life and times of Sir Henry Sidney who commissioned the Roll – particularly on his time in Ludlow and his legacy that we can still see today. From 1560 to 1586, Sir Henry was the Lord President of 'The Council in the Marches of Wales', which was a form of regional government for Wales and its border counties from 1483 to 1689. The President acted as the monarch's representative, and the Council's administrative centre was Ludlow Castle.

The Heraldic Roll provides a valuable insight into this period during the sixteenth century when Ludlow has been described as the 'Capital of Wales and the Marches'. However, the impressive ruins of Ludlow castle stand witness to a much longer period of 600 years, during which the town and castle had an important role in national affairs and politics. Founded in the late eleventh century, in the period after the Norman Conquest of England, its location gave Ludlow a strategic importance from the outset; as one of the line of castles along the Welsh Marches it contributed a defensive barrier, as well as providing a secure base for conquest into Wales. First built by a Norman knight, Walter de Lacy, Ludlow was owned by his direct descendants before passing, through marriage, first to the de Geneville family, then into the hands of the Mortimer family based nearby at Wigmore. Ludlow's importance increased in 1328 when Roger Mortimer was raised to the rank of earl, taking the title Earl of March, during the period of nearly four years that he was the virtual ruler of the country. On the death of the last male Mortimer in 1425, the vast inheritance, including Ludlow, passed to his nephew, Richard, Duke of York. Ludlow was now the home of a duke who challenged for the throne of England. When Richard's son, who had been brought up in Ludlow, won the throne and was crowned Edward IV, Ludlow became a royal castle, remaining in the ownership of the Crown for 400 years, and the base of the Council.

After the abolition of the Council in the Marches of Wales in 1689, the castle very quickly declined into a ruinous condition. The roofs were stripped, leaving the interior open to the weather; the stone was plundered for use elsewhere, and trees and ivy colonised the walls. The castle was acquired from the Crown in the late eighteenth century by the Earl of Powis (whose descendants still own it), saving it from further plunder and decay. Gradually, the overgrowth was stripped back, and the ruins stabilised, enabling visitors today to walk amidst the buildings and be transported by the stones back to the medieval splendour of earlier centuries.

How Ludlow Castle developed firstly into a royal castle and then into the centre for the Council is told in Chapter 11 of this book, through the lives of its owners and their families whose coats of arms feature on the Heraldic Roll. Biographies of all the other people whose coats of arms are on the Roll follow, together with information about the heraldry.

There is a straightforward introduction to heraldry to help the general reader understand some of the references, while the appendices provide a detailed glossary of heraldic terms and a full heraldic description (*blazon*) of the coats of arms. The appendices also include detailed information on the painting technology of the Roll, and the family trees of the Mortimer and de Lacy families.

# 1. What is the Roll?

THE LUDLOW CASTLE Heraldic Roll is a pictorial record of the heraldic decoration placed in the newly enlarged and restored Chapel of St Mary Magdalene (otherwise known as the 'Round Chapel') in the inner bailey of Ludlow Castle. Wording on the Roll itself says that it was '... set forth by the appointment of the right honourable the lord president Sir Henry Sidney knight of the noble order & lord deputy of Ireland and one of her majesties most honourable Privy Council.'

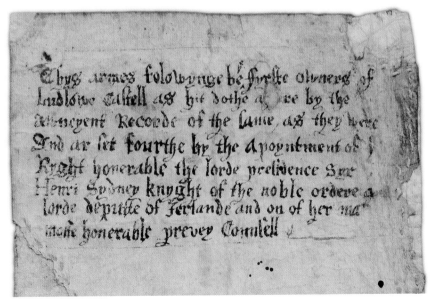

Opening text of the Roll: *Thys armes folowynge be ye Fyrste owners of Ludlowe Castell as hit dothe apere by the awncyent Recorde of the same as they were And ar set fourthe by the Apoyntment of ye Ryght honerable the lorde presidence Syr Henri Sydney knyght of the noble ordere & lorde deputte of Ierland and on of her ma(jesties) moste honerable prevey Counsell*

1

The Roll consists of 42 painted coats of arms with accompanying text. It begins with the arms of 11 of the owners of the castle, from its founder Walter de Lacy in the eleventh century to Queen Elizabeth I in the sixteenth. These include arms of the Mortimer family, Earls of March, through whose descent Ludlow became a royal castle under Edward IV. Next are depicted the arms of the 22 members of the Council in the Marches of Wales, appointed in 1570 and still serving in 1574, which the Roll specifies were placed on the left side of the chapel. It concludes with the arms of nine of the Presidents of the Council appointed from 1473–1560, which were placed opposite, on the right side of the chapel. The end of the Roll is damaged, and it seems certain that it originally included the arms of the four presidents who immediately preceded Sir Henry Sidney, which were also displayed on the right side of the chapel.

The chapel was completed early in 1574, but the Roll not until sometime after 1576, and possibly as late as 1580. From the record drawn up by the eighteenth-century Shropshire antiquarian, William Mytton, it appears that after the chapel decoration was completed dates of death were added to the text under each individual's arms, and that this practice continued up to the end of Sir Henry Sidney's presidency in 1586. The last date of death recorded on the Roll is that of Nicholas Bullingham, Bishop of Worcester in 1576. The next recorded by Mytton is that of Nicholas Arnold in 1580, which gives a possible date range for the Roll of 1576–80. However, another councillor, George Phetiplace, died in 1577, so a closer date range of just 1576–77 seems quite likely. Since the Roll would almost certainly have been made at the instigation of Sir Henry Sidney it seems likely that it was commissioned around the time the chapel was completed and before he went to Ireland in 1575. It is known that the text was added to the Roll by a different individual after the arms had been painted. Given the comparatively poor execution of the text it seems unlikely to have been subject to the personal supervision of Sir Henry, and therefore was probably completed before his return from Ireland in 1578.

The purpose of the Ludlow Roll is uncertain. We think – partly because of the quality of the painting – that Sir Henry Sidney probably commissioned it for his own personal record, or possibly for the Council's archive. Nothing is known about where it has been kept or its ownership prior to 2003. The making of a record copy may not have been an unusual thing to do. There is a surviving contemporary example of a heraldic roll from Adlington Hall, Cheshire. Here, in 1581, Thomas Legh refurbished the Great Hall, decorating the ceiling with 186 coats of arms of local families in order of precedence. In Chetham's library, there is a manuscript, formerly owned by Legh, which includes a detailed, painted record of these arms. This would seem to have been made for Legh's own reference and enjoyment.[i]

The Ludlow Castle Heraldic Roll is written on parchment. It is over four and a half metres long, yet just ten centimetres wide. It is constructed of seven lengths of parchment each around 75 centimetres long, sewn together with linen thread. Parchment is made from animal skin, usually sheep or calf. This was prepared by a wide variety of methods, including soaking in lime and water to remove the hair. It was then stretched on a frame to dry and finely scraped to produce a smooth surface suitable to write on. Parchment was the main writing material used in medieval Europe for all books and documents until the advent of printing on paper in the 1470s. It is considerably stronger than paper and so, although it quite quickly ceased to be used in book production, it remained commonly used for official documents, particularly those for permanent record such as title deeds, certificates and grants. Despite paper gradually superseding parchment for record-keeping over the centuries, parchment continued to be used into the early twentieth century for title deeds. It is still occasionally used, mainly for decorative official documents such as royal grants, certificates and grants by the College of Arms. Until January 2017 parchment was always used for the archive copy of Acts of Parliament. After much debate, Parliament agreed that Acts should no longer be preserved on parchment but be printed on archival paper with, as a concession to the traditionalists, a parchment cover.

## CONDITION & ANALYSIS

The Ludlow Roll was found to be in fairly good condition, with most of the text and many of the images still being clear and vibrantly coloured. Much of the parchment shows little evidence of damage from light exposure, which indicates it will have been mainly kept rolled up and not on open display. However, it has clearly been frequently unrolled and rolled over its lifetime. This gradual attrition has unfortunately resulted in serious cracking and flaking of the painted surfaces, with the consequent partial loss of some of the colours, and with particular paint layers, such as blue, being more affected than others. The Roll has also suffered periods of neglect, during which it has been exposed to damp conditions and attack by hungry rodents. The pattern of damage from the areas eaten by the rodents indicates that the Roll had lain partially unrolled with the exposed sections awkwardly folded – a picture of neglect. The areas lost are on both edges of the Roll, and have resulted in the partial loss of some text and images. The arms most seriously affected are those of Henry VIII, Elizabeth I and Sir Henry Sidney. This damage was skilfully repaired a few years ago by its then-owner, Marian Gettleson, using patches of parchment carefully sewn in place with linen thread to match the original. Fortunately, water damage and staining has been slight; however, this has particularly affected one area, resulting in the almost total loss of the colours on the arms of Sir James Croft.

Overall, the Roll was in quite a fragile state when purchased – although, in many aspects, in remarkable original condition. It was clear that, for its continued preservation and any future handling, the Roll would need to be conserved. Prior to this a pigment analysis was undertaken by Stephen Rickerby and Lisa Shekede, both highly-experienced wall painting conservators (*see Appendix 1*). The purpose of the pigment analysis was twofold: firstly to provide insight into the production of the Roll, and secondly to inform the conservators as to the physical and chemical composition of the materials used, in order to understand the deterioration processes affecting them and to inform conservation interventions. For example, the flaking nature of some paint layers and the presence of an aqueous binder meant that often only a 'non-aqueous' process could be recommended. The conservation work was done by Elizabeth Bowerman and Kaori Takahashi Hilton, conservators at Herefordshire Archives Service. All the painted surfaces and text were stabilised and consolidated by applying binders of either a high quality gelatine dissolved in water and Ethanol; or *Klucel G*, a cellulose binder, dissolved in pure Ethanol which was used on areas where a 'non-aqueous' process was required.

The pigment analysis revealed that the Roll was produced by two different individuals. The first, a highly skilled arms painter, carefully set out the outline of the shields in ink, and then painted each using a wide and sophisticated palette of colours, often employing expensive pigments. The inscriptions were then added by a second individual with considerably less precision of style and layout. The script is in the style of the black letter typeface used in printed books of the time. Red was used for the first letter of each piece of text, and for some capitals and a border around the text. It is curious that the scribe's work is relatively unrefined in comparison to the skill and precision of that of the painter. If a professional clerk, the scribe may have been unused to that style of script or was perhaps elderly.

Gelatine is carefully applied to Walter de Lacy's arms to stabilise the flaking pigments.
© *Herefordshire Archives and Record Centre*

The conservators, Lisa and Stephen conclude:

The Ludlow Castle roll of arms was incontrovertibly a lavish and prestigious commission, produced using a rich and diverse palette. While this did not include gold or silver, the rare and almost prohibitively expensive blue pigments, ultramarine and azurite – which at this time would more usually have been replaced by cheaper, synthetic copper- and cobalt-based substitutes – are abundantly present. The execution of the painting was also carried out with great skill and precision by a painter evidently well versed in heraldic painting and adept at blending colours and adjusting pigment volume ratios to obtain a range of different effects. There is no doubt that the roll was intended to reflect the prominence of its powerful commissioner, Sir Henry Sidney, Lord President of the Council in the Marches of Wales.

The palette has fortunately been preserved in an almost pristine condition despite the fact that many of the paint materials employed are susceptible to fading and other forms of alteration. The fact that the roll can now be viewed and appreciated in much the same state as it was first created makes it a particularly rare survival.

## Who was the Painter of the Ludlow Roll?

It is not known who executed the painting of the arms in the Round Chapel at Ludlow in 1574, or who painted the Ludlow Roll. If not the same person, both would have been skilled professionals – probably either members of the College of Arms or of the London Company of Painters and Stainers. Given the quality of the Roll it is unlikely that anyone of lesser skill would have been employed to paint the chapel. Details of the arms of the previous owners and some of the early Presidents will have been researched by a herald from the College of Arms. Indeed, the Roll specifies that records were used to determine the arms of the castle owners, and that research failed to provide details of the arms of the first President, Bishop John Alcock.

Sir Henry Sidney's accounts contain frequent payments to the heralds, and to other painters and craftsmen for painting, engraving or enamelling arms on furnishings, clothes or plate. In the 1570s Sir Henry was commissioning work from the herald Robert Cooke, Clarenceux King of Arms (the senior officer of the College of Arms with jurisdiction south of the River Trent), who researched and, in part, fabricated Sidney's family pedigree. Sir Henry was also using the London painter-stainer, Robert Greenwood, for many commissions, including supplying the garter knights' arms on cloth and metal for use in his St George's Day garter celebrations in Ireland in 1577. These unfortunately didn't reach their destination, fetching up at the bottom of the Irish Sea.

Robert Greenwood seems to have been well connected with the College of Arms. In his will of 1585 he refers to 'my good friend' Robert Cooke, whom he appointed executor along with two other senior heralds, Edmond Knight (Chester Herald) and Robert Glover (Somerset Herald). Greenwood also included bequests of a gold mourning ring to 'his old friend' Richard Lee (Richmond Herald), and a pair of gold bracelets enamelled with Greenwood's arms to Cooke's daughter, Catherine.

There are several tantalising references to payments for painters in Sir Henry's accounts. On four occasions between October 1572 and October 1573, an unnamed painter working in Ludlow Castle was paid a total of £6 – a reasonable sum, but hardly enough for the chapel work which entailed 46 coats of arms. Greenwood could charge as little as 20d for one coat of arms, but between 10s and 13s 4d for arms executed in oils. In the same year Greenwood also received a payment of £3 for 'making and painting of arms', but there is no reason to suppose that this had any connection to work in Ludlow.[ii]

Given Sir Henry's character and connections it is probable that he would have used London craftsmen for the chapel research and decoration; however, there were also skilled painters in the provinces. In the Tudor period there was increasing demand not just for the production of family pedigree rolls but also for portraits, which often included arms, as well as painted wall decoration in domestic houses. The presence of the Council in the Marches of Wales in Ludlow will have generated business for a range of craftsmen, including painters. John Knight, a London painter from a prolific family of painter-stainers (and related to the herald, Edmond Knight) seems to have thought a Ludlow base also desirable for business. He owned a house in Broad Street and another in Mill Street, which were sold on his death in 1616.[iii] There is also one known painter from Ludlow – Richard Adams – who was said to be 'skilful in heraldry'. Early in his life he became assistant to Thomas Jones of Fountain Gate, Tregaron. Jones was a prominent 'herald bard' who compiled many Welsh pedigrees which Richard Adams painted. Adams worked mainly with Jones perhaps as early as 1575, but certainly from 1580, and produced many fine pedigrees. Adams is also recorded as doing work in Ludlow between 1604 and 1616, and may have returned to the town after Jones' death. His work in the castle included work in the chapel and renewing the arms over the gate and in the garden house. He is last recorded in 1616, employed by the council to paint heraldic banners for the elaborate ceremony which took place in Ludlow on the occasion of the creation of Charles, son of James I, as the Prince of Wales.[iv]

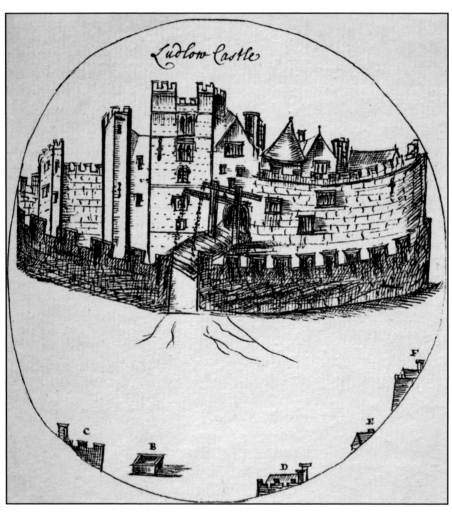

Ludlow Castle inner bailey with prison buildings and coach house in the outer bailey, from *The Account of the Official Progress of His Grace Henry the First Duke of Beaufort (Lord President of the Council in Wales, and Lord Warden of the Marches) through Wales in 1684*, by Thomas Dineley. *H910.8WAL/DIN © Hereford Cathedral Library*

# 2. Ludlow Castle Chapel and its Heraldic Decoration

O N THE EVE of the sixteenth-century religious upheavals, Ludlow Castle had two chapels: one dedicated to St Mary Magdalene in the inner bailey and the other dedicated to St Peter in the outer bailey. Both chapels were served by priests attached to the Hospital of St John the Baptist, which was situated near Ludford Bridge at the bottom of Lower Broad Street. The chapel of St Mary Magdalene, with its unusual circular nave, was built c.1150 by Gilbert de Lacy (d. after 1163). The circular nave is a form which was inspired by the Church of the Holy Sepulchre in Jerusalem, and adopted particularly by the Knights Templar.[i]

The Chapel of St Peter was completed in c.1328, in thanksgiving for Roger Mortimer's daring escape from the Tower of London five years earlier. A chantry was set up for two chaplains, later provided by the Hospital of St John in Lower Broad Street, to say mass there for the souls of the King, Queen Philippa (wife of Edward III), Queen Isabella, the Bishop of Lincoln, Mortimer himself and Joan his wife, their heirs and ancestors.[ii]

Depiction of ancient Jerusalem, from Sebastian Munster's *Cosmographia* (Basel, 1550), L.5.10, p. 1014 © Hereford Cathedral Library

It is not clear from the records in what way each chapel was used over the decades, but it is likely to have varied. When new, St Peter's may have been used in preference to the old chapel of St Mary Magdalene, or may have been predominantly a chantry chapel for the Mortimers.

In 1458 Richard, Duke of York, granted the chapel of St Mary Magdalene to the Hospital of St John the Baptist (which also serviced St Peter's chapel) on condition that it provide priests to say mass there for Richard, his wife, Cecily, and his family. The grant specifies that the majority of daily services, including Sunday services, were to be conducted in the round chapel of St Mary Magdalene, while only those on Thursdays and Fridays were to be held in St Peter's chapel. Less than 20 years later, when Prince Edward, the young son of Edward IV was resident, the opposite was the case, with daily services being said in St Peter's for the household, while St Mary Magdalene served as a private chapel for the prince.[iii] The chapel may also have been used by the Prince's Council – out of which grew the permanent Council in the Marches of Wales based at Ludlow Castle.

In churches in the late fifteenth and early sixteenth centuries, it became increasingly common to provide a private pew for the local lord and his wife, usually in an elevated position, creating a two-tiered space. In castles and large houses it was also desirable for the lord to have access to this space from his private apartments. When the chapel was a separate building, this was usually achieved by creating a new wing or walkway attaching to the chapel. The round chapel in Ludlow Castle was altered in this way early in the sixteenth century for use by its royal residents: Arthur, Prince of Wales (the eldest son of Henry VII) and, 20 years later, Mary (daughter of Henry VIII) as Princess of Wales. A floor was inserted in the round nave, projecting over the chancel screen and containing a pew which overlooked the chancel, and was probably reserved for use by royalty

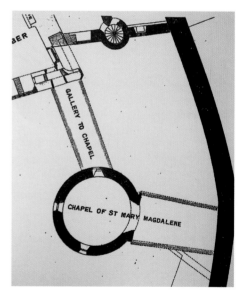

Plan showing walkway from the council chamber and the extended chapel, from *William St John Hope*, 1908

and the President of the Council in the Marches of Wales. Doorways were inserted at both levels and two windows inserted at ground level for extra light.[iv] A two-tiered walkway was also built to link the apartments to the chapel. There is no archaeological evidence for the design of the walkway. It was most probably a wooden structure in the form of an open loggia at ground level with a covered passage above (of which there are a number of known contemporary examples, as at North Wyke in Devon, and Shurland in Kent). At the upper level a covered passage led from a room adjacent to the Great Hall, which was used as the Council Chamber and which reflects a similar arrangement at Henry viii's palace of Hampton Court. This could serve as both a private and processional entrance to the chapel.

Since the Council in the Marches of Wales represented royal government, and all but two of its presidents appointed before 1560 were bishops, the form of services in the castle chapels would certainly have conformed to the requirements of the time. However, with the dissolution of the Hospital of St John in 1538, and the consequent loss of the chapels' regular clergy, services probably only took place when the Council was resident.

The Protestant Reformation that began under Henry viii and was consolidated in the early years of the reign of his daughter, Queen Elizabeth, resulted in considerable changes to the form of services and the internal layout and decoration of places of worship. The Protestant reformers required that idolatrous imagery be removed or whitewashed over, while the display of Royal Arms, which became popular under Henry viii, was permitted and encouraged. Statuary, relics and fittings were removed from chantry chapels and shrines dedicated to individual saints. The chancel was no longer to be the preserve of the clergy but used by the laity to receive communion at a new free-standing table replacing the stone altar at the east end. An Order of 1561 required that a board displaying the Ten Commandments be placed above this table, and the display of other Biblical texts was permissible. There is a rare survival of a Commandments board of this date in St Laurence's, Ludlow.

In 1560 Sir Henry Sidney was appointed Lord President of the Council in the Marches of Wales. He arrived at the Council's administrative base in Ludlow with a clear view of the importance of his office and of the status of the Council in the locality, so set about improving and modernising the castle to reflect this. The chapel of St Mary Magdalene in the inner bailey received his full attention in 1573, shortly after his return from his first term of office as Lord Deputy of Ireland.

At that time the layout of the chapel had not changed since its construction in the twelfth century. It consisted of a round nave with an entrance on the west side, with a columned, decorated arch on the east side, leading into a chancel consisting of a square space with a semi-octagonal sanctuary at its east end. Across this arch was a wooden screen. This was an essential feature of the medieval church, and would have divided the chancel, where the clergy performed the services, from the worshippers in the nave.

Sir Henry rebuilt and arranged the chapel to conform to the practices of the Elizabethan church, and provided decoration to reflect the prestige and importance of both the Council and Ludlow Castle itself. To achieve this, the chancel of the chapel was rebuilt, heightened and extended up to the castle wall, while the round nave was retained.

There is a contemporary official account of all the building work carried out by Sir Henry Sidney, which describes the work on the chapel:

> For making, repairing and amending of the Chappell within the said Castle ceiling and glazing and tiling of the same with fair and large windows: wainscotting, benching and making of seats and kneeling places and putting up of her Majesties arms with diverse nobleman's arms together with all the Lord President's and council round the same.[v]

We cannot be certain of the actual design of the rebuilt chapel, but it seems likely that the walls of the new chancel were panelled (wainscoted) – and that, given the limited space, benches with kneeling places rather than stalls were fitted against the walls to the left and right of the entrance. A separate seat may only have been provided for the chaplain and senior official present. The President may have sat here or in the elevated pew jutting into the chancel, accessed by the covered walkway from the Council Chamber. A wooden altar table was placed at the east end against the castle wall. The coats of arms of the Council Members and former Presidents, together with inscriptions, were painted on the wall panels, in imitation of the arms of Knights of the Garter displayed on the stalls of St George's Chapel, Windsor.

Robert Commander, who was chaplain to Sir Henry as President of the Council, recorded in detail the coats of arms which decorated the chapel, in a large commonplace book (or scrapbook) which is now held by the British Library.[vi] He writes that the 'chapel of the castle of Ludlow, a foul ruinous place, was well repaired & beatified to the praise & honour of Almighty God'. He would have witnessed the progress of the work, and records the exact

The castle chapel by Thomas Dineley, 1684. The only known depiction of the castle chapel as enlarged by Sir Henry Sidney. In front of it is a poor depiction of the fountain (which was almost eight feet in diameter) for the spring water supplied to the castle in 1566. From *The Account of the Official Progress of His Grace Henry the First Duke of Beaufort (Lord President of the Council in Wales, and Lord Warden of the Marches) through Wales in 1684*, by Thomas Dineley. H910.8WAL/DIN © Hereford Cathedral

dates of the completion of the decoration. First, in January 1574, the coats of arms of ten of the owners of the castle, from Walter de Lacy to Henry VIII, were 'placed upon the Principall Pylleres of the Queenes Majesties Chappell of Ludlowe within hir said castle.' There is considerable uncertainty as to what these principal pillars refer to, since the use of the word 'pillar' implies a free-standing feature; however, it seems clear from later accounts (such as Thomas Churchyard's, below) that the owners' arms were prominent within the display in the chancel. It is possible that pillars supported the pew projecting into the chancel, and that the owners' arms were placed on these, and would thus have been seen on entering or leaving the chancel (*see inside cover*).

Commander does not mention the arms of Queen Elizabeth I but it was common for these to be displayed centrally on, or above, the screen below the chancel arch, or in another prominent place.

On 23 January 1574, the arms of Sir Henry Sidney and all the other members of the Council in the Marches of Wales appointed in 1570 were placed on the left-hand side of the chapel. Finally, on 2 February 1574, the arms of all the former Presidents of the Council since 1473 were placed on the right-hand side of the chapel. Commander also records the text of verses in praise of the Queen, composed by Simon Thorneton, the Ludlow schoolmaster, which was displayed at the entrance to the chapel. These verses may have been composed for use in a celebration or service of dedication on the completion of the work. It was usual for the school, along with town and church dignitaries, to take part in such events which often included specially composed recitations or dramatic performances. That there was indeed such a celebration seems very likely since accounts for February 1574 include the purchase of banqueting dishes, linen for cloths and napkins, and a large quantity of muscatel wine – all at Sir Henry's personal expense.[vii]

The display of these coats of arms in the chapel would have been both colourful and impressive. The new Tudor nobility were keen to show off their power and importance by adorning their buildings and possessions with heraldic shields and emblems. Sir Henry Sidney is known to have included his arms in stone, paint and glass on many building works, public and private, with which he was associated.

Sir Henry's lavish decoration of the chapel was much admired. In 1587 Thomas Churchyard, a soldier poet, described the chapel in glowing terms in his poem 'The Worthiness of Wales':

> A chapel is, most trim and costly sure
> So bravely wrought, so fayre and firmly fram'd
> That to world's end the beautie may endure;
> About the same are armes in colours such
> As fewe can shewe in any soyle or place;
> A great device, a work most rare and ritch
> which truly shewes the armes, the blood and race
> of sondrie kings but chiefly noblemen

Shrewsbury born, Thomas Churchyard had a Ludlow connection through his mother, Margery Cooke, whose parents had endowed St Laurence's

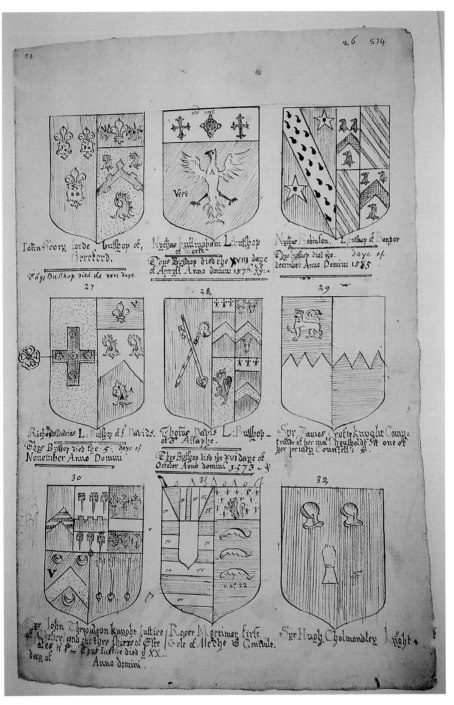

Revd William Mytton's drawing of some of the arms in the castle chapel, c.1735.
MYT/3/574 © Cadbury Research Library, Special Collections, University of Birmingham

and were buried there. Churchyard published a considerable number of works, but also had an active military career including serving as a mercenary for Sir Henry Sidney in Ireland.[viii]

Arms of council members were also displayed in the council chamber and continued to be made and put up, sometimes in the chapel but principally in the council chamber, until the abolition of the Council in 1689. One of the last Presidents of the Council was Henry Somerset, Duke of Beaufort. In 1684 he went on an official tour of Wales, which was recorded by Thomas Dineley, an antiquarian, who accompanied the Duke. Dineley describes and illustrates some of the arms displayed in the chapel and council chamber, and includes the only depiction that we have of the Round Chapel complete with the chancel constructed by Sir Henry Sidney.[ix]

For a time, most of the arms remained *in situ*, and fortunately were drawn and described in about 1735 by the Shropshire antiquarian William Mytton (1693–1746). Mytton records over 250 arms still on display in the castle, and a further 55 which had been removed to the Bull Inn in Corve Street, Ludlow.[x]

Eighteenth-century travellers often commented on the armorial decoration of the chapel, which was still visible despite the building's increasingly ruinous state. In 1768, when John Dovaston of The Nursery, near Oswestry, visited the castle, some arms could still be seen, although the roof of the chapel had collapsed. Despite this the covered walkway from the council chamber to the chapel was still intact. Drawings of the castle were made by the Shrewsbury architect, Thomas Farnolls Pritchard, in 1765 when the Earl of Powis applied to the Crown to lease the castle. The drawings show the chapel without the chancel; and in Pritchard's written survey, dated 1771, he records that Sidney's chancel had been completely taken down.[xi] It would seem that, up to this time, items from the fabric and fittings were being regularly removed. William Hodges, in his history of the castle published in 1794, recounts that some years previously, Miller Page, a former owner of the Bull Inn in Corve Street, enriched himself by plundering and selling the old materials of the castle, and acquired the coats of arms on panels described by William Mytton, using them as wainscoting for the rooms of the Bull Inn. These panels remained in place until the 1920s when they disappeared, possibly sold and exported to the United States.[xii] All the other arms described by Mytton are dispersed and lost.

# 3. Robert Commander, c.1532–1613 Chaplain to Sir Henry Sidney

I T IS THANKS to the survival of a commonplace book in the British Library, written by Robert Commander (or 'Commaundre') that we have the exact date of the placement of the arms in the chapel at Ludlow Castle, as well as some additional detail of the decoration of the chapel. The book contains about 800 pages and is entitled *The Booke of Heraldrye and other thinges togither with the Order of Coronacions of Emperours, Kinges, Princes, Dukes, Byshoppes, Earles and other Estates.* It reveals the depth of Commander's interest in heraldry, royal and noble genealogy, and history. A large portion of the book is devoted to a guide to creating and deciphering the elements found on coats of arms, followed by details of heraldic form and precedent in ceremonies, particularly funerals. In the 1570s Christopher St Lawrence, Baron Howth, described Sir Henry Sidney as having, in his retinue, gentlemen excelling in their knowledge of noblemen and their heraldry, who no doubt will have included Robert Commander. The book is also a cornucopia of diverse notes and titbits including laudatory and scurrilous verse, critical comments on current hair and clothes fashions, slang terms for vagrants, lists of armour and armaments, and naval ships and accounts of voyages of exploration.[i]

Robert Commander's origins are unknown. Commander was an uncommon surname, with families found mainly in the village of Bishops Tachbrook, Warwickshire and in London at this time. A Robert Commander was a King's scholar at Eton in the 1540s and was admitted to King's College, Cambridge in 1548 at the age of 16. He left Cambridge under a cloud, without a degree, accused of destroying a good many books in the college library. Later in life Commander was noted as a Protestant fanatic, which, if this scholar is the same person, could perhaps ring true. His spell in Cambridge coincided with the time when the new King Edward vi's government was introducing a strict Protestant order which Commander may well have espoused. Any library of the time is likely still to have been well-stocked with books reflecting both the old order and the new.[ii]

What is certain is that by 1558 Robert Commander was ordained and living in the parish of St Mary, Bristol. He was married to Agnes Folliet and six of their children were baptised there between 1561 and 1567.[iii] We know from a letter of 1582 that at least three of these children had survived into adult life: Owen, Giles (who was apprenticed in London and caused his father anxiety because of his misbehaviour) and James, who was a servant to Edmund Molyneux, personal secretary to Sir Henry Sidney. Molyneux was the author of a fulsome biography of the Sidney family included in Holinshed's Chronicles, a popular work of the time.[iv]

It is not known when Robert Commander was appointed as chaplain to the Lord President of the Council. Possibly as early as 1560, but certainly by 1567 he was with Sir Henry Sidney when he was Lord Deputy of Ireland. While in Ireland, Commander was given a living attached to Christ Church Cathedral, the Rector and Prebendary of Kilmactawley, County Dublin, and Vicar of Bodenstown, County Kildare.[v] He remained in the employ of the President and Council until Sir Henry's death in 1586. Commander wrote a full account of Sir Henry's death, and all the ceremonies surrounding his funeral journey from Worcester to Penshurst where Commander had the honour of conducting the funeral service.

After Sidney's death Robert Commander concentrated on his living in Tarporley, Cheshire. He had been appointed rector of the parish by 1567, and it is probable that around this time his wife and family moved to Tarporley where another two children, Raph and Grace grew up. After Agnes died in 1598 Commander married Elizabeth Hill of The Foorde (now Fordhall Farm), Shropshire. She died a few years later, with Robert outliving her for a further seven years, dying in his eighties in 1613.[vi]

OPPOSITE: Robert Commander's commonplace book describing the arms placed in the Queen Majesty's Chapel of Ludlow and 'sett owte in cullors of Armes there by the procurement of the right honerable Sir Henrye Sydney knight.' Egerton MS 2642, fol. 273r © The British Library Board

# A Table of all the firste founders

and owners of the castell of Ludlowe in
the Countie of Saloppe in the marches of
walles as they were lynally matched in
mariage, and so placed vpon the honorable
wylles of the auncient male lyne chappell
of Ludlowe within her said castell And sett
in to in ordors as armes there by the comaund
ment of the right honorable Sir Henry
Sydney knight of the noble order of the
garter Lord president of walles beinge of
her matie Counsell & marches of the same
Anno domini 1573.

at Syr Walter Lacye furst owner of
Ludlowe Castle as appereth by Recordes.

Geffrye Geneuyle matched with Lacye

Sir Mortymer furst Earle of Marche matched
to Geneuyle

Leonell Duke of Clarence matched with Westmer

-monde Earle of Marche matched with Clarence

Richard Earle of Cambridge matched wth Marche

-hard Duke of yorke matched with westmerland

Edwarde the iiijth matched with woodvyle
of Rypers

-ury the vijth matched wth Elizabeth of England
daughter to king Edwarde the fourthe

Henrye the viijth matched with Anne Marchiones
of Penbroke daughter of Sir Thomas Bulleyn
knight Earle of wiltshire and Ormond

## The Names of all suche of the Q
matie Counsell in the marches & princi
palitie of walles, as they are placed in the
Chappell of Ludlowe vppon the faniary
Anno domini 1573.

first Sir Henrye Sydney knight of the noble order of the
garter, Lord president of this counsell.

John Story, Byshopp of Herefor

T Wylso

Portrait of Sir Henry Sidney, aged 44, wearing the collar and garter of the Order of the Garter, by Arnold van Bronckhorst. His arms with crest and supporters are displayed above. *NT486274 © National Trust Images*

# 4. Sir Henry Sidney, 1529–86

A man of comely and great stature, a liberal man, wise, and an orator, in setting forth any cause, very severe and upright in judgement and yet a friendly gentleman to his own friends, very courteous, and free of his own nature, a lusty feeder and surfeiter, which was a great pity in so great a personage.

**Christopher St Lawrence, Baron Howth**[i]

SIR HENRY SIDNEY came from a fairly modest landowning, county family which, in the mid-fifteenth century, increased its status and wealth through a marriage into the Brandon family, Dukes of Suffolk. Through this connection Henry's father, William, entered the Court of Henry VII. There he gained notice, lands and honours, largely through his military and diplomatic service, being knighted in 1513. Sir William also advanced at Court where, in 1538, he was appointed by Henry VIII to be chamberlain of the household to the infant Prince Edward. Consequently Henry, who was just nine years old, became a constant companion to the Prince, sharing his education and remaining close to Edward for the remainder of his short life. When Edward succeeded his father as King Edward VI, Henry continued in his household as a Gentleman of the Privy Chamber and attended him during his last illness, reporting that the young king died in his arms.[ii]

When Edward became king in 1547 he was only nine years old and therefore government had to be conducted through a regent acting on his behalf with the Privy Council. From 1550 this hugely powerful role was effectively held by John Dudley, Earl of Warwick whose son, Robert, and other close family members also held posts at Court. Warwick obviously saw Henry's close friendship with the King as potentially useful, and married him to his only daughter, Mary, early in 1551. Henry was now linked to a family who dominated the Court and royal politics for much of the rest of the century.

This alliance quickly bore fruit when King Edward conferred a knighthood on Henry who was knighted in a grand ceremony at Hampton Court in October 1551, at which John Dudley also received the title of Duke of Northumberland. At the same time Edward granted the Penshurst estate in Kent to Henry's father, William. This addition to the existing family property in Kent, Sussex and Hampshire, granted in Henry VIII's reign, provided his son with a fairly substantial inheritance on William's death in 1554. Penshurst Place remained in the family, and is the seat of Henry's descendant, Viscount De L'Isle.

For a while then, Sir Henry was closely involved at the heart of royal government – but this was soon to end in near-disaster for the whole family. Edward died in 1553, aged 16, and the Dudley faction, which had championed strong Protestant church reforms, was faced with the prospect of a Catholic queen in the person of Henry VIII's eldest daughter, Mary. Shortly before he died Edward nominated as his successor his cousin Lady Jane Grey, who had been married to Dudley's youngest son, Guildford, a few weeks before. Dudley tried to insist that the King's wishes be respected and Jane be made queen, but this attempted coup collapsed after a few days and Mary succeeded to the throne. John Dudley, his son, Guildford, and daughter-in-law, Jane, were executed for treason, while Dudley's other sons – John, Robert, Ambrose and Henry – were imprisoned in the Tower of London.

Fortunately, Sir Henry managed to distance himself from the plot, was swiftly pardoned by Queen Mary and even served in her government. He was sent on the diplomatic mission to Spain to broker Mary's marriage to King Philip. There he established a warm personal relationship with Philip, which was undoubtedly a factor in procuring the release of John, Robert and Henry Dudley from the Tower in the autumn of 1554, with their remaining brother, Ambrose, joining them a couple of months later. At about the same time, King Philip agreed to be godfather to Henry's first son. This son was christened Philip, no doubt with the intention both to flatter and to curry favour with the royal couple.

During Mary's reign another family alliance helped boost Sir Henry's career, and gave him his first contact with Ireland where he was to serve intermittently for the next 22 years. His brother-in-law, Thomas Radcliffe, Earl of Sussex, was appointed Lord Deputy of Ireland in 1556, and took Sir Henry with him as his deputy in the post of Vice-Treasurer. Henry remained in Ireland until the accession of Queen Elizabeth in 1558 when the Dudley family – particularly in the person of his brother-in-law,

Portrait of Lady Mary Dudley by circle of Hans Emworth. This was possibly
painted around the time of her marriage to Sir Henry Sidney in 1551.
*NT486275 © National Trust Images*

Portrait of Robert Dudley, Earl of Leicester, brother-in-law of Sir Henry Sidney, by Steven van der Meulen, c.1564. Above on the right are his Arms with Order of the Garter. On the left (and probably added later) are his arms as Knight of the Order of St Michael.
*acc. no. 14.1996 Photo: Waddesdon Image Library, Public Catalogue Foundation*
*© Waddesdon (Rothschild Family)*

Robert – was once again in the ascendancy. Elizabeth and Robert had been friends since childhood and, by the time of her accession, Robert Dudley was a firm favourite who quickly became one of the most powerful and influential members of her Court. Honours for his family quickly followed with his sister, Mary Sidney, becoming one of the Queen's most favoured ladies-in-waiting, and her husband, Sir Henry, being appointed Lord President of the Council in the Marches of Wales on 10 May 1560.[iii] This post was highly prestigious, effectively heading up the regional government as the Queen's representative in Wales and the English counties on its border. The Council's main work was in keeping the peace and dispensing justice throughout the area, and also ensuring that royal orders and legislation were carried out. Its administrative centre was at Ludlow Castle where Sir Henry was often resident, remaining Lord President of the Council for the rest of his life.

Although the Presidency represented a prestigious post, Sir Henry also hoped for an office closer to the Queen's Court, and certainly aspired to a peerage. At first, he was indeed favoured by Elizabeth. In May 1564 he was installed a Knight of the Garter at a ceremony in St George's Chapel, Windsor, becoming a member of that elite group of only 24 founded by Edward III. The following year Elizabeth gave Sir Henry another major office, sending him to Ireland as Lord Deputy. He remained in Ireland for the next six years, keeping in touch with his Welsh affairs through his Vice-Presidents – first William Gerard and then Sir John Throckmorton. So, for these years, and again from 1575 to 1578, Sir Henry held the two highest provincial offices of state, representing the Queen over most of her Western realm, which gave him immense patronage and influence. It also excited much envy and rivalry at Court, which ultimately worked against him.

Sir Henry always hoped that further honours would follow, but it wasn't to be. In 1572 he was seriously considered for a baronage; however, his wife, Mary, in a private letter to the Secretary of State, William Cecil, asked that the matter be dropped because their income did not match that required to sustain a title.[iv] This lack of wealth was to dog Sir Henry throughout his career. By the standards of many of his contemporaries at Court he had indeed comparatively modest means and was frequently financially embarrassed. However, he spent lavishly – as he felt befitted his status in both personal and official affairs. He regularly exceeded the allowance given to his offices by the Crown, and often covered some of this overspend from his own resources.

In both Wales and Ireland Sir Henry proved himself an energetic and able administrator. While serving in Ireland, in addition to the main task of advancing English rule and authority on the island, he set about enhancing his public and often personal prestige through building works, public ceremony and propaganda. He repaired and enhanced Dublin Castle (the seat of royal administration), and was instrumental in rebuilding and enhancing Christ Church Cathedral which was often used on ceremonial occasions. Further afield he provided better roads and new bridges, and improved the buildings and fortifications in many towns. Whether travelling through the country or attending government he is recorded as being richly dressed and conducting all with elaborate pomp and ceremony.

Irish affairs were always complex since they involved dealing with the multiple and often rebellious Irish clans, as well as accommodating the interests of English settlers and trying to maintain peace. Further difficulties could arise caused by conflicting Irish interests at Court, which on more than one occasion resulted in the Queen favouring a particular clan in opposition to the settlement or treaty that Sir Henry was trying to achieve, thus undermining his authority. However, his main conflict with the Queen was over money. Elizabeth was always concerned to keep costs down and required Ireland to be less of a burden on the Exchequer. Sir Henry was confident he could achieve this, but instead accumulated a huge deficit and was accused of extravagance. He was recalled in 1571, thoroughly exhausted and disillusioned, and found his reception at Court on his return less than welcoming. However, he still had the important support of Robert Dudley, the Earl of Leicester, as well as one of Elizabeth's most senior privy councillors, Francis Walsingham, and the Dudley-Sidney faction was still reckoned a formidable force at Court.

For the next four years Sir Henry was very active as President of the Council in the Marches of Wales, and in addition devoted his considerable energy to substantial building works both at Ludlow and Penshurst. As in Dublin, the works at Ludlow were intended to boost his personal prestige, as well as that of the Council. However he was not content and wished to redeem his record in Ireland. So, rejuvenated, he began a campaign to persuade the Queen to reinstate him. Unsurprisingly, his successor as Lord Deputy had not fared any better in Ireland, and Sidney put forward a proposal for taxation reform in Ireland, which, after an initial large outlay, he claimed would yield a net profit to the Crown. The Queen was won over and Sir Henry set out for Ireland once again in September 1575.

Sir Henry Sidney as Lord Deputy of Ireland receives the submission of Turlough Lynagh O'Neale with much ceremony. *The Image of Irelande*, by John Derrick (London, 1581) © Edinburgh University Library

Needless to say, Sir Henry's taxation reforms met with strong opposition from Irish clansmen and English settlers alike, fuelling resistance to the Tudor policy of the Anglicisation of the island. In this period Sir Henry made another important family alliance through the marriage of his daughter, Mary, to Henry Herbert, Earl of Pembroke, a leading figure in Leicester's party and perhaps the most influential nobleman in Wales.

However, this alliance didn't spare Sir Henry the Queen's increasing displeasure. Rather than increasing the Crown's income through taxation, his Irish expenses simply spiralled. His opponents at Court fed rumours accusing him not only of extravagance in Ireland but also of diverting income to his personal gain. He was warned by Philip Williams in 1577 that his opponents at Court, 'labour to settle in opinion in her majesty's and (privy) council's head that (...) you are grown a great riche man.'[v]

Sir Henry was recalled in September 1578, feeling aggrieved and once again under a cloud. He spent much of his last years at Ludlow engaged

Miniature of Mary Herbert, daughter of Sir Henry Sidney, by Nicholas Hilliard.
© *National Portrait Gallery*

on his personal affairs, and was not seen often at Court. At about the same time his wife, Mary, retired as lady-in-waiting to the Queen. It also probably suited Queen Elizabeth, who was wary of factions at Court, to have Dudley and his brother-in-law remain at a convenient geographical distance. Sir Henry was not without friends at Court though. His eldest son, Philip, was also well-regarded, and his subsequent marriage to Sir Francis Walsingham's daughter formally allied the Sidney family to Elizabeth's Secretary of State.

Despite his previous record, in 1582 Sir Henry was once again considered for the post of Lord Deputy of Ireland. This time he made his acceptance conditional upon the Queen appointing him with an enhanced title of Lord Lieutenant of Ireland, granting him a peerage endowed with suitable land

Henry Herbert, 2nd Earl of Pembroke who succeeded his father-in-law, Sir Henry Sidney, as Lord President of the Council in the Marches of Wales.
© *Amgueddfa Cymru – National Museum Wales*

grants, and withdrawing the accusations of his extravagance in Ireland.[vi] The Queen did not choose to meet his terms and Sidney remained in Ludlow. It obviously rankled that his work and achievements in Ireland were neither appreciated nor acknowledged. In 1583 he wrote an autobiography which, after several redrafts, he sent in letter form to Sir Francis Walsingham. His detailed account, which he calls a 'tragical discourse', is almost entirely concerned with vindicating his record of service in Ireland, which represented only a quarter of his time in royal service. Throughout the account he shows how deeply aggrieved he was not to have received higher favours and honours from the Queen, despite the fact that as Lord Deputy of Ireland and Lord President of the Council in the Marches of Wales he had governance of a huge swathe of the kingdom.

In his final years, during which he largely devoted himself to his interests in Wales and the Marches, Sir Henry continued to display the same energy which had always marked his public and private life. In 1581 the new building to accommodate the justices was completed at Ludlow Castle, and a major remodelling of the King's Tower at Penshurst was completed a few years later. He also turned his attention to St Laurence's church. In 1580 he provided a fine memorial to his daughter Ambrosia (who had died at Ludlow in February 1575), which is lavishly decorated with family coats of arms. The monument is situated in the chancel, in a highly prestigious position close to the high altar where there was also seating for the President and other nobles. By this time his son Robert's former tutor, John Bust, was rector. Sir Henry took advantage of this connection to regulate the music and liturgy of the parish church. By an Order of June 1581 he set out instructions for the choir and organist.[vii] With the style and standard of music to his satisfaction, in the following year Sir Henry spent St George's Day at Ludlow and there celebrated the Feast of the Order of the Garter in an elaborate civic ceremony (which, as a knight of that order, he was required to do each year).

Having shared the education of a royal Prince, Sir Henry was noted as an extremely cultured and well-read man. He had a particular interest in history and the preservation of antiquities, along with the promotion of national culture. In Ireland he encouraged the writing and publication of a history of the island, and the translation into English of Gerald of Wales' chronicle of the conquest of Ireland. In Christ Church Cathedral, Dublin, he also commissioned a restoration of the tomb of Strongbow, the leader of the twelfth-century Anglo-Norman invasion of Ireland, in what was surely

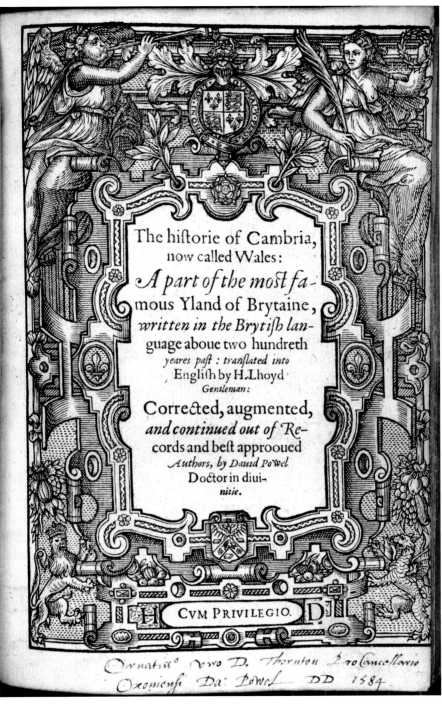

The historie of Cambria,
now called Wales:

*A part of the most fa-*
mous Yland of Brytaine,
*written in the Brytish lan-*
guage aboue two hundreth
*yeares past : translated into*
Englith by H.Lhoyd
*Gentleman:*

Corrected, augmented,
*and continued out of Re-*
cords and best approoued
*Authors, by Dauid Powel*
Doctor in diui-
*nitie.*

CVM PRIVILEGIO.

Title page of David Powell's *Historie of Cambria, now called Wales*, 1584. This history of
Wales in English was produced under the patronage of Sir Henry Sidney.
Powell's *History of Cambria*, L.III.19 © *Hereford Cathedral Library*

an act of propaganda as much as of antiquarianism. He embraced the new developments in map-making by employing Robert Lythe to survey and map the country, which also aided the task of conquest.[viii]

After his return from Ireland in 1578 Sir Henry was able to devote himself to similar projects in Wales. Christopher Saxton's maps of Wales were produced under his patronage in 1579. In 1583, at the time he was writing his own memoirs, he commissioned David Powell, a Welsh cleric, to prepare and research a history of Wales in English, which incorporated a translation of the early Welsh chronicle *Brut y Tywysogyon*. Powell's *Historie of Cambria, now called Wales* was published the following year, with a fulsome tribute to Sir Henry included in the book's dedication, recording that he 'alwaies hath beene (...) more inclined and bent to doo good to his countrie, than to benefit or inrich himselfe, as Wales and Ireland beside his owne can bear witness.'

# 5. Governance of Wales, and the Council in the Marches of Wales

I N ORDER TO understand some of the references in this book as well as the emergence and role of the Council in the Marches of Wales, it is necessary to provide a brief background to how the governance and administration of Wales had developed in the medieval period during the centuries before the creation of the Council.

Before the Norman Conquest of 1066, while England had developed into a single, unified state, this had not happened in Wales. The country was still divided into several separate, smaller kingdoms or principalities, which expanded and contracted depending on the respective strength of the rulers and the marriage alliances that they made. By the eleventh century, four main kingdoms had evolved: Gwynedd in the north, based on the mountainous security of Snowdonia and the agricultural fertility of Anglesey; Powys in the central area (although at this point Powys had been taken over by Gwynedd); Deheubarth in the south-west; and Morgannwg or Glamorgan in the south-east. In many ways it is best to consider each of these as groupings of power, as the extent of their territory was constantly evolving, with no fixed boundaries.

This fragmented political structure was one factor that made it more difficult for the Normans to conquer Wales; another was the mountainous and fragmented geography. But the chief factor informing their lack of a decisive push to conquer the whole of Wales was that it was not a priority of the English Crown, with a succession of monarchs happy to accept recognition of their overlordship. This situation led to a piecemeal takeover of parts of Wales, with control of some areas passing back and forth for a period that lasted 200 years. It was only when the conquest and control of

Wales became a priority for Edward I in the 1270s and 1280s that conquest was completed and native rule in Wales ended.

At times during this period of 200 years, Anglo-Norman lords were given a free hand to seize what lands they could from the Welsh princes. Not surprisingly, the lands that were targeted and won were those that were most accessible – along the border from the Dee estuary down to the Severn estuary, and all along south Wales to Pembrokeshire. Although Anglo-Norman control was never secure, a series of lordships developed that became known as the Welsh Marcher Lordships.

During the thirteenth century, two princes of Gwynedd – first Llywelyn ab Iorwerth then his grandson, Llywelyn ap Gruffudd – succeeded in establishing their power over the rest of native Wales, as well as taking back control of several of the Marcher Lordships. Indeed, Llywelyn ap Gruffudd was recognised by the English Crown as the 'Prince of Wales' in 1267. However, after Edward I inherited the throne, this relationship broke down and Edward determined on the final conquest of Wales, which was achieved by 1282 following the death of Llywelyn.

Edward I's settlement of Wales in the 1280s did not incorporate Wales into the governance of the kingdom of England. Instead, it created the Principality of Wales, which ran from Anglesey in the north through west Wales and into Carmarthenshire. The shires of the Principality were organised into groups centred on Caernarvon in the north and Carmarthen in the south, with Flint attached to the royal administration of Chester. The Principality was governed directly by the King or the Prince of Wales through his appointees, headed both in the north and the south by a justiciar and chamberlain; however, the shires of the Principality stood quite separate, both geographically and constitutionally, from those of England.

Edward I also accepted, used and extended the existing administrative structures of the Marcher Lordships, although these were quite different from the Principality of Wales in their development and origin. The Anglo-Norman lords who were first settled in the border regions had been given extensive powers – both in recognition of the need to provide a defensive barrier against Wales, and in order to take opportunities for the conquest of more land. In addition, as they conquered and took control of districts in Wales, the new lords assumed the powers of the native rulers. Consequently, the Marcher Lordships, although ultimately held of the Crown, were independent franchises. The function of government in each lordship was the sole responsibility of its Marcher Lord, who exercised almost regal powers

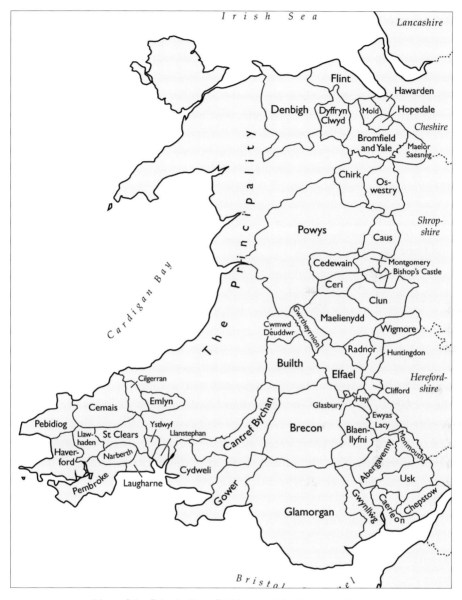

Map of the Principality of Wales and Marcher Lordships

within their lordship: the lord, and not the king's sheriff, was responsible for the legal system, including power of life and death; he could impose his own taxes, build castles without needing royal permission, and raise his own army. Royal officials had no authority in Marcher Lordships. There are many examples of Marcher Lords standing up for their rights, strongly proclaiming that the king's writ did not apply in their lordship, including one case when the unfortunate messenger was forced to eat the King's message – wax seals and all! Not surprisingly, the strongest Marcher Lords attempted, and sometimes succeeded, in withdrawing their lordships from the jurisdiction of the adjoining English shires of Herefordshire and Shropshire in order to make them into Marcher lordships.

When those Marcher Lordships that had been created by Edward I in the 1280s are added to those conquered from the Welsh during the previous 200 years, and to those withdrawn from the English shires, there were over 50 independent Marcher Lordships that separated the English shires from the Principality of Wales, running throughout south Wales to Pembrokeshire. As early as Magna Carta in 1215 there had been recognition of the existence of the laws of the Welsh, the laws of the Marches and the laws of the English.

Such a diversity of laws, governance and legal structures need not in itself have been a cause of disorder. However, by the fifteenth century this was seen as one factor in the increasing lawlessness of Wales and the Marches. Other factors were also relevant, such as the increasing absenteeism of the Marcher Lords (by this point more and more Lordships had been accumulated by a small group of great earls and dukes of England, whilst a number had passed into the ownership of the Crown). The aftermath of the rebellion of Owain Glyn Dwr and the associated destruction of many border areas at the start of the 1400s had also contributed to the unease and insecurity. Despite repeated attempts to remedy the situation nothing was achieved. A petition to Parliament in 1449 maintained that even in the royal territories of the Principality the population 'dayly habundeth and encreseth in misgovernance'.

This is the context in which Edward IV began to create first a household council to manage the estates of the infant Prince of Wales, and subsequently to give it an increasing role in tackling the law and disorder that was perceived to have become endemic in the Principality of Wales and the Marcher Lordships.

## The First Council and its Development into the Council in the Marches of Wales

In 1471, Edward IV established a household and council for his infant eldest son, Edward, Prince of Wales, with responsibility for Wales and Chester. Two years later the council was enlarged when the three-year-old Prince took up residence in Ludlow Castle (Ludlow being chosen as it had become

Edward IV: having been brought up at Ludlow Castle, in turn he sent his eldest son, Edward, Prince of Wales to live there. © *National Portrait Gallery, London*

a favourite home of Richard, Duke of York, and was where his son Edward IV was brought up). As the Prince himself was a child, and thus a figurehead signifying the royal authority of the Council, a president was appointed to run the Council, the first being John Alcock, Bishop of Rochester, Lord President from 1473 to 1483. During this period, although the Council was still primarily part of a royal magnate's household, its royal connection and local presence created opportunities for it to be used in other ways, and it began to acquire further ad hoc political and legal powers. For example, in

1476 the Council was given a 'Commission of oyer and terminer' (the power to make inquiry into all treasons, felonies and misdemeanours) within the Principality of Wales, the Marches and adjacent English shires. In the same year, Edward IV arranged a conference at Ludlow between the Council and the Marcher Lords to discuss the punishment of crime in Wales and the Marches. A few months later, a commission was issued to the Prince to appoint judicial commissions in Wales, the Marcher Lordships and the four border shires, with powers to punish criminals, and to enquire into negligent officials.

This first period in the history of the Council came to an end when, on the unexpected death of Edward IV in 1483, Prince Edward left Ludlow to travel to London for his intended coronation, which never happened. Instead, his uncle was crowned Richard III, only to be defeated at Bosworth in 1485, following which the victorious Henry Tudor was crowned Henry VII. There is no evidence for the existence of a Council in Ludlow during this and the following period, confirming that its function had not involved any established machinery of either governance or justice.

The Council re-appeared in 1493 when Henry VII gave his eldest son, the seven-year-old Prince Arthur, powers similar to those of Prince Edward and, like him, exercised by others on his behalf. This time, though, the Council was given powers to hear and redress grievances by appeal to the Princes' Council from the courts of Marcher Lords and the officials of royal Marcher Lordships. There is no evidence as to whether the Council exercised these powers. However, when Prince Arthur died in Ludlow in April 1502, the Council this time did not expire with him, but continued a public function separate to running a royal household.

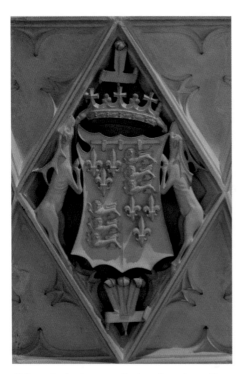

Prince Arthur's arms displayed on the ceiling above his tomb in Worcester Cathedral. The supporters are two harts (a royal badge), with the three feathers of the Prince of Wales below, and the crown above

Only two months after the death of the prince, in June 1502 the Council, under the presidency of Bishop William Smyth of Lincoln, was given a commission of *oyer* and *terminer* in north and south Wales, Chester, the Marches and the four English border shires of Shropshire, Worcestershire, Herefordshire and Gloucestershire. Thirty years after the first creation of a Princes' Council, the royal rights had become permanently delegated to ensure law and order throughout Wales and the English border land. Unfortunately, due to a lack of evidence, it is not possible to assess how effectively the Council discharged its functions in the 22 years after 1502.

It was not until 1525 that there was another royal household in Ludlow, when the Princess Mary resided there for three winters. The requirement for a re-energised Council to manage the Princess Mary's household coincided with further crucial developments in royal policy. The role and powers of the Council were again gradually increased as Henry VIII's chief adviser, Cardinal Wolsey, appreciated the scope the Council offered to assert royal authority in the areas furthest from London. The Council in the Marches of Wales was given powers like those of the Council in the North, with a hierarchy of officials to carry out its business (a total now of 340 people when combined with the members of the Princess' household). The Council began to act as a court of law, exercising both criminal and civil jurisdiction, hearing cases both in its own right and as appeals from manorial courts. There are indications, though, that it was not always effective, particularly after the departure of the Princess Mary's household in 1528, when complaints surfaced that the President, John Veysey, Bishop of Exeter, was not up to the task of imposing law and order.

Since its inception in 1471 as a council for the household and estates of the child Prince of Wales, the Council had existed for over 60 years only as a result of royal instruction – a 'prerogative court'. A series of Acts of Parliament in 1534, 1536 and 1543 made significant changes not only to the status of the Council (giving it statutory powers), but also to the judicial structure of the Marches and Wales. The Act of 1534 gave the Council the formal and statutory powers to hear suits and also to supervise and intervene in the judicial proceedings in Wales and the Marches. The 1536 and 1543 Acts of Union (of England and Wales) abolished the governance and judicial structure of the Marcher Lordships and the Principality of Wales. In their place a new structure of county governance throughout Wales was established, with the over 50 Marcher Lordships incorporated either into those new counties or the border counties of England, creating a defined boundary between England and Wales. For the first time, Wales was governed in the same way as England, including through the introduction of the systems of justices of the peace, and reform of the Courts of Great Sessions in Wales. These changes considerably increased the importance of the role of the Council. The Act of 1543 included the provision for the appointment of a President of the Council, the Council itself, officers and clerks, using language that both established the court whilst also acknowledging its previous existence.

These governance and administrative reforms were driven through by Thomas Cromwell who had succeeded Cardinal Wolsey as chief adviser to Henry VIII. In response to the complaints about the ineffectiveness of the Council in the late 1520s/ early 1530s, in 1534 Cromwell also appointed one of his associates as Lord President. Rowland Lee, Bishop of Coventry and Lichfield was given a clear remit to exercise effectively the new powers of the Council. Lee undertook his task with vigour and ruthlessness for nine years until his death in 1543, gaining a deserved reputation for a personal reign of terror throughout the Marches and Wales.

The final years of Henry VIII's reign and the turbulent short reigns of first his son, Edward VI, then his eldest daughter, Mary I, led to a succession of Presidents of the Council who served for only a short time as people fell in and out of favour with the changing ruling factions. The accession of Elizabeth I, however, brought a period of stability that saw the Council at the height of its powers and influence. Throughout virtually all her reign there were only two Presidents: first, Sir Henry Sidney from 1560 to 1586, followed by his son-in-law, Henry, Earl of Pembroke from 1586 to 1601.

THE PRESIDENCY OF SIR HENRY SIDNEY, 1560–86

On 10 May 1560 Queen Elizabeth I issued instructions for the conduct of her Council in the Marches of Wales for 'the continuance of quietness and good government of the people and the inhabitants within the Dominion and Principalitie of Wales, and the Marches and good administration of justice'. She appointed as President her 'trusty and well beloved servant Sir Henry Sidney', knowing his 'approved wisdom and experience and assured discretion and dexterity in executing of justice'.[i] The instructions set out in detail the role and powers of the President and Council and its officers. Sir Henry was to be by far the Council's longest serving President, retaining the office until his death in 1586, 26 years later.

Sir Henry Sidney's authority as President of the Council in the Marches of Wales was partly determined by his status at Court, which, for different reasons, prevented him from being very effective in the post despite his long tenure. Armed with Elizabeth's new instructions for the Council, he started strongly, working with his deputy Sir John Throckmorton and able fellow councillor, William Gerard, to address the main problem of increased and unnecessary litigation which was overwhelming the court. Orders were put in place to divert business as appropriate to local courts, and to reduce the large number of superfluous clerks, lawyers and court officials. Implementation of these orders, which were initially effective, lapsed as Sir Henry, then highly in favour with Queen Elizabeth, was sent on diplomatic missions to France and Scotland. He was then appointed Lord Deputy of Ireland in 1565, where he remained for six years, which largely occupied his energies.

So, until his return in 1571 the Council was led by his deputy, first John Throckmorton, followed by Hugh Cholmondeley who initiated some useful reform in speeding up the process of examining complainants and reducing the number of lawyers attending the courts. During Sir Henry's absence there were continual complaints of delays in justice, excessive fines, partiality and corruption, laxity in levying fines and keeping accounts, and extravagance of the household at Ludlow. For the next four years after his return, Sir Henry was largely concerned with council business, but made little impact on these abuses. Complaints persisted and the Queen issued renewed instructions to the Council in 1574.

The following year Sir Henry was once again posted to Ireland. In his absence there was a serious attack on the reputation of the Council and on Sidney's allies, Sir John Throckmorton and William Gerard. This was made by an eminent Welsh lawyer, Dr David Lewis, who complained that law and order had broken down throughout the whole country, and that Sir Henry and the Council were both ineffective and too lenient. Throckmorton and Gerard were called by the Privy Council to answer complaints against them. Gerard gave detailed evidence in his defence and outlined proposals for reform. He said that in Wales the Council was neither 'reverenced, feared or their proceedings esteemed'. He criticised his fellow councillors, saying that many were concerned for their self-interest alone and that the more able were rarely involved in council business. Generally, the Council's business was conducted by fewer than half a dozen councillors, three of whom the Queen's instructions named and specified to be in constant attendance.

The remainder were chosen and invited to attend by the President and would thus tend to be his associates. Over 1,200 court cases came to the Council's court each year, 90% of which Gerard estimated were frivolous and baseless. He proposed that more able councillors be appointed and that the Council should travel more frequently through Wales with the assize judges, and thus bring justice directly to the people. He also suggested that property cases should be reduced in favour of criminal cases in order to better maintain peace; and that at least one of the justices should understand Welsh to speed up cases and guard against false translation.[ii] As a result, revised instructions for the Council were issued in 1576 incorporating some of Gerard's suggestions. Sir Henry seemed content with this moderate reform of the Council and was once again secure in his post, but when Gerard joined him in Ireland as Lord Chancellor in 1577 the Council was left open to his opponents.

Sir Henry's most vocal opponent on the Council was Sir James Croft of Croft Castle, Herefordshire, which is close to Ludlow. In 1570 Croft was appointed to the Council and made Controller of the Royal Household. His position in Court, combined with his influence and family connections in the locality, made him a powerful opponent. With the appointment of William Whitgift, Bishop of Worcester, to the Council and vice presidency in 1577, Croft gained a valuable ally. Whitgift devoted much of his energy to enforcing the recusancy laws in Wales (in particular the pursuit of Catholic priests), and alienated Sir Henry by not sufficiently consulting him on council business. Although Sir Henry returned the following year, his failure in Ireland left him vulnerable to attack. He still had strong support in the Council from those also allied to the Earl of Leicester's faction (notably his son-in-law, Henry, Earl of Pembroke), but his opponents also had the ear of the Queen. Both Croft and Whitgift directly attacked Sir Henry for his conduct in the Council, and for his apparent laxity and leniency in pursuing recusants, all of which resulted in him receiving a reprimand from the Queen. In a postscript to this letter Sir Francis Walsingham advises Sidney 'to walk warily for your doings are narrowly observed and her majestie is apt to give ear to any that shall yll you'.[iii] Despite this, Sir Henry retained sufficient authority and support in the Council for the rest of his tenure.

In both Ireland and Wales Sir Henry was noted for qualities of firmness and sympathy for the native population. He spent much of his last years in Ludlow 'in the sweet marches', and considered Wales to have been 'a happy

SIRIAMES·CRAFTS                    CONTROLER

Sir James Croft, adversary of Sir Henry Sidney on the Council in the Marches. He is
shown holding his staff of office as controller of Queen Elizabeth's household.
*NT 537581 © National Trust Images/ John Hammond*

place of government (...) for a better people to govern, or better subjects to
their Sovereign, Europe holds not'.[iv] Although he arguably accomplished little
as President, Sir Henry served during a period when the Council was at its
most prominent and influential. His successor as president was his son-in-
law, Henry, a Welshman and a Welsh speaker, who would immediately be
immersed in what was ultimately the insuperable task of Council reform.

## Decline and Abolition of the Council

The problems that Sir Henry experienced during his presidency stemmed, ironically, from the considerable powers that the Council had been given, combined with confusion over its jurisdiction. It was the wide-ranging powers of the Council in this period that drew attention to problems and anomalies that were inherent in its role, and which ultimately led to its decline and abolition in the following century. It had been given powers of criminal jurisdiction and oversight of other courts in Wales and neighbouring parts of England, with the power to hear appeals. The Council also had a freedom to interpret law similar to the Star Chamber in London, and was one of the few courts empowered to use torture; it had jurisdiction over civil cases and it took on aspects of the Court of Chancery and of the Court of Request (the poor man's court), both based in London. One purpose of the court was to enable people living a long distance from London and in a poorer region to have equal access to the law. And, indeed, the court was popular with the oppressed poor who, it was said, 'flocked to it.' In practice, this generated opposition as it was claimed that the court's fees were lower than those at Westminster – much to the annoyance of lawyers who practised in the latter, as they lost business to Ludlow.

Much of the opposition to the Council in the Marches of Wales developed from the problems of conflicting jurisdictions, which was a general problem in a period during which each court's jurisdiction had not been defined, either in terms of types of legal cases or geographical extent. The Council also clashed with the Ecclesiastical Courts, which had jurisdiction over morals and matters of conscience, when the former began to hear matters concerning breaches of contract, debt, slander, scandal, misconduct and sexual morals.

The fines levied by the court also became a source of contention, as some payments formed part of the expected bonuses of the various salaried officials. Fines were also expected to help finance the Council's own costs, including the upkeep of Ludlow Castle. All this gave judges an incentive to fine heavily to ensure that their own salaries were paid. Also, the more cases the court handled the greater its income – a source of grievance both for those being fined and for competing jurisdictions that lost income.

Although primarily a court of justice, the Council had other functions as an administrative body, particularly in relation to military matters. The President of the Council was *ex-officio* Lord Lieutenant of all the counties in his charge except Gloucestershire, making him responsible for ensuring that

Seal matrix of the
Council in the Marches
of Wales. Engraved in
or after 1660 to replace
a seal matrix destroyed
in the Civil War. It is
possible that Sir John
Charlton of Ludford
House paid for it. Steel
with ivory handle.
© *Shropshire Council,
Shropshire Museums*

the counties contributed to the armed forces. To assist him, he appointed deputy-lieutenants in each county, and the Council had a say in the appointment of sheriffs, justices of the peace, and other local functionaries.

At the start of the seventeenth century, after the death of Elizabeth I and the accession of James I, several attempts were made to restrict both the legal scope of the Council and the geographical area of its jurisdiction. The attempts either failed or were quickly overturned, although the Council did lose permanently its power to use torture. Despite this mounting opposition, the presidency of William Compton, Earl of Northampton from 1617 to 1630, brought another period when the court flourished, with a large volume of business and high income.

Opposition to the Council and its court began to increase again in the 1630s with attempts to limit its jurisdiction. For example, in 1636 Archbishop Laud ordered the Council to suspend its jurisdiction over sexual cases. Inevitably, the Council became drawn into the political conflict between Charles I and Parliament, particularly when the King's Privy Council used the Council in its unpopular campaign to enforce the collection of taxes for the raising of royal troops. Its association with the personal rule of Charles I and his arbitrary use of the Star Chamber and Privy Council against his opponents ensured that the Council attracted some of the hatred being generated towards the monarchy at the time. When Charles I was finally forced to call a Parliament, in 1641 the Act for the Abolition of the Star Chamber was passed, which included clauses that 'repealed and absolutely revoked and made void' the legal jurisdiction of the court of the Council in the Marches of Wales. Significantly, the Act did not abolish either the Presidency or the Council itself, only their judicial powers. However, although the Council technically remained in existence, there is no evidence that it functioned during the years of the Civil War and the Protectorate of Oliver Cromwell which followed the execution of Charles I.

The restoration of Charles II to the Crown brought about the re-establishment of the Council by royal proclamation in 1661, and the appointment of a new President. As there are few surviving records, little is known about the judicial activity of the court in this period. However, the period was characterised by people competing and jockeying for position as a means of thus securing an income. Mostly this led to absentee office-holders who never visited Ludlow, appointing in their stead lesser-paid deputies, and bringing the Council into disrepute. Finally, in 1689, 'An Act for taking away the Court holden before the President and Council of the Marches of Wales' was passed, stating that the 'proceedings and decrees of that court have by experience been found to be an intolerable burthen to the subject.' Although it technically had an existence separate from that of the court, the Council effectively also ceased with this Act.

The Council had first developed as a response to the confusion of the multiple structures of the Principality of Wales and more than 50 Marcher Lordships, and the subsequent breakdown of law and order. In turn, the Council had also, in time, come to be seen as inefficient and an unnecessary anomaly. In the medieval period, royal governance had been mobile out of necessity – partly because the exercise of kingship was personal (requiring the presence of the king), and partly because it was not practical for the king and his Court to stay in one place for too long. By the seventeenth century a process of centralisation on London was underway, making unnecessary a devolved structure – particularly one that overlapped with, and duplicated, the county-based systems to administer justice.

# 6. Sir Henry Sidney and the Enhancement of Ludlow Castle

I N MAY 1560, when Sir Henry Sidney was appointed Lord President of the Council in the Marches of Wales, Queen Elizabeth I stated in her instructions setting out the powers of her Council that she was, 'credibly informed that not only Ludlow castle but also other of our castles, houses and edifices there are in great ruin and decay'. She ordered that, henceforth, all income deriving from the fines raised in the courts was to be solely devoted to repairs and new buildings as required.[i] With this secured funding, Sir Henry, with considerable energy and enthusiasm (and at some personal expense), set about repairing and enhancing Ludlow Castle. He wanted both to reflect its prestige and importance as the administrative centre of the regional Royal Government of Wales, but also to provide it with the comforts and amenities of a residence fit for Tudor nobility. Over the 26 years of his presidency, all areas of the castle received his attention and it is clear that these improvements were much admired by contemporary writers.

There is a contemporary, official account of all of the building work undertaken by Sir Henry Sidney at Ludlow Castle, which gives no dates for the work; however, it has been possible to understand the sequence of some of the work carried out from other sources. Early works to the castle may have included general repairs, such as lead roofing, and also the enhancement of the approach to the castle, which provided such an important first impression to visitors. A 'fayre lardge stone bridge' four-and-a-half feet high and 30 to 40 yards long was constructed, spanning the castle ditch. The bridge consisted of one large arch in the middle flanked by two smaller arches at each end.

View of the Castle and Town from Whitcliffe, by Thomas Dineley, from: *The Account of the Official Progress of His Grace Henry the first Duke of Beaufort (Lord President of the Council in Wales, and Lord Warden of the Marches) through Wales in 1684*, by Thomas Dineley. *H910.8WAL/DINTh © Hereford Cathedral Library*

## WATER SUPPLY

One of the first problems to be tackled was the creation of an adequate water supply for the large household:

> Making a conduit of lead to convey the water into the same castle of Ludlow the space of a mile and more in length, for making a goodly large fountain of lime and stone and lead with her Majesties arms and diverse other arms on, conveying the water in lead from the same fountain to the garden and diverse other offices in the house and from thence into the Castle Street within the same town of Ludlow and there making a fountain of lime and stone.[ii]

By 1560, it seems that the ancient well in the castle was unable to provide any water, meaning that two men with horses were employed to fetch water daily from the river Teme instead. Unsurprisingly, there were complaints that at times of tempest and flood this water was, 'so muddied as to be unhealthsome'.[iii] A further complaint was that the costs of feeding the horses – and, more particularly, feeding the men – were burdensome and that a piped, spring water supply would be both healthier and more cost-effective. A generous natural spring was identified in Priors Halton, on the edge of Whitcliffe Wood, on land owned by Charles Fox, Secretary to the Council, and by the spring of 1566 pipes had been laid from there to a large stone fountain or reservoir placed close to the Castle chapel. The fountain was seven-and-a-half feet in diameter, lined with lead and decorated with the coat of arms of Elizabeth I, and almost certainly those of Sir Henry Sidney.[iv] The water supply then continued to a similar reservoir placed in the Castle Square, for use by the residents of Ludlow. As recompense to Charles Fox for maintenance access to the pipe across his land he was awarded two deer annually from the Council's allowance of deer supplied from the Royal Forest of Bringewood close by.[v] The water source at Priors Halton proved to be a very abundant spring and continued to supply water to Ludlow into the twentieth century, and still supplies farms in its vicinity to this day.

## The Outer Bailey – New Facilities for the Judicial Court

Not only was Ludlow the administrative centre of the Council it was also a location for conducting the Council's judicial business, hearing and judging cases, and holding and processing prisoners. The considerable court business was all conducted in the outer bailey, while the buildings of the inner bailer were reserved for the Council and domestic use. By 1570 work had begun on converting and extending St Peter's chapel in the south-west corner, to a new use as a courthouse and records store. In November the Clerk to the Council, Thomas Sherer, complained that the court records and archives were being poorly housed and were vulnerable to damp, and asked that work on the building be improved and completed. The upkeep and security of records was of importance to Sir Henry Sidney who, at much the same time, had provided a dry and secure room in Dublin Castle for keeping the records. Work was quickly approved and St Peter's was enlarged, with a court room at first-floor level, accessed by external steps, and with two rooms for storing and processing records below.[vi]

Remains of St Peter's chapel in the outer bailey, converted into a court for the Council in the Marches of Wales by Sir Henry Sidney, with a store for keeping records underneath

Prisoners were looked after by the castle porter, and the facilities for both porter and prisoner were much improved. The porter's lodge at the front gate was enhanced with new or refurbished chambers and a kitchen, larder and buttery. The area of the prison which was adjacent to the lodge on the left of the entrance was extended with the construction of a 200-yard-long wall enclosing a space to allow the prisoners to exercise. The porter also served as gaoler, and was to provide meals of meat and drink sufficient to ensure the prisoners' 'competent and convenient livelihood'. Prisoners had to pay for the meals themselves at a rate of 8d for meals at the best table or 6d at the second. The porter also received other fees from his prisoners. They were charged 2s 6d on arrival, and those charged with the highest offences – treason, murder or felony – were to be detained in irons and charged another 2s 6d when these encumbrances were removed.[vii]

Beyond the prison, a sizeable area was enclosed by a nine-foot-high wall which was 200 yards in length and reserved for a wood yard. There, wood was cut and prepared for various uses, though mainly for providing heat for the household and court. This area of the castle continued to be used for wood and the working of stone into the nineteenth century when the area was leased out to private individuals.

THE INNER BAILEY

The inner bailey contained most of the domestic buildings and the private and public apartments, including the Great Hall where public ceremonies and entertainments would take place. Adjacent to the Great Hall on the east side was the council chamber which was connected to the chapel by a covered corridor and, beyond that, private apartments for the President and his family.

Here, Sir Henry modified and modernised the existing buildings, and built extra lodgings and offices to provide for the Council and court officials, justices and household staff, to increase their comfort both while at work and leisure. The council chamber and private apartments received his greatest attention. New lead was provided for the roof, stairs were repaired or newly built, and large, stone mullioned windows were inserted in the council chamber and many other rooms, which greatly increased the light.

The 'great parlour' in the private apartments was modernised with the addition of wooden wall panelling, a new floor and a very large oriel window on the north side, looking out across the Teme valley towards Bromfield. Accounts survive for the 1570s when Sir Henry and his family were largely resident in Ludlow, illustrating how richly furnished these apartments were. Among the items purchased for Ludlow were Flemish tapestry wall hangings, 'turkey work' embroidered cushions and chairs, and a bed of state with rich hangings embroidered with coats of arms and garlands worked in silver, gold and coloured silks threads. Sir Henry also commissioned a portrait of himself and 'other noblemen' to adorn the walls of the apartments.[viii]

In 1574 work on remodelling the chapel was completed (see Chapter 2).

While the castle would have had sundials for timekeeping, it would seem that it lacked a clock. In May 1577 Sir Henry, who was serving in Ireland at the time, instructed his

Interior of the first-floor Council Chamber showing one of the large and fair windows added by Sir Henry and the doorway into the passage leading to the Chapel

deputy Sir Andrew Corbett to provide a clock, 'being a thing most necessary'. From an illustration drawn by Dineley in 1684 it appears that this clock may have been placed in the chapel, directly above the main entrance. Thomas Higges, who also took care of the clock in the church, was employed to look after it at an annual salary of 13s 4d (after a complaint from Higges, this was later raised to £1).[ix]

The Great Hall remained in the grand medieval style, having an open, central hearth with a louvre in the ceiling directly above for smoke to escape. During the Christmas celebrations in 1580, when the hall would have been filled with people feasting and celebrating, a fire broke out which prompted the installation of a proper fireplace and chimney for better safety, as well as 'for the better avoiding of smoke and the clean keeping of the house'.[x] The large, traceried window in the middle of the façade overlooking the inner bailey was blocked up, and a fireplace with an elaborate double flue constructed in its place.

Accommodation for the Judges, completed in 1581

The following year, 1581, saw the completion of a large building to provide accommodation and offices for the justices when attending the courts. It is on the south side of the inner bailey beside the keep and overlooking the outer bailey, and is in fine Tudor style with large windows and a gabled roof. This building was probably the last major work done by Sir Henry.

## Gardens and Leisure

While Ludlow Castle was predominantly a workplace for the Council in the Marches of Wales it was also a residence principally for the President and his household – and also, at times, members of the Council when in attendance. Sir Henry often travelled with his wife and children, and while he modernised their apartments he also improved the castle's facilities for leisure and recreation.

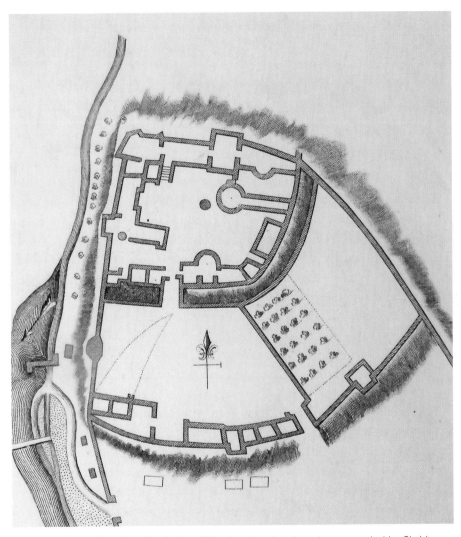

Stukeley's plan of Ludlow Castle in c.1721, showing the chapel as extended by Sir Henry Sidney and the gardens laid out to an orchard and bowling green.
© *Shropshire Council, Shropshire Museums*

Sir Henry had a keen interest in garden design. He would have known the great gardens created by Henry VIII at Hampton Court, and may have advised his brother-in-law, Robert Dudley, on the design of the elaborate and costly garden created at Kenilworth Castle for the visit of Elizabeth I and her household in 1576.[xi] In the 1560s he undertook an ambitious remodelling of the garden at his family home, Penshurst Place in Kent. This involved considerable earthworks to create a large level area around the house, which he filled with formal beds, walls and terraces. It was probably after this, in the early 1570s, that Sir Henry turned his attention to the garden at Ludlow Castle which was on the east side of the outer bailey to the right of the castle entrance.

By 1560 someone was already regularly employed to look after the castle garden. The layout and extent of the garden are unknown, though it may have included a bowling green, since there are references to playing bowls in the castle from this time.[xii] It is not known if the planting and layout of the garden were changed by Sir Henry, but he did refurbish existing garden buildings and provide new garden seats. He also created a new garden feature outside the castle wall on the north side, consisting of, 'a large walk enclosed with pale and timber', and containing, 'a fair and large seate (...) with a house over the same' (a sort of gazebo from which one could enjoy views across the Teme and Corve valley).[xiii] This feature may have been influenced by 'The Pleasance' at Kenilworth Castle, which was divided from the main garden by a wall, and contained a building and large area for recreation – though all on a much grander scale. Looking at the terrain outside the castle today it is difficult to see where a 'large walk' might have been, but it is possible that it led out from a door in the north wall of the garden.

The gardener at Ludlow Castle was also responsible for looking after the area reserved for 'tennis plaie'. This was probably an open, grassed area, but Sir Henry upgraded it by providing, 'a fair tennis court in the castle paving it with free stone' suitable for playing Real Tennis, the game beloved and popularised by Henry VIII. The court was walled, and paved with low, wooden, roofed galleries on two sides, and would have provided sport for all. It was built within the garden against the castle wall, immediately to the right of the main entrance (where the café and castle ticket office are now).

There were other opportunities for sport outside the castle. Access to royal forests and the supply of venison was strictly controlled. On Sir Henry's appointment in 1560, Elizabeth I sent instructions to all her forest keepers that the Council was to be allowed a total of 12 deer per annum, to

Entrance to the inner bailey with inscription over the gate celebrating the completion of Sir Henry's work on the castle in 1581

be provided from any of the royal forests or chases within Wales and the English counties on its border. As a special concession, the President and other Council members were permitted, if they wished, to hunt for these deer themselves. Since the nearest royal forest was at Bringewood just outside the town it is likely they availed themselves of this privilege from time to time. At other times they would have hunted with hawks and dogs in other woods and parks in the locality. A falconer was employed, and hoods and bells supplied for the hawks. New kennels were built at the castle for the greyhounds and dogs in 1574, at a time when Sir Henry and his family were resident for long periods. The children were also regularly provided with bows and arrows and gloves, and may have joined in the sport.[xiv]

The work on the castle during Sir Henry's presidency was significant and extensive, and was also typical of the energy and desire he displayed throughout his career to improve and aggrandise all with which he was

associated. Over the entrance to the inner bailey there is a fine, stone carving containing the arms of Elizabeth I, with those of Sir Henry underneath. Both inscriptions record the date of completion, 1581, but under Sir Henry's arms there is also a rather poignant inscription in Latin: **hominibus ingratis loquimini lapides**. When Sir Henry was Lord Deputy of Ireland he also oversaw significant repairs to Dublin Castle in the 1560s, which were marked by a stone inscription similarly placed over the inner entrance. This plaque contained a verse in praise of Sir Henry, saying that the stones, due to their endurance, would speak of his fame forever.[xv] By 1581, however, Sir Henry was out of favour and had little influence at Court, which he

The stone-carved arms over the entrance to the inner bailey

bitterly resented. So, as at Dublin, the buildings were used as a metaphor of Sir Henry's true worth, the inscription in Latin at Ludlow declaring, 'To ungrateful men these stones do speak'.

# 7. The Sidney Family and Castle and Town Life

THROUGHOUT THE YEARS that Sir Henry Sidney was Lord President of the Council in the Marches of Wales, and Lord Deputy of Ireland, his wife, Mary, and family often travelled with him and thus were occasionally resident in Ludlow Castle. Henry and Mary had seven children: three sons and four daughters. Only one of their daughters, Mary, survived into adulthood. Although all three sons survived their father, both Philip and Thomas died as young adults, leaving only the middle son, Robert, to inherit the family estates and enjoy a long life. In James I's reign Robert also gained what had so sorely eluded his father: a title. In 1603 he was made Baron Sidney of Penshurst: then, in 1605, Viscount L'Isle, and finally, in 1618, Earl of Leicester, the lapsed title of his uncle and namesake, Robert Dudley.

Sir Henry's eldest and most celebrated child was Philip. He was a poet, scholar and soldier who became one of the most admired of Queen Elizabeth's courtiers, regarded by many as the perfect example of the Renaissance gentleman. He was one of the most influential literary figures of the Elizabethan age, particularly noted for his romantic poetry and prose harking back to the medieval ideals of chivalry and courtly love, which won him considerable fame in both Britain and Europe. He died in 1586 at the age of just 31, only a few months after his father, as a result of a leg wound sustained in the Battle of Zutphen in Holland. Such was Philip's celebrity that he was granted the exceptional honour of a state funeral and was buried in St Paul's Cathedral.

Philip was five years old when his father became Lord President of the Council in the Marches of Wales, in 1560. His eldest sister, Margaret, had died in infancy, and his surviving sister, Elizabeth, was just a baby. Another sister, Mary, was born in the following year at the President's

Portrait of Philip and Robert Sidney, c.1573 (artist unknown).
© *Shropshire Council, Shropshire Museums*

house at Tickenhill, near Bewdley. Mary was later to marry Henry, Earl of Pembroke, and became her brother's literary executor, publishing and promoting his work, while also being an admired author in her own right. Her husband succeeded her father as Lord President, so her association with Ludlow Castle was lifelong.

After Sir Henry returned from Ireland in 1571 his wife and children spent prolonged periods at Ludlow. By this time Elizabeth had died, aged eight, in Ireland, and Philip, who had attended Shrewsbury School in the 1560s, was now studying at Oxford and engaged at Court. So, the children who accompanied their parents in Ludlow were Mary (b.1561), Robert (b.1563), Ambrosia (b.1566) and Thomas (b.1569).

The family spent most of 1573–74 in Ludlow, at the time the chapel was being rebuilt. Household accounts for these years give a flavour of life for the family in the castle. Apart from clothes and education (Simon Thorneton, the Ludlow schoolmaster, was tutor to the children) much of the expenditure was on entertainment. Players visited at Christmas and Easter, and performed the popular story of Robin Hood especially for the children. Musicians were included in the household and, dressed in livery clothes, would have played in the Great Hall and private apartments. Special payments were made to minstrels and singers who performed for the children on May Day morning and Midsummer's Day. The children were often entertained by a juggler called Stony, and Sir Henry employed a jester, Will Sheynton, who, suitably attired in motley, entertained children and adults alike. One other very large item of expenditure in these years was for apothecary bills. Ambrosia was increasingly unwell and in the care of Dr Guilio Borgarucci, who was physician to the royal household. Despite the use of a diverse range of remedies, – including wormwood, sarsaparilla, camomile and *cardus benedictus* – Ambrosia died, aged nine, at the castle in February 1575, and was buried in St Laurence's church.[i]

Although much of the Sidney family's personal expenditure was principally through London merchants, Ludlow tradesmen benefited as well. A huge sum was spent annually on clothing for the family, equivalent of several thousand pounds in today's money. Robert Wright, a Ludlow tailor, made clothing for both Sir Henry and the children, and livery clothes made of frieze (a woollen cloth) for 55 of Sir Henry's retainers. A Ludlow mercer, Mr Crowther, provided green silk and taffeta, russet fustian, and gold and silver trimmings for a suit of clothes for Robert.[ii] Sir Henry regularly used a Ludlow goldsmith, Andrew Sonnybank, for a wide variety of

A   When thus this thrice renowmed Knight, hath captiue made and thrall,
The furious force of franticke foes, and troupe of rebells all,
When he by marshall feates of armes, hath nobly them subdude,
To Princes Dome: whose heauy wrath, their treasons haue renewde,
When he their glory and their pride, hath trampled in the dust,
And brought to naught which doe pursue, the bloudy rebells lust:

60

O Sydney worthy of tryple re-
nowne,
For plagyng the traytours that
troubled the crowne. 1581.

by conquest thus hath wonne, the honour of the field,
e vnto our Soueraygnes Courte, report thereof doth yeld
nclude when honor braue, his trauells to requight
the him with eternall fame, meete for so great a knight
these thinges are done and past, then doth he backe reuart
yn:where he is receiued, with ioy on euery parte.

Sir Henry being greeted by Dublin City Council outside the city gates, from *The Image of Irelande*, by John Derrick (London, 1581). He is accompanied by an attendant carrying the sword of state, a sergeant at arms with his mace of office, a herald, men in livery and trumpeters. Sir Henry would have been greeted on arrival at Ludlow in a similar way.
© *Edinburgh University Library*

work: engraving arms on silverware, making silver and gilt tankards and serving dishes, and making and mending jewellery. Sonnybank had had a lucky escape in 1569 when he was convicted for shooting and killing Thomas Tushingham, by misadventure, while practising archery at the town butts (which were on the Linney below the castle). He received a pardon from the Queen after six months' incarceration. One wonders whether Sir Henry had a hand in his pardon.[iii]

The Council in the Marches of Wales brought not only business but also prestige to Ludlow, and the town council were at pains to foster good relations through the regular giving of gifts. On the arrival of the Lord President, the town council would ride out dressed in their 'best attire', to the outskirts of the town at Rocks Green, Overton or Old Field at Bromfield to greet him. Here, they would present him with an ox, a fat boar or a hogshead of muscatel wine, and escort him into town.[iv]

Regular gifts of wine, claret, salmon, fresh fish and sugar were sent to the President, and occasionally to other Council members, and to the judges when holding their courts. In March 1581 a gallon of wine was sent daily to the castle for Sir Henry for a full week after his arrival. At Christmas, the town council would provide an ox and gifts of money to the household staff in the castle, from the butler and cook to the fire maker and kitchen boys, and in return the council would receive a gift of venison. The bailiffs and councillors with their wives would sometimes be entertained at the castle. Regular banquets would be held at the town council's premises, the New House (which stood near to where the Buttercross now is), for a variety of castle residents: the president's men, senior officials and their wives, but rarely for the President himself. When Mary Sidney joined her husband in Ludlow in September 1582 the town council sent to the castle the ingredients for a banquet upon her arrival: capons, turkeys, chickens, pigeons, rabbits, sugar and marmalade, cakes, and wafers, cheeses, comfits, filberts, damsons, plums, pears, apples – and to drink: sacke, wine and claret.[v]

At times the castle couldn't accommodate all the people attending the President, and the town was expected to provide the extra beds and bedding needed. In order to meet the expenses of the gifts (an ox would cost £10) and bed-hire a levy was raised from the householders within the town walls, and those who refused to pay were duly punished. So, perhaps for some of Ludlow's inhabitants the presence of the Council was a mixed blessing.[vi]

# 8. The Death and Heraldic Funeral of Sir Henry Sidney

I N 1586, AFTER spending Easter in Ludlow, Sir Henry moved to Tickenhill, near Bewdley, an official residence of the Lord President and one much favoured by him. Towards the end of April he left Tickenhill and travelled by barge along the Severn to Worcester where he was taken ill. It was thought he had caught a chill on the water. He was tended in the Bishop's Palace by an elderly servant, Robert Barbor (alias Griffith), one of the *pursuivants* or messengers of the Council. Sir Henry Sidney died there a week later on 5 May 1586.[i]

Robert Commander, chaplain to the President and the Council, gives an account of his death, his funeral procession from Worcester to his family home, Penshurst in Kent, and his burial there:[ii]

> *H*e died in the palace of the Bishop of Worcester upon Thursday a quarter & half quarter of an hour after three of the clock [22 minutes past three] in the morning being the 5th of May, AD 1586. His body was removed out of the said palace into the cathedral church of Worcester where his bowels were interred in the Dean's chapel, where the body of Sir Rice ap Thomas was also interred, over against Prince Arthur's chapel on the same 5th day of May at about 8 o'clock. His heart was buried at Ludlow by [beside] his daughter Ambrosia Sydney with great solemnity & a funeral sermon by Mr John Buste, parson of that Town.

St Laurence's burial register records that Sir Henry's heart was buried in the chancel on 8 May, where it was placed either within or close to Ambrosia's tomb. The service would have been conducted with due ceremony, perhaps attended by members and officials of the Council, but certainly by the Aldermen and Town Councillors, who also paid the costs of the burial of 28s 8d.[iii] John Bust, who conducted the service, had been tutor to Robert Sidney, Sir Henry's second son. Bust was appointed Rector of Ludlow in 1580, probably through Sir Henry's patronage, but had quite a turbulent career, falling out with his parishioners and being accused of neglect of duty. He was not forgotten by his pupil, Robert, who gave Bust the living of Penshurst in 1596, where he remained its rector for the rest of his life.

Sir Henry's body remained in Worcester for six weeks while, by the Queen's instructions, William Dethick, Garter King of Arms, made arrangements for Sir Henry's funeral, which was to be conducted with all the heraldic ceremony befitting a Knight of the Garter. A funeral carriage, heraldic banners and shields had to be made, and accommodation for all those accompanying the body to Penshurst (and their horses) arranged at each stopping place.[iv]

A large party assembled in Worcester on the evening of 14 June and attended a funeral service in the Cathedral, with a sermon delivered by Dr Godfrey Goldsbrough, one of the cathedral canons, followed by a 'solemn dinner'. The funeral cortège set off from Worcester the next morning, led by 50 poor men from the city dressed in black gowns, who accompanied the corpse on foot to the city boundary. All the church bells in the city rang out a funeral toll as the carriage, with 140 horsemen dressed in black, passed by. The poor men were followed by 40 mounted yeoman, then by a trumpeter and a standard-bearer carrying a large banner decorated with the cross of St George, the Sidney family motto (*Quo Fata Vocant*) and heraldic supporters, a chained porcupine and crowned lion. Behind them came 24 gentlemen in black cloaks, including Robert Commander and another chaplain. Next came the group accompanying the corpse, led by Nicholas Dethick, Windsor Herald, followed by John Rudyard carrying the Great Banner of Sir Henry's arms. Beside Rudyard was John Devawe, Sergeant at Arms of the Council in the Marches of Wales, carrying his silver gilt mace of office. Then came the carriage with Sir Henry's coffin, led by William Dethick, Garter King of Arms. Both heralds wore hooded black coats under their colourful heraldic coats of office. The carriage was covered in black velvet decorated with the heraldic devices of Sir Henry, and flanked by four horsemen carrying banners of the Sidney arms. Behind the carriage Sir Henry's horse was led by Christopher Wrenne, his Master of Horse. There then followed some members of both the Council in the Marches of Wales and Ludlow's town council – and, at the rear, the servants of all those taking part.

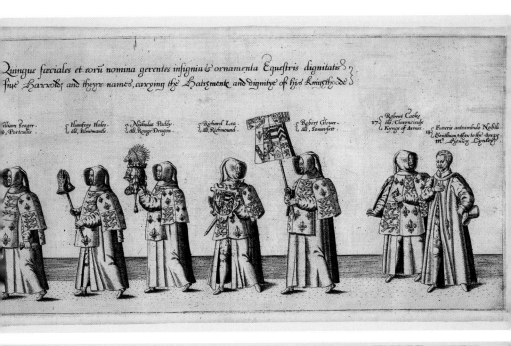

Quinque fæciales et eoru nomina gerentes insignia & ornamenta Equestris dignitatis
siue Harrolds and theyr names, carrying the Hatzments and dignitye of his Knighthoode

...illiam Seager .
& ..., Portcullis .

& Humfrey Hales .
& als, Blewmantle .

& Nicholas Paddy .
& als, Rouge Dragon .

& Richard Lea .
& als, Richmound .

& Robert Glouer .
& als, Somersett .

17 & Robert Cooke
& als, Clarencieuxe
& Kynge of Armes .

18 & Funeris anteambulo Nobili
& Gentilman assisto to the corpse
Mr Henry Lynley .

Corpus Velutacro contectu peristromate et elatu a
16 ipsius famulis · Veluti partes angulares Supportata
a 4 nobilibus amicitia & beneuolentia ipsi coniunctissimis ·
Aplustra insignium, Subuecta ʼa 4 consanguineis ·

19

The corps was couered wth veluet and caryed by 14
of his yomen · The corners of the Paull wexe
houlden by 4 Gentlmen his deere louinge freindz
The Banrolls wexe caryed by 4 of his neer kynredd

6

Mr Hen: Sidney .

Mr Tho: Dudley .

Mr Edw: Wootto .

Mr Edm: Walsingham .

Mr Edm: Packenham .

Mr Foulke Gryuell .

Mr Edwʼ Dyer .

Mr Wil: Sidney .

Sir Philip Sidney's state funeral, 1587. Heralds carry the funerary objects, including helm with crest and mantle, shield and sword and armorial coat. The coffin is accompanied by family mourners carrying banners of arms. © *by permission of the Folger Shakespeare Library*

Leaving Worcester, the cortège travelled to Penshurst, stopping overnight at Evesham, Chipping Norton, Oxford, High Wycombe, Kingston upon Thames and Croydon on the way. In each village or town they passed through the church bells tolled and people lined the route to view the spectacle. Throughout the journey gifts of money were given to the bell ringers, and alms were distributed to the poor (which, at Oxford, included some poor scholars).

In Penshurst church a hearse was made, which Commander describes as, 'a very stately hearse enrailed about and set full of banners & pencells & escutcheons of arms both of his own and also of the Lady Mary Sydney his wife, daughter to John Duke of Northumberland.' This hearse was a low, wooden enclosure within which the coffin was placed during the service, and about which chief mourners might sit. Its frame and floor were completely covered in black velvet fringed in silk and taffeta and decorated with heraldic shields. Posts or metal brackets were fixed to the frame to display the heraldic banners and funerary objects.

On arrival at Penshurst on 21 June, Sir Henry's coffin was taken from the house to the church in formal procession with a large company of mourners all dressed in black cloaks accompanied by Windsor and Chester Heralds and Garter King of Arms, carrying the funerary objects: an armorial coat, a steel gilt helm, a crest carved in wood and gilded with a mantle of velvet decorated with knobs and tassels attached, a gilt sword with velvet scabbard and a target or shield of arms.

Robert Commander lists the chief mourners in the procession as:

> Sir William Fitzwilliams knight, his brother in law, as chief mourner & some time Lord deputy of Ireland as now he is, & by the Earl of Huntington, his brother in law, and by the Earl of Pembroke, his son in law, Sir Henry Harrington & Sir Henry Bagnoll, knights, Jacques Wingfield Esq., Master of her Majesty's ordnance in Ireland, Mr Wootton Esq., Mr Mountacute Esq., & of the Council of the Marches of Wales, Mr Fabian Phillipps, Robert Towneshed & Henry Towneshed Esq with diverse other gents of his kindred & gentlemen of worship of Kent & elsewhere. Also the Sergeant at Arms attendant at her majesty's Council in the Marches, Mr Jon Devawe, & all the officers of the [Ludlow] household.

Sir William Fitzwilliams was acting as chief mourner in the absence of Sir Henry's eldest son, Sir Philip Sidney.

Sir Henry was then interred in his father's chapel. He was laid to rest beside the grave of John Dudley, Earl of Warwick, his brother-in-law, who had died at Penshurst shortly after his release from prison in 1554. The service was conducted by Robert Commander and the funeral sermon was given by Revd Dr Thomas White, who was vicar of St Dunstan-in-the-West, London, and a noted preacher.

The service in the church did not entirely go to plan, in that it was somewhat marred by a brawl in which William Dethick, the Garter King of Arms, 'beat the minister in his church' (though whether Dr White or Robert Commander, or one of the other two chaplains in attendance, is not recorded). Dethick had recently been appointed Garter King of Arms, a position his father had also held. He was considered a skilful and experienced herald, but was already noted for his aggressive behaviour and was known to be not above underhand dealing and corrupt practices. In 1603 a royal commission reported on his actions and character, and cited the attack on the minister at this funeral as an example of his violence. He was duly removed from office.[v]

Robert Commander concludes his account:

> After he was interred & all the obsequies & funeral Sermon done, there was made a very great Funeral dinner in this knight's house for their estate and all others that came thither at that time & more money was then given to the people. So[he was] interred by Mr Robert Commander, the chaplain of the household in Wales, where the said Noble knight had governed by the space of 26 years and an half to the glory of Almighty God, the honour of his Prince & the profit & welfare of the Commonwealths of England and Ireland etc.

In his will, written five years earlier, Sir Henry specified that his funeral and burial costs should be no more than £1,000. In the event, with the cost of the draper's bill for black velvet cloth for the hearse and mourners' clothes being over £700 alone, the total was £1,570 19s 7d. This equates to around £320,000 in 2019, a very considerable amount. Sir Henry also specified that a monument to him be erected in Penshurst Church, but it does not appear that this was ever carried out.

### Sir Henry Sidney's Heart Burial

When Sir Henry's heart was buried at Ludlow it was encased in a small lead container or 'heart case' with his arms cast on the lid in the form of a pheon encircled by a garter. The outside of the container was inscribed with:

## HER ♥ LITH ♥ THE ♥ HARTE ♥ OF ♥ SYR ♥ HENRYE ♥ SYDNY ♥ L ♥ P ♥ ANNO ♥ DMNI ♥ 1586

The practice of burying the heart, separately to the body, was an ancient one. Since it is associated with the soul and affections, the heart was often buried in a place special to the deceased. The practice continued to be popular among noble and royal families in the mid-sixteenth century. Both Henry VIII and Edward VI had their hearts buried separately.

Sir Henry's heart case has a curious history. At some unknown date it was removed from the church, possibly at the time of the church reordering in the 1750s, and seems to have come into the possession of Revd Dr George Coningsby, rector of Penscombe and Bodenham. He was a great collector of antiquities, who died in 1766, a very wealthy man. Apart from his collection and property bequeathed to a number of people, he left his considerable library to Balliol College, Oxford, with a gift of £300 to pay two Fellows to catalogue the books. One of the executors of his will was his 'friend Thomas Harris of Leominster, attorney', into whose possession the heart case then passed. When Harris sold his house in Leominster he seems to have left the object behind for the new owner, Edward Coleman. He, in turn, sold it to Samuel Nicholas, postmaster of Leominster, in August 1794.[vi] What happened thereafter is not known, but the heart case was acquired by the British Museum at an unknown date and is on permanent display there.

The lead heart case with engraved inscription in which Sir Henry Sidney's heart was buried in St Laurence's, Ludlow, 1586. The lid is cast with the *pheon* of Sir Henry Sidney, encircled with the Garter and with the initials 'HS' above the shield, and the letters 'LP' on each side of the shield. *British Museum PET OA.4280* © *Trustees of the British Museum*

# 9. The Display of Heraldry

I N 1573, WHEN Sir Henry Sidney commissioned 46 coats of arms to be displayed in the newly completed chancel of the Chapel of St Mary Magdalene in Ludlow Castle, he was following the fashion for heraldic display. The number and significance of the gentry had increased in the Tudor period. This created an interest amongst new and old families for researching their genealogy, and so confirming their status in society. In response to this demand, the College of Arms, which had been founded earlier by charter by Richard III in 1484, was incorporated as a separate institution in July 1555. The principal herald was Garter King of Arms, who had overall jurisdiction over England, Wales and Ireland. There were also two provincial Kings of Arms: Norroy, who dealt with arms north of the Trent, and Clarenceux, south of the Trent. In addition there were lesser officers known as heralds and pursuivants. The heralds licensed arms and were tasked with both investigating and authenticating a family's pedigree and design of arms. They did this by sending two or three heralds to visit each county to survey all those with claims to bear arms. The heralds produced an official pedigree and coat of arms for each family, with these recorded in visitation books which were kept by the College of Arms. This all fed into a fashion for the display of arms in stone, glass and paint, which provided a visual record of an individual's lineage and personal status for all to see and take note. In 1569 there was a visitation of Shropshire conducted by the herald Robert Cooke, Clarenceux King of Arms, who had advised Sir Henry on his pedigree and arms.

Sir Henry Sidney was typical of this new class, coming from a fairly modest landowning county family which had accrued lands and honours through serving the Tudor monarchs. From an early age, Sir Henry's place at the heart of Henry VIII's court and his close companionship with the king's

Extract from the pedigree roll of Sir Philip Sidney, commissioned by Sir Henry from the herald Robert Cooke, Clarenceux King of Arms, c.1580. Sir Henry and Mary Sidney's arms are in the centre joined by a red circle with his four sisters on either side. Beneath are the arms of Sir Philip and his sister, Mary Herbert, Countess of Pembroke. Other arms are of relatives in the Fitzwilliam, Harrington, Dormer and Radcliffe families.

*Sir Philip Sidney pedigree roll, MS. Eng. b. 2152(R) © Bodleian Library, University of Oxford*

son, later Edward VI, instilled in Sir Henry a sense of entitlement and worth. This resulted not only in an expectation of high honours and titles but also a desire to establish a suitably worthy pedigree which could be displayed on his coat of arms. Sidney tasked the herald, Robert Cooke, Clarenceux King of Arms, to research a pedigree from the family papers. He duly provided a lineage back to a fictitious Sir William Sidnei, Chamberlain to Henry II – about 150 years earlier than any lineage supported by the documents. Sir Henry had married well. His wife was Lady Mary, eldest daughter of John Dudley, 1st Duke of Northumberland who, at the time of their marriage, was the most powerful courtier in the land. Lady Mary was able to display an impressive collection of quarterings from her father. It is certainly not easy to establish the provenance of some of the quarterings on Sir Henry's arms, and it appears that Cooke ignored, or at least bent, the rules to satisfy Sir Henry's ego.

Although the display of arms was fashionable, Sir Henry seems to have taken this to excess. Not only did he erect arms at his residences, he displayed arms on every public project with which he was involved. As Lord Deputy of Ireland, his arms were displayed on new building work at Dublin Castle. They were also to be found on building projects across the country with examples surviving from Kinsale, County Cork, Athlone, Westmeath and Roscommon, and Johnstownbridge, County Clare. Apart from self-promotion these arms, often displayed in conjunction with the royal arms, would also have served as propaganda signalling the expanding control of royal government over Irish clans.

Similarly, as Lord President of the Council in the Marches of Wales, Sir Henry erected arms in buildings throughout Ludlow Castle and on public projects in Ludlow and Shrewsbury.

### Display of Patrons Arms

Approaching Ludlow Castle in 1581, one would have seen, on the gatehouse of the inner bailey, a brightly-painted display of heraldry between fluted columns with Ionic capitals. The two Latin inscriptions tell us that it was created in 1581.

Beneath the royal arms and the major Latin inscription, there are four Latin words: HOMINIBUS INGRATIS LOQUIMINI LAPIDES ['To ungrateful men these stones do speak'.] The inscription thus records both the completion of his scheme of works and possibly Sir Henry's disillusionment at the end of his career.

At the top the Tudor royal arms are supported by the English lion and Welsh dragon. Sir Henry's arms are below. The two shields are set in a curious architectural frame which has an arch above the royal arms to contain the crown, and at the top of each side are two small triangular frames, each

Arms over Ludlow Castle Gate drawn by William Mytton, c.1735. The inscriptions read:
ANNO DOMINI MILLESIMO QUINGENTESIMO OCTAGESIMO CO[M]PLETO, ANNO REGNI ILLUSTRISSIME AC
SERENISSIMAE REGINAE ELIZABETHAE VICESIMO TERTIO CURRENTE, 1581 [*Completed in the year of
our Lord fifteen hundred and eighty, in the twenty-third year of the reign of our illustrious and
serene Queen Elizabeth, 1581*]; and below: HOMINIBUS IN GRATIS LOQUIMINI LAPIDES. ANNO REGNI
ELIZABETHAE 23 [*To ungrateful men these stones do speak. In the 23rd year of Queen Elizabeth*].
THE 22ND YEAR CO[M]PLET OF THE PRESIDENCY OF SIR HENRY SIDNEY, KNIGHT OF THE MOST NOBLE
ORDER OF THE GARTER ETC 1581.

MYT/3/546 © Cadbury Research Library, Special Collections, University of Birmingham

containing a royal badge. These are the fleur-de-lys and the rose on a crown used from the reign of Edward III, and perhaps most commonly employed by Henry VIII (who possessed, for example, a silver bowl and cover with a crown on top, garnished with crowns of gold, and red and white roses, which passed to Elizabeth I). These arms and badges indicate the royal ownership of the castle, while the lower arms indicate Sir Henry's role as President of the Council in the Marches. Surmounted by his crest of a porcupine, and with supporters, the shield is quartered Sidney and an unknown coat.

The arms displayed on the gatehouse comprise those both of Sidney and the royal arms representing the President, appointed by the Queen, and his feudal superior or patron. Similar displays occur lower in the social hierarchy. For instance, a house in King Street, Ludlow (which was rebuilt for Thomas Hankey, one of Sir Henry's servants and steward of the Council at Ludlow), contained the arms of Sir Henry Sidney displayed over a fireplace.[i] Another surviving example in the Marches of the display of a patron's arms is on the gatehouse of Trevalyn Hall, in Denbighshire, built in 1576 by Sir John Trevor, a member of the cadet branch of the Trevor family. The entrance to the house was decorated with the arms of his patron, Thomas Sackville, Lord Buckhurst, later Earl of Dorset (1536–1608). The display over the entrance at Trevalyn is similar to that on the tomb of Richard Harford, at Bosbury, Herefordshire, made by John Gildon in 1578. This tomb carries the arms of his patron, William Paulet, 1st Marquess of Winchester (d.1572).

In a similar way, Sir Henry's arms in Beaumaris parish church, Anglesey, adorn the tomb of his secretary, William Thwaites, who died in 1566. When Sir Henry was appointed Lord Deputy of Ireland in 1565, he found himself stranded on the Welsh coast for two months waiting for the winds to be favourable for the sea crossing. Two attempts to send horses, wine, furniture and baggage over resulted in serious or total loss before the weather changed, and Sir Henry and his wife successfully reached Dublin in early January. By this time William Thwaites was seriously ill and was left behind on Anglesey where he died. Sir Henry was greatly affected by his death, and ensured that he took care of his widow, providing her with a pension and, upon her death in 1572, taking over the wardship of their daughter, Ursula.[ii]

SIR HENRY AND THE HERALDRY OF OFFICE

Among Mytton's manuscripts there is a drawing representing a structure at the upper end of the Council Chamber of the castle, in the solar wing from which steps led to the chapel. This strange structure is of uncertain use but may have represented a canopy for Sir Henry's seat as President. In front of a centre window were the royal arms and supporters. There were four pilasters: two bearing the letters 'E' and 'R', while the outermost bore the Tudor rose and the portcullis. Here the initials 'E' and 'R' (for 'Elizabeth Regina') are used in addition to the royal arms combined with the two badges. The portcullis is used instead of the fleur-de-lys (as used on the gatehouse). This badge, originating in the Beaufort family, came to the royal family through Margaret Beaufort, mother of Henry VII.

Between the pilasters, on the left, were the arms of France and the arms of North Wales, both crowned. Between the pilasters, on the right, were the arms of Ireland and of South Wales, also crowned. The panelling of the upper part, on which the shields of France and Ireland are placed, was painted red, and the lower part, beneath the other shields, was blue. These represent the possessions of the English monarchy. Below the pilasters was a moulding and cornice, and beneath this the arms of Sidney in the centre with his family

The canopy over the President's chair in the council chamber decorated with the arms of Queen Elizabeth I, drawn by William Mytton, c.1735.
*MYT/3/626 © Cadbury Research Library, Special Collections, University of Birmingham*

badges, the *pheon* representing Sidney and the ragged staff representing Warwick. The collection of shields expressed not so much Sir Henry's personal power as that of the monarchy over the areas the Council and the President (or Viceroy) had authority. The porcupine, the family or personal crest, of Sir Henry does not appear.

Another official item that had the royal arms engraved upon it was the seal of the Council (*see p. 45*). The only seal matrix to survive is the final matrix engraved in 1660 (a seal matrix is the metal object, engraved in intaglio, used for impressing the design into wax on or attached to documents). A new seal matrix would usually be made for each monarch, so the one used in the time of Sir Henry was destroyed on the death of Elizabeth I and a new one created for James I. This, in turn, was destroyed in the Civil War.

The other ceremonial object associated with the Council was the sword of state, recorded in a drawing by William Mytton, which survives in the collections of the National Trust at Powis Castle, Montgomeryshire. The shape and design suggest a fifteenth-century date. It may have been carried in procession before Arthur, son of Henry VII and Prince of Wales; or one of the earlier Yorkist Princes – either Edward, son of Edward IV, or Edward, son of Richard III (who died in 1484). Certainly, one of these two earlier Princes of Wales possessed a ceremonial sword for the Earldom of Chester, which is now in the British Museum (*reg. no. SLAntiq.364*). This bears the arms of the Princes of Wales, the ancient Kingdom of North Wales (according to the English heralds) and the Duchy of Cornwall on one side, and on the other side the Earldom of March, the Earldom of Chester, and a damaged and an unidentified coat (*Argent a chief azure*).

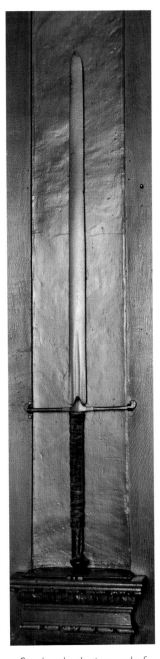

Steel and velvet sword of state of the Council in the Marches of Wales, late fifteenth-century, on display in Powis Castle.
*Photo © Jeremy Hall*

It is difficult to find a display of arms associated with the Council of the North, created by Henry VIII as a partner organisation to the Council in the Marches. At the King's Manor, York, the site of the Council of the North in the sixteenth century, there are royal arms over the entrances, but these were put up by Lord Sheffield in the early seventeenth century (though there were probably earlier examples).

One of the best contemporary displays associated with the Council of the North survives in the great chamber at Gilling Castle, Yorkshire. Here, there are three large windows, commissioned by Sir William Fairfax, a member of the Council of the North from 1577 to his death in 1597. They show shields of the Fairfax family. One panel is signed by Baernard Dininckhoff, a Bohemian glass painter who had settled at York, and is dated 1585. The royal arms are set in the most important place, with the Fairfax arms, slightly larger, below them. Around the walls a forest of 22 painted trees are hung with the shields of 400 Yorkshire gentry. Alas, no armorial or other sixteenth-century glass survives at Ludlow; however, in 1574–75, Sir Henry did arrange the purchase of glass with arms 'of my lord's pedigree', probably for Penshurst.

## Sir Henry and Garden Heraldry

Sir Henry put up the royal arms elsewhere in the castle, notably on the fountain that he created to bring fresh water into the castle and town from the countryside to the west of Ludlow. This displayed the arms of Elizabeth I and other unknown arms. Almost certainly Sir Henry's arms would have been there, and possibly those of Fox. Sir William St John Hope (who excavated Ludlow Castle in the early twentieth century) found the footings for the fountain in the bailey midway between the kitchen and the chapel. Raised on an octagonal step, circular within, the fountain would have provided a centrepiece for the inner courtyard or garden. Fountains as garden features with heraldic display may have been introduced into England from Italy or France. The fountain at Wilton House, Wiltshire includes a stone with the Sidney porcupine carved on it. This is a survival from the earlier fountain constructed after 1577 when Mary married Henry Herbert, 2nd Earl of Pembroke (who was to succeed Sir Henry as President in 1586). Between 1615 and 1621, Mary (later the Dowager Countess of Pembroke) was to build a house at Houghton Conquest, Bedfordshire, the ruins of which still display Dudley/ Sidney badges on the exterior.

A notable surviving example of garden heraldry is the frontispiece for the garden seat made for Queen Elizabeth when she visited Kenilworth, Warwickshire (the seat of Robert Dudley) in 1575. It has Doric pilasters and shell-headed alcoves; however, instead of the usual roundels and ox heads in the metopes (the rectangular elements filling the spaces between triglyphs in a Doric frieze), there is the Earl of Leicester's ragged staff (for Warwick) and cinquefoils (for the Beaumonts, Earls of Leicester).

## HERALDRY IN CHURCHES

In churches the royal arms were displayed as a sign of loyalty, and to represent the headship of the Church by the monarch, after King Henry VIII had declared himself Supreme Head of the Church of England in 1531. The title was repeated in the Act of Supremacy in 1534, and reaffirmed by Elizabeth's Act of Supremacy of 1559, through which she was given the title of Governor of the Church of England. The royal arms were often set up in parish churches above the rood beam at the entrance to the chancel, in place of the Crucifixion with the Virgin Mary and St John – 'In place of the cross, they put up the Arms of the King of England', in the words of the Catholic priest and polemicist, Nicholas Sander (1530–81). The royal arms signalled the royal control of the Church. Examples exist in the churches of Rushbrooke, Suffolk, (Henry VIII), Westerham, Kent, (Edward VI), and Lower Quinton, Gloucestershire, and Greens Norton, Northants, (both Elizabeth I). A local example exists at Claverley, Shropshire, where the royal arms are now hidden behind the organ.

When he reconstructed the chapel of St Mary Magdalene, Sir Henry put up 'her Majesties arms with divers nobleman's arms, together with all the Lord Presidents and counsellors rounde aboute the same'. This indicates the centrality of Elizabeth's arms to the display.

In St Laurence's Church, Ludlow, there is a board painted with the Ten Commandments, purchased by the churchwardens in March 1561. In addition to the three letters 'IHS' (representing Jesus), this includes the royal badges of the rose and the fleur-de-lys. In January 1561 a Royal Order required churches to put up tables of the Ten Commandments. The purchase probably owed nothing to Sir Henry, but the churchwardens presumably thought it best to acquire a board with royal badges. The fleur-de-lys was a French badge. Prominent on the French royal arms, it may have come into English royal use with Edward II's marriage to Isabella of France, and was certainly more common after Edward III's claim to the French throne in 1337.

Ambrosia Sidney's tomb in St Laurence's Church, Ludlow, 1580

## The Tombs of the Sidneys

Coats of arms were also displayed on many sixteenth- and seventeenth-century tombs and tomb fittings, and there are many examples from Presidents and Councillors on the Roll.

The most extravagant display of the family arms surviving in Ludlow is on the tomb of Sir Henry's young daughter, Ambrosia, erected in 1580 in the chancel of St Laurence's Church. It is a table tomb surmounted by a pedimented architectural panel. The frame contains an inscription in gold, above which are the full arms of Sir Henry with garter, helm and supporters, a collared and chained porcupine and a crowned lion. Below is the family motto 'QUO FATA VOCANT', [*where destiny calls*]. On the left side of the inscription are the arms of Sir Henry impaled with the arms of his wife Mary surmounted by the chained porcupine and surrounded by the family motto. On the right side, within a garter and surmounted by a ducal crown, are the arms of Ambrose Dudley, Earl of Warwick, after whom Ambrosia was named. These shields are repeated on three panels on the side of the tomb.

The tomb of Sir Henry's father, William Sidney (presumably erected by Sir Henry and his mother in 1553) still survives at Penshurst, Kent. It has a fine display of heraldry, with enamelled shields from a monumental brass workshop (the so-called Fermour workshop, named after the Fermour brasses found in the churches at Easton Neston in Northamptonshire, and at Somerton in Oxfordshire). Sir Henry was buried at Penshurst, but there is no evidence that he specified arms on his tomb, which does not survive. On the leaden heart case to contain his heart, installed in the tomb of his daughter Ambrosia, the Sidney *pheon* alone was surrounded by the Garter (*see p. 68*); and it was by the *pheon* alone that he was represented in the early seventeenth-century book in the Antiquaries showing the arms of the Presidents of the Council in the Marches of Wales.

## Sir Henry and the Garter Knight Celebrations

Apart from these permanent monuments, Sir Henry had personal and family arms regularly embroidered or engraved on household plate, clothes, bedding and furniture. On several occasions he also commissioned heraldic banners and hangings displaying the arms of all the Knights of the Garter, to be made for the annual ceremony on St George's Day (23 April).[iii]

Sir Henry was installed as a Knight of the Garter on 14 May 1564, and an enamelled plate with his shield of arms was placed on the back of his stall at St George's Chapel in Windsor.

As a member of this Order he was required to either attend the monarch at the St George's Day ceremony at the Court, or celebrate it in like manner wherever he was. The knight was bound to erect the arms of his companions in a nearby chapel or church in imitation of the choir stalls in Windsor, and to attend services and ceremonies corresponding to those staged at Court. During his service in Ireland and Wales there were many occasions when Sir Henry was absent from Windsor, so had to make his own arrangements. Accounts survive of several of the ceremonies that he held in Dublin, Drogheda, Shrewsbury and Ludlow. In Dublin in 1578, he rode dressed in scarlet garter robes from the castle to Christ Church Cathedral. He was accompanied by a herald and a pursuivant (junior herald), the Sergeant at Arms carrying the mace, the Knight Marshal with a guard of honour carrying the sword of state, and over 120 nobility, gentry and city councillors and officials on foot. The choir of the cathedral was decorated with a blue cloth affixed with the arms in metal of all the garter knights, and a stall was set up for the Queen as if she were present. Sir Henry made obeisance to this stall three times, and made an offering at the altar as required by the ceremony. After the service the company processed back to the castle where they received a gun salute and a 'royal feast' was prepared. So many attended that tables and candlesticks had to be borrowed, an extra 160 trencher plates were purchased and 80lbs of hops were used to provide drink for all.[iv]

A similar service took place in St Chad's, Shrewsbury, in 1581 and St Laurence's, Ludlow in 1582 when Sir Henry and his company were attended by the councillors, officials and trade guilds of the town. At Ludlow, banners displaying the arms of the garter knights and an altar cloth made of red and white squares of camblet (a ribbed, woven textile) each embroidered with a garter, were made, and singing men from Hereford (possibly from the cathedral) came to swell the ranks of the choir. The town council contributed to the costs and also provided 20 sheep and an ox for the feast, and drink for the singers. This special occasion was obviously much prized by the town, since 80 years later the banners were still preserved in the town council chamber with an inscription recording the event.[v]

There are two books on heraldry that Sir Henry might have read or had knowledge of: *The Accedens of Armorie* by Gerard Legh (1562), and *Works of Armorie* by John Bossewell (1572). It has been observed how writers on heraldry in the sixteenth century supposed that the bearing of arms made a positive contribution to virtue. The charges on shields – such as the lion and eagle – represented the strength and fierceness of those represented

QVO ME FATA VOCANT

Sir Henry Sidney's Garter stall plate (21cm x 16.5cm), of copper alloy and enamel, 1564, fixed to his stall-back in St George's Chapel, Windsor. © *St George's Chapel, Windsor*

by the arms, and symbolised virtue in those who had originally won the coat. Both the porcupine (which the Sidney family may have adopted from King Louis XII of France) and the *pheon* were presumably intended to represent the strength, fierceness and tenacity of the owner. The reasons for the adoption of these two specific devices by the Sidney family, probably in the fifteenth or early sixteenth century, are not known. Most of the representations of Sir Henry's heraldry are concerned to represent his status acquired through his marriage, and his assumption of his wife's genealogy. His display of the royal arms was due both to his status as President of the Council and his loyalty to Queen Elizabeth.

# 10. Introduction to the Heraldry of the Roll

THE LUDLOW CASTLE Heraldic Roll contains a rich and fascinating collection of coats of arms. However, it is not a completely full and accurate record, as some of those who appear as previous owners of the castle never actually enjoyed that position, and some of the previous Presidents of the Council are omitted altogether. That said, most of the coats of arms on the Roll have been painted very accurately, with only a few exceptions. Comparison with Mytton's eighteenth-century descriptions of the original shields has generally shown that, where there are discrepancies, the sixteenth-century Roll is the more accurate. In just one or two cases, however, Mytton's descriptions have been useful in confirming inaccuracies on the Roll itself.

This introductory section is intended to enable the reader to make sense of the descriptions of the coats of arms. Arms are 'blazoned' (that is, described in heraldic terms) according to rules; and rules govern the way in which individual coats of arms are marshalled or arranged together on a single shield. This section also shows how both English and Welsh arms sometimes deviated from the normally accepted rules of heraldry during the Elizabethan period. To assist the reader, heraldic terminology has been largely avoided when commenting on individual coats of arms. Full blazons of all the arms are given in Appendix 2, and there is a glossary of the terms used in the blazons in Appendix 3.

## THE INTRODUCTION AND ORIGINAL PURPOSE OF HERALDRY

Since the earliest times, men have employed symbols to express themselves. Ancient Greeks and Romans used a variety of emblems as insignia for their armies and, much later, we have the colourful shields recorded on the Bayeux

Tapestry. In the twelfth century, however, we see the introduction of a more formalised system of hereditary devices based on a shield. The earliest known example of a coat of arms which conformed to the new system was that of Geoffrey of Anjou who was knighted by king Henry I in 1127, and at around this period heraldry as we know it then spread rapidly across Western Europe.

The fact that true heraldry didn't develop until the twelfth century immediately raises an interesting question: the first coat of arms on the Roll is that of Sir Walter Lacy who died in 1085 (1). So, we must assume that Walter himself was never aware of the coat of arms that is now associated with his name. The family chose their arms in the twelfth century, and the earliest appearance of the arms of this branch of the Lacy family occurs on a seal of Walter de Lacy (d.1241) son of Hugh de Lacy (d.1186) (*see p. 95*). So the family projected the arms backwards onto their ancestors. The same thing can be seen on some Welsh coats of arms (*17 Davies, 22 Arnold, 27 Price*) whereby descent is often claimed from quite distant ancestors or Welsh heroes.

Initially, heraldry was mainly used to help to identify heavily-armoured knights at tournaments or in battle. Younger sons altered the arms slightly to make them distinct, but they could still be easily recognised as belonging to the same family. Moreover, other quite distinct families sometimes chose coats of arms that were very similar to those of a family with whom they had strong ties through marriage, tenurial overlordship or some other connection. In this way, a lord's recognisable 'affinities' might amount to a formidable team on the battlefield.

Much had changed, however, by the Elizabethan era. A person's coat of arms was now less vital for identification purposes and had become most important as an indication of his social status – based, to a significant extent, on the quality of one's ancestral pedigree. To see how this worked, it is necessary to understand how coats of arms were grouped together in 'quarters'.

## IMPALEMENT, QUARTERING AND THE INHERITANCE OF COATS OF ARMS

A married man may display his wife's coat of arms alongside his own on a single shield. His arms are normally placed on the left side (**A**) and his wife's on the right side (**B**), and the two arms are said to be 'impaled'. The man's and woman's coats of arms are not cut in half and put together; rather, each complete coat is squeezed into half of the shield.

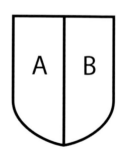

Generally speaking, any children of the marriage would simply inherit their father's arms and not their mother's.

However, if the wife's father dies leaving no surviving sons, she becomes (together with any sisters) a 'heraldic heiress'. Being now a senior representative of the family, she inherits her family coat of arms. Her husband may then cease to 'impale her arms' with his and, instead, place them on a small 'escutcheon of pretence' (B) in the centre of his own shield (A).

The children of the marriage inherit both their father's (A) and their mother's arms (B) (normally, with the father's coat placed in the top left corner) and will quarter them together like this:

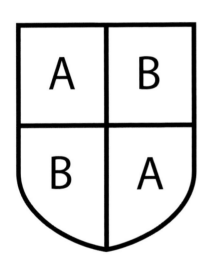

William Gerard's coat of arms (*above right*) has the Gerard arms in quarters 1 and 4, and the arms of Ince in quarters 2 and 3. His arms would therefore be described, simply, as 'Quarterly Gerard and Ince'.

Further coats of arms may be added through subsequent marriages to heiresses. These are always called 'quarters' even though there may be more than four of them. The quarters are numbered row by row from left to right (*see overleaf, left shield*). No. 1, in the top left, is almost always the patriarchal coat, but exceptions do occur for various reasons. If the quarterings do not fit easily into a rectangular pattern, the first quarter is repeated at the end (*see overleaf, right shield*).

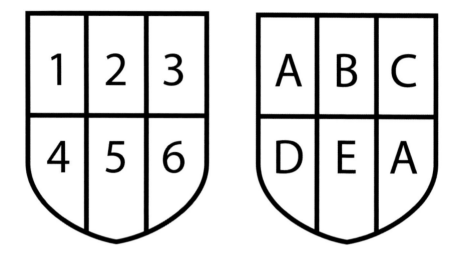

Although there are some official rules about quarterings, there has never been any restriction on the number of quarterings that can be included on a coat of arms. For this reason it is common to find several versions of a person's arms, which include more or fewer quarterings, or even different quarterings, partly depending on the whim of the owner, but also on the situation. A person entitled, for instance, to 24 quarterings may sometimes choose to include just the first and no others, for the sake of simplicity and impact.

### The Coats of Arms of Bishops
Before the Reformation, bishops did not marry and it was normal to impale the bishop's personal arms with those of his diocese or see, with the diocesan arms on the left and the bishop's own arms on the right. This practice continued after the Reformation. Eleven of the people named on the Ludlow Roll were bishops, and there were an additional two on the missing end of the Roll. Five of them have their personal arms impaled with that of their bishopric (*13 Scory, 15 Robinson, 16 Davies, 17 Davies, 39 Lee*), while another five show the bishop's arms alone (*14 Bullingham, 36 Smyth, 37 Blyth, 38 Veysey, 40 Sampson*). No shield is drawn for John Alcock, Bishop of Worcester (*35*).

### Breaking the Rules
In the sixteenth century many of the major families could claim many quarterings. Despite clear rules relating to the inheritance of coats of arms through heiresses, monarchs (as the official granters of arms) were in a position to ignore the rules and do as they pleased. Edward iv's queen,

Elizabeth Woodville, came from relatively humble stock on her father's side, so her quarterings were re-ordered to emphasise her mother's much more impressive pedigree (*8 Edward IV*). The less-impressive Woodville arms were demoted from the first to the last quarter. In the next century Anne Boleyn's coat of arms was even more drastically re-organised. Henry VIII created three new quarterings for his wife, and the relatively humble family coat of Boleyn was replaced by a new quartered coat that displayed the peerages to which her father had been elevated (*10 Henry VIII*).

WELSH COATS OF ARMS

There are several coats of arms on the Roll representing Welshmen. Welsh genealogy is made very difficult by the extended use of patronymics, whereby a person's full name would include the name of his father and maybe some other ancestors, such as Ellyw ab Iorwerth ap Gruffudd. The change to the use of surnames was adopted unevenly, so it is often difficult to identify a specific individual with any certainty. Also, Welsh quarterings did not always follow the usual rules of English heraldry. If a man could reasonably claim familial descent from some significant earlier Welshman – possibly through a female line or maybe just by long-established family tradition – that might be enough to warrant including a quartering to represent that person (*see in particular 17 Davies, 22 Arnold, 27 Price*).

SOME TECHNICAL TERMS

As mentioned earlier, when describing the coats of arms that appear on the Ludlow Roll, heraldic language has been kept to a minimum. There are just a few basic terms and ideas that it will be helpful to know and understand.

Firstly, the 'geography' of a coat of arms. 'Dexter' (which means right) refers to the left-hand side of the shield as we look at it, and 'sinister' (which means left) is on the right side. One has to imagine a knight holding his shield in front of himself – as we look at him, his right is our left.

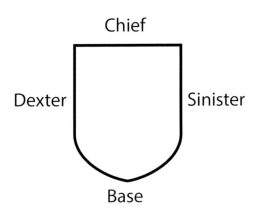

Chief

Dexter

Sinister

Base

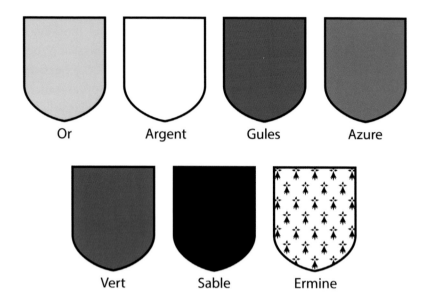

| Or | Argent | Gules | Azure |

| Vert | Sable | Ermine |

## Field, Charges and Ordinaries

The basic underlying colour or pattern of a shield is called the 'field'. Usually the field is a single colour (*see above*), but sometimes it is split into two or more sections of different colours, or it may even comprise a repeating pattern of colours. Onto this field are placed 'charges', of which the most basic are geometric figures called 'ordinaries' (*see below*).

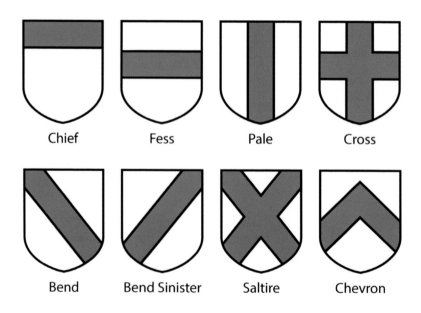

| Chief | Fess | Pale | Cross |

| Bend | Bend Sinister | Saltire | Chevron |

## Differencing Arms for Cadency

The way of changing a coat of arms to 'difference' it for younger sons had changed significantly by the time the Roll was created. While the eldest son kept his father's coat of arms, they were changed (differenced) for younger sons. In the medieval period a coat of arms was differenced by changing colours, or altering or adding charges, so that the resulting shield was different, but identifiably similar, to the main arms. In around 1500 a new system was introduced whereby a man's sons bore the father's arms differenced by the addition of a small extra component – a 'charge', as shown here:

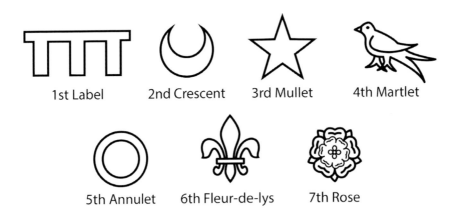

1st Label     2nd Crescent     3rd Mullet     4th Martlet

5th Annulet     6th Fleur-de-lys     7th Rose

The idea was that the eldest son would remove the label when his father died, and he then became head of the family. It was expected that younger sons would retain their marks, but the system was cumbersome and ambiguous when applied to grandsons. It was never obligatory, but was widely used for sons and occasionally for grandsons.

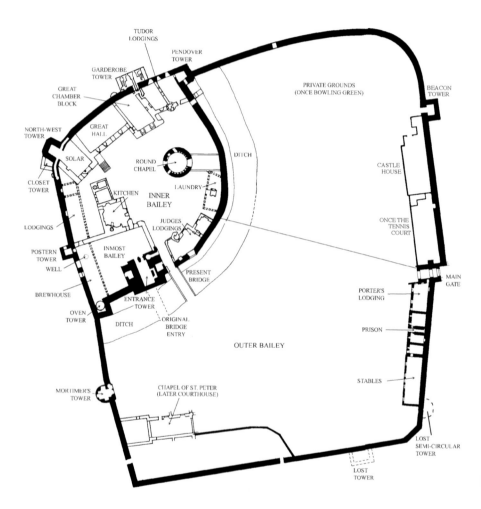

TUDOR
LODGINGS

PENDOVER
TOWER

GARDEROBE
TOWER

GREAT
CHAMBER
BLOCK

PRIVATE GROUNDS
(ONCE BOWLING GREEN)

BEACON
TOWER

NORTH-WEST
TOWER

GREAT
HALL

SOLAR

DITCH

ROUND
CHAPEL

CASTLE
HOUSE

CLOSET
TOWER

LAUNDRY

KITCHEN  INNER
BAILEY

LODGINGS

ONCE THE
TENNIS
COURT

JUDGES
LODGINGS

POSTERN
TOWER

INMOST
BAILEY

WELL

PRESENT
BRIDGE

MAIN
GATE

BREWHOUSE

PORTER'S
LODGING

ENTRANCE
TOWER

OVEN
TOWER

ORIGINAL
BRIDGE
ENTRY

PRISON

DITCH

OUTER BAILEY

STABLES

MORTIMER'S
TOWER

CHAPEL OF ST. PETER
(LATER COURTHOUSE)

LOST
SEMI-CIRCULAR
TOWER

LOST
TOWER

Plan of Ludlow Castle

# 11. Ludlow Castle and Biographies of the People Listed on the Roll

T HE RUINS OF Ludlow Castle are an evocative reminder of its important role not just in the history of the Welsh Marches but across the whole of England and Wales. Ludlow Castle is situated on the fringes of the Welsh Marches, and consequently ownership of the castle and control of the surrounding area was of significant strategic importance, with the Crown often taking a keen interest to influence that ownership. First developed as a frontier fortress, it later became a palatial castle for the wealthiest lords to entertain royalty, before coming into the ownership of the Crown when the then owner of the castle, Edward, Earl of March was crowned Edward IV. Edward had spent much of his childhood at Ludlow, and the castle remained a favourite possession of the Yorkist and early Tudor kings. As a royal castle it became the base for The Council in the Marches of Wales, sustaining its active use long after many other castles had been abandoned to the elements.

The story of Ludlow Castle is dominated by the lives and actions of the lords and families who owned it. For this reason the following section weaves together the history of the castle and the development of the buildings with the biographies of the owners of Ludlow Castle, whose coats of arms are depicted on the Roll. The development of the castle was sporadic, depending not just on the wealth of the owners but also the defensive requirements of the castle and its relative importance to them. Some of the owners were more focussed on their lands and possessions in Ireland, or their involvement in the great affairs of state in England. Others spent heavily to modernise and extend the castle to reflect their own wealth and importance.

OVERLEAF: Ludlow Castle by Julius Caesar Ibbetson, 1791.
© Manchester Art Gallery, UK/ Bridgeman Images

Ludlow is situated near to the border with Wales, with ancient routes passing both north-south and east-west. As such, one might expect it to have been an important site throughout history. However, until the Norman period after 1066, the evidence for its occupation is patchy. There is plenty of evidence for Iron Age, Roman and Saxon settlement in the wider area, but hardly any in Ludlow itself – though a reference to a place called 'Lude' in the Domesday Book is seen by some as evidence for the existence of Ludlow in the late Anglo-Saxon period.

By contrast, the arrival of the Normans following the Conquest of 1066 can be clearly seen. Whatever the use of the location had been before, Ludlow was an obvious place for the Normans to build a castle. The castle, as a massively fortified home for the lord and his followers, was an innovation by the Normans, compared to the more communal fortifications of the Iron Age period, the Romans and the Anglo-Saxons. The natural ridge of high ground, defended on three sides by the River Teme, was an ideal location to build a castle to dominate and subdue the local area. The location also provided a defensive barrier towards Wales, and was well placed for military access for further conquest when the time was right. The building of the Norman castle at the end of the ridge sparked the development of Ludlow.

# 1 Sir Walter Lacy, d.1085

S IR WALTER DE Lacy (the title 'Sir' is a later, erroneous addition) was a Norman nobleman from Lassy in France, who came to England in 1066. King William placed him in the central and southern Marches alongside William fitz Osbern, Earl of Hereford, probably as second-in-command.

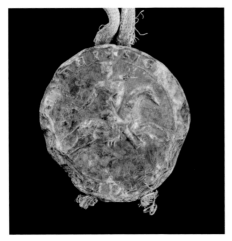

The earliest appearance of the arms of this branch of the Lacy family is on a seal of Walter de Lacy, (d.1241) son of Hugh de Lacy (d.1186) on a grant to Craswell Priory, c.1225–50. *Chantry Grant to Craswell Priory, HCA482.* © *Hereford Cathedral*

Walter received lands in Herefordshire, Worcestershire and Shropshire, establishing a castle at Weobley, with another important manor at Stanton Lacy, which included Ludlow. William, as the closest confidant of the king, was given extensive powers within his territory, to secure the boundaries with Wales and to pacify the local area. Whilst William lived, he fulfilled this role well: having put down a rebellion in 1069 led by the Saxon magnate, Edric the Wild, he launched an attack into south Wales and built a string of castles along the border from Chepstow up to Wigmore. Within a short while, however, he was killed whilst campaigning in Flanders in 1071. William was succeeded by his son, Roger; however, Roger had all his lands in England confiscated when he was involved in a failed rebellion against the king in 1075.

THE COAT OF ARMS
I Arms of Lacy

Walter de Lacy would never have seen this coat of arms. He died in 1085, well before heraldry as we know it swept across Western Europe. These are the arms adopted by his descendants much later, and have been projected backwards.

Roger fitz Osbern's fall from power provided an opportunity for Walter de Lacy to advance. Walter remained loyal to the king, helping to ensure that the revolt failed, and was probably rewarded with more lands. Furthermore, the abolition of the fitz Osbern earldom resulted in a significant rise in status for Walter, as he now held his lands directly from the king as a tenant-in-chief.

It is Walter who is generally credited with the earliest developments of a castle at Ludlow, and it may well be that it was his enhanced status after 1075 that triggered his determination to build a castle befitting his new standing. According to family legend, Walter's death in 1085 was as a result of falling off scaffolding whilst inspecting a church that he had endowed – St Guthlac's in Hereford. Walter was succeeded by his son, Roger, who was involved in two failed rebellions as a result of which he was deprived of his lands in England and Normandy. The king allowed his lands to pass to his brother, Hugh de Lacy, who died childless sometime before 1115.

Little is generally known about the early building work undertaken at Ludlow Castle; however, archaeological analysis shows that the first significant phase of its development took place in the late eleventh century. Combining this with historical sources, it seems most likely that this development took place between Walter's increase in prominence following Roger fitz Osbern's disgrace, and Roger de Lacy's exile.

Ludlow Castle is typical of how castles developed and evolved over centuries as building techniques improved, defensive features were enhanced, and the occupants wanted more comfortable accommodation. Thus, the castle that was first built at Ludlow occupied a much smaller site than it does now, originally comprising just the inner walled area that is now the inner bailey within the dry ditch accessed by a bridge and gatehouse. Walter and Roger de Lacy constructed the walls and towers at Ludlow from stone at the outset, unlike many other castles which were first built in timber then changed later to masonry construction when time and money allowed. The settlement of Ludlow began to develop around this time.

On Hugh de Lacy's death, the barony (including Ludlow Castle and the emerging borough of Ludlow) reverted to the Crown. Although there was a male claimant – Gilbert de Lacy, son of Hugh's exiled brother Roger – Henry I ignored his right, probably as he was the son of a known traitor. First, the king arranged for the inheritance to pass to a de Lacy heiress, Sybil, who was most probably the daughter of Roger and Hugh's sister, Agnes, by Geoffrey Talbot. He then arranged the marriage of Sybil to one of his most

The Norman Keep and curtain wall built by Walter de Lacy and his son Roger de Lacy in the late eleventh century (the top floor of the keep was added later)

loyal and capable supporters, Payne fitzJohn, a minor baron whom Henry I promoted to a position of great power in the Welsh Marches, making him Sheriff of Herefordshire and Shropshire, with a key role in securing the border. When Payne, after some 20 years as Lord of Ludlow, was killed in 1137 whilst pursuing a Welsh raiding party, King Stephen arranged for Sybil to marry one of his supporters, Joce de Dinan. However, the king had first to besiege Ludlow Castle in 1139, in order to eject Gilbert de Lacy who had used the disruption to seize Ludlow for himself, claiming it as his rightful inheritance.

The feud between Gilbert and Joce for control of Ludlow continued during the period of civil wars during Stephen's reign, with Hugh Mortimer (d.1181–85) of Wigmore joining with Gilbert. At one point, Hugh was captured by Joce and imprisoned in Ludlow, being freed only when his wife paid a huge ransom to secure his release. By about 1150, Gilbert had succeeded in taking control of Ludlow. However, although he had finally won his inheritance, Gilbert did not stay long to enjoy it. In late 1159 he set out as a Templar for the Holy Land, where he is last heard of in 1163, when he was Preceptor of the Templars in the county of Tripoli, helping to defeat the Saracens at the Castle of Krak.

During this period of civil war, Ludlow Castle underwent further significant developments in order to improve its fortification and defensive capability, and to meet the religious needs of its occupants. Another storey was added to the Entrance Tower (now the Keep), possibly in anticipation of the siege by the king in 1139, or during the conflict between Joce and Gilbert.

The Round Chapel dedicated to Mary Magdalene built by Gilbert de Lacy in the 1150s

This created a building that could function as a substantial defensive tower, with suitable accommodation also for the lord and his family. In the 1150s, Gilbert built the unusual round-naved chapel of St Mary Magdalene, heavily influenced by the designs typical of the Order of the Knights Templars, indicating perhaps a long-standing interest in going on crusade.

The de Lacy family continued to hold Ludlow Castle during the second half of the twelfth century and well into the thirteenth century. There were, however, significant periods when it was in the hands of the Crown due at times to suspicions about the loyalty of the de Lacys and at other times because of the large debts that they owed. Little is known of Gilbert's eldest son, Robert, who only held Ludlow for a short time, as he had been succeeded by his younger brother, Hugh (d.1186) by 1162. It was Hugh who was granted the former kingdom of Meath in Ireland, which was to become the primary focus of the de Lacy family's power, as the value of the Meath lands was far greater than their lands in England and Wales. Hugh was killed in Ireland in 1186, whilst inspecting a castle he had built. With his eldest son, Walter (d.1241), under-age, Ludlow remained under the control of the Crown until formally granted to Walter in 1190.

Like his father, Walter spent much of his time in Ireland where he was implicated in actions against the Crown during the reigns of both King Richard I and King John. Because of this, Ludlow was confiscated and held by the Crown for lengthy periods. A consequence of his long life was that both his son and grandson died before him, leaving the inheritance to be divided between his two surviving granddaughters. At the time of Walter's death in 1241 both girls were probably minors, so the barony reverted to the Crown. Three years later Henry III arranged the marriage of the elder sister, Maud to one of his favourites, Peter de Geneva, instructing the sheriff to make an equal partition of the de Lacy lands between Maud and her husband on the one hand, and her younger sister, Margaret on the other, whose portion was to remain in the king's hands. Later the same year, Margaret married John de Verdun. The borough of Ludlow was thus divided between the two sisters (remaining under divided ownership until 1356), though the portion that contained the Castle was granted to the elder sister, Maud. Her first husband having died in 1249, Maud married Geoffrey de Geneville in 1252.

Despite the de Lacys' absence in Ireland much of the time, and with Ludlow Castle often in the hands of the Crown, the later part of the twelfth century saw considerable expansion and development of the castle grounds and buildings. The most significant development entailed a large area to the south and east of the original buildings being incorporated into the castle, making the overall footprint four times as large. This was achieved by building a new, ditched curtain wall that arced round from the south-west corner of the original building to the north-east corner. Significantly, a new eastward-facing entry gateway re-orientated the castle away from the south-facing original gatehouse, and looked instead now toward the market, church and borough that were developing along the ridge. It is likely that the walls and entrance gateway of this new outer bailey were completed before Henry II's sequestration of Ludlow in 1177, with Mortimer's Tower and another tower added in the early 1200s to improve the defences. With the original castle now functioning as an inner bailey, the access to it through the Entrance Tower was blocked off, and a new entrance was cut through the wall alongside the keep.

The addition of a new curtain wall in the late twelfth century created an outer bailey that increased the size of the castle four-fold

## 2 Geoffrey de Geneville, 1225/33–1314

### 1st Baron Geneville

G EOFFREY WAS AN Anglo-French noble from the Champagne region of France, who had family connections with Eleanor of Provence, wife of Henry III. Geoffrey came to England in 1251 and a year later married Maud de Lacy, heiress jointly with her sister Margaret of the de Lacy estates, with Maud's portion of Ludlow including the castle. Geoffrey became a friend and trusted advisor to the king's son, Lord Edward, (later Edward I) and played an important role as a supporter of the royal family in the conflicts with the baronial opposition led by Simon de Montfort. In the second half of 1264, Simon de Montfort captured Ludlow Castle, but Geoffrey had retaken it by

THE COAT OF ARMS
*2 Geoffrey de Geneville & Maud de Lacy*
*Dexter: Geneville / Sinister: Lacy*

The things that look like moustaches on the Geneville arms are horse *barnacles* or *brays*. Closing a barnacle around the mouth of a horse instantly causes it to calm down and be docile. Similar devices are still used today but are called twitches.

May 1265 when he was part of the group which engineered Lord Edward's escape from captivity in Hereford, providing him with shelter in Ludlow Castle. Maud and Geoffrey had also inherited half the de Lacy lands in Ireland, where Geoffrey played a key role to bring together with the royalists those who had previously supported de Montfort, ensuring significant support from Ireland in the critical victory by the royalist army at the Battle of Evesham in 1265.

There was a strong crusading tradition in the de Geneville family, so it was not surprising that Geoffrey and his brother accompanied Prince Edward on his crusade in 1270. After his return, Geoffrey was appointed Justiciar of Ireland, spending much of his subsequent career in that country, or on diplomatic missions to France and the Papal Curia.

In the legal proceedings of 1292 Geoffrey de Geneville and his wife, as the 'heir of Walter de Lacy', for a time successfully claimed a franchise at their manor of Stanton Lacy and town of Ludlow 'by conquest'. They were asserting for themselves the royal right to fully administer the system of criminal justice in their lordship, including the right to hang a convicted person, and to try under their right all civil causes within their jurisdiction. Geoffrey and Maud were in effect attempting to establish for themselves the rights, powers and income of a Marcher Lordship. They may have succeeded for a time, but it is unlikely that it continued for long.

Like his grandfather-in-law, Geoffrey lived to an old age (probably into his eighties), and as with Walter de Lacy he outlived both his sons. Spending much of his time in Ireland or on diplomatic missions, Geoffrey and Maud had given their lands at Ludlow to their second son Peter in 1283 (the eldest, Geoffrey, having already died). However, Peter died in 1292 leaving three young daughters, aged six, five and one. To avoid splitting the inheritance in the way that the de Lacy inheritance had been split between his wife and her sister, Geoffrey placed his two younger granddaughters, whilst still children, in the nunnery at Aconbury. This ensured that the eldest granddaughter, Joan de Geneville, became sole heiress.

Aged 15, in 1301 Joan married the 14-year-old Roger Mortimer, heir to the barony of Wigmore, thus bringing Ludlow Castle into the ownership of the Mortimer family which dominated the next period of its history.

The late twelfth-century expansion of the castle, with the addition of the large outer bailey, had created space for development within the inner bailey. The de Genevilles took the opportunity to create more 'modern' and luxurious living accommodation, building a first-floor Great Hall, constructed

*From the left*: Solar block and Great Hall built by Geoffrey and Peter de Geneville in the late thirteenth century, and Great Chamber Block to the east of the Great Hall with Garderobe tower behind – built by Roger Mortimer in the 1320s

over a large undercroft, together with a two-storey Solar Block (living space and bedrooms), which was attached to the western side of the Great Hall. Both additions were built in stone against the safe northern curtain wall, with work probably starting in the late 1280s under the control of Peter de Geneville, and completed after his death by his father. Further works were started in order to increase the height of the new Solar Block and adjoining wall tower with a new closet tower attached, and new kitchens in the inner bailey. Although started by Geoffrey de Geneville, it is possible that this second phase of works was not completed until after Roger Mortimer assumed ownership of the castle.

## 3 Roger Mortimer, 1287–1330
### 1st Earl of March

THE MORTIMERS HAD become powerful Marcher lords based, since the 1070s, a short distance from Ludlow at Wigmore. By the end of the thirteenth century, the Mortimers were becoming the greatest of the Marcher Lords. In part, this position was attained by their longevity as a family, surviving in the end for over 350 years, during which time

other families died out or fell out of favour with the Crown; indeed, it has been noted by A.C. Reeves in *The Marcher Lords*, that the survival of the Mortimers was both a 'political and biological feat'.

In the period following his marriage to Joan de Geneville in 1301, Roger Mortimer's early career was characterised by success as a military leader, and as an able administrator who was loyal to the Crown. He commanded forces at Bannockburn in 1314, helped put down rebellion in Wales, and served terms as both King's Lieutenant and Justiciar in Ireland. His personal life

---

THE COAT OF ARMS
*3 Roger Mortimer, 1st Earl of March & Joan de Geneville*
*Dexter: Mortimer / Sinister: Geneville – surmounted by an earl's coronet*

There are many small variations in the Mortimer coat of arms. Despite it having been painted about 250 years after Roger died, the version of his arms on the Roll is almost identical to the earliest examples to be found, including that in the window in St Laurence's Church in Ludlow commemorating Roger's sister Maud. The only difference is that the number of horizontal bars here is six, while it is more common to find seven in early examples.

was settled, with many indications of a strong relationship and partnership between Roger and Joan de Geneville in the management of their estates. He was well placed to play a leading role in national affairs when circumstances pushed him into a course of action that would spiral out of control.

By 1320, when Roger returned from a period in Ireland, Edward II was under the growing influence of the Despenser family – father and son both named Hugh. With a deserved reputation for unscrupulous greed, they were becoming a threat to all the Marcher Lords, and to the Mortimers in particular. When hostilities broke out, the Mortimers were in effect putting themselves in alliance against the king. Forced to surrender to the king at the start of 1322, Roger Mortimer and his uncle, Roger Mortimer of Chirk were sent to the Tower of London. They were both condemned to death; however, for reasons that are not fully understood, the sentences were subsequently reduced to terms of life imprisonment. Along with the former's other properties, Ludlow was confiscated to be held by the Crown for over four years.

In August 1323, having drugged the guards, Roger escaped from the Tower, fleeing to France where his presence was accepted by the French king who was the brother of Edward's queen, Isabella (Mortimer's uncle, Roger of Chirk, did not escape and subsequently died in the Tower in 1326). In England, Isabella was becoming increasingly alienated from the king, isolated and demeaned by the Despensers. When, in 1325, Edward II allowed her to lead a diplomatic mission to her brother's court in France, Isabella openly came out against her husband and his associates, refusing to return to England. A close alliance developed between Queen Isabella and Roger Mortimer (such that by 1326 it was being claimed in England that they were lovers), and together they developed a scheme to return to England. Landing in Suffolk in September 1326 with a small army, Roger and Isabella captured Edward II, who was forced to agree to abdicate in favour of his 14-year-old son, Edward III. The traditional version of events is that Edward II was murdered at Berkeley Castle in 1327 at the instruction of Roger and Isabella, though this has been challenged by some historians evidencing that Edward II lived in exile on the Continent as a hermit into the 1340s.

For the next nearly four years Roger was at the height of his powers, influence and wealth, and was, alongside Queen Isabella, the dominant figure in England. However, Roger and Isabella did much to provoke the resentment and animosity of the nobles. Roger made a critical mistake in not having an official position in the governance of the country – he was never officially regent, nor was he ever a member of the council established to direct the government during the minority of Edward III. Instead he used his relationship with the queen and the young king to appoint his allies to the great posts of the kingdom and to manipulate and control events. In 1328 Roger was raised to the rank of earl. Given his vast estates and lordships, his relationship with the queen and young king, and his role in ruling the country, this was not surprising. What did surprise people at the time, however, was the title that he chose – Earl of March – as there was no precedent for this; all earldoms related to specific counties, never a whole region. This reflected not only Roger's ambition but also his recognition that the Mortimers' power derived from their dominance in the Welsh Marches.

The forced abdication of a king to be replaced by his heir who was a minor had never happened before. Caught up in new and unique events amidst the turmoil of power and royalty, Roger inevitably made mistakes that led to increasing resentment of the ways in which he enriched himself, to opposition to his political actions, and ultimately to his downfall. In particular, the young king chafed under Roger's control. Approaching the age of 18, Edward III wanted to rule in fact not just in name, so began to support action against Roger. This enabled his own close allies to capture Roger in Nottingham from where he was taken to London, tried for treason, condemned and executed at Tyburn in 1330.

It is possible that in the first phase of his career Roger was responsible for completing the building works at Ludlow Castle begun by the de Genevilles. The castle certainly benefited from his success and wealth in the last phase of his career, when he was determined that Ludlow should reflect his hard-won status and provide palatial accommodation to entertain the royal family. To commemorate his escape from the Tower of London, he built a chapel in the outer bailey, which was dedicated to St Peter in thanksgiving for his freedom that he gained on the Feast of St Peter in Chains – 1 August.

Having completed the works to the Great Hall and the Solar Block on the castle's west side, Roger constructed the Great Chamber Block on the east side, and the Garderobe Tower (so called as each room had its own en-suite toilet, or garderobe – a great luxury at that time). Roger's work made the North Range one of the finest sets of buildings in the country, and transformed the castle into a palatial residence. There are some accounts suggesting that Roger visited Ludlow with the queen and the young king in this period (though, unfortunately, the presence of the king at Ludlow cannot be confirmed). There is a popular story that Roger built the Great

Garderobe Tower built by Roger Mortimer in the 1320s

Chamber Block to solve the problems caused by his possible relationship with the Queen. If the queen visited Ludlow, the Lady of the Castle would have to give up her own (the castle's best) rooms to her social superior; a somewhat awkward situation if the queen was also your husband's lover. According to this story, Roger overcame the dilemma by building the new block, thus allowing his wife to remain in her rooms, the queen to have the new apartments, whilst Roger himself diplomatically slept with the guards. There is no evidence that this happened, and it is virtually impossible that the Great Chamber Block could have been built in the timescale, but it makes for a good story.

In the aftermath of Roger's execution, the Mortimer family were not treated as harshly as they might have been. Roger's wife, Joan de Geneville, was exempted from the confiscation of Roger's titles, property and estates, thus keeping her inheritance of Ludlow Castle. Roger's heir, Edmund (d.1331), was soon given back the family seat of Wigmore together with Maelienydd and other Marcher Lordships. Edmund, however, died just a year after his father's execution, leaving a child of only three years old to inherit. As the young Roger (d.1360) grew up, he was gradually allowed to assume some of his inheritance. When only 18, he distinguished himself in Edward III's wars in France, being knighted by the Black Prince (Prince Edward, heir to the throne) and fighting at the Battle of Crecy. In 1348, still only aged 20, he was honoured by being selected as one of the founding members of the king's new 'Order of the Garter', becoming an increasingly important commander and ally of the Black Prince. In 1354 the judgement on his grandfather was annulled, and all the Mortimer lands and titles were restored to him, and he thus became the 2nd Earl of March.

Roger's life ended abruptly whilst still young, when he was killed on campaign in France in 1360, aged only 32. Two years before his death, however, Roger completed two actions that had significant long-term implications for Ludlow. Firstly, he succeeded in uniting what had become the two separate Lordships of Ludlow when he agreed an exchange of lands with William de Ferrers who had inherited the de Verdun half of the de Lacy inheritance. Secondly, he engaged his six-year-old son, Edmund, to a granddaughter of the King – Philippa, daughter, only child and heir of Edward III's second surviving son, Lionel of Antwerp, Duke of Clarence. This marriage brought the Mortimers within the royal family and Edmund's children into the line of succession for the throne. The Mortimer claim to the throne would have significant consequences for Ludlow Castle and the town.

## 4 Lionel of Antwerp, 1338–68
### 1st 'Duke' of Clarence'

L IONEL WAS THE second surviving son of King Edward III. Aged four, he was married in 1342 to the ten-year-old Elizabeth de Burgh, the daughter and sole heir of the deceased William de Burgh, third Earl of Ulster, and heiress from her grandmother of the Clare estates in England and Wales. The marriage was consummated in 1352 and produced only one child, Philippa.

It is a mystery why Lionel is included on the Roll in this section of owners of the castle, as there is no documentary evidence that he ever owned Ludlow Castle. The only known connection is the betrothal in 1358 between his daughter Philippa and Edmund Mortimer (d.1381), while both were still children. When Edmund's father died in 1360 (with Edmund still aged only eight), Lionel, therefore, was his future father-in-law. However, there

THE COAT OF ARMS
*4 Lionel, Duke of Clarence & Elizabeth de Burgh, 4th Countess of Ulster*
*Dexter: the royal arms (quarterly France Ancient & England) with a label for*
*difference / Sinister: Burgh (Ulster) – surmounted by a ducal coronet*

Lionel was the second surviving son of King Edward III. Edward III claimed the crown of France and, as it was the more ancient kingdom, he placed the French arms in quarters 1 & 4, demoting the English arms to quarters 2 & 3. In early times the coat of arms of France (*France Ancient*) included a continuing pattern of gold fleurs-de-lys on a blue field. The French subsequently reduced the number of fleurs-de-lys to three and Henry IV followed suit around 1405, the revised version being referred to as *France Modern*.

The sons of Edward III all bore labels across the top of their shields and these were differenced to distinguish one from another. Lionel's label included small red rectangles called cantons. Although it is possible to make out the label on Lionel's coat of arms on the Roll, there is no sign of the difference mark. This is also true of his daughter's arms in No. 5. The royal arms in Nos. 6 & 7 are descended from Edmund of Langley so would have had three red balls on the labels. These differences are not evident on the Roll either.

Lionel's wife Philippa de Burgh was Countess of Ulster in her own right. It is possibly no accident that the arms of de Burgh with a red cross on a gold background are very similar to the earlier arms of Lacy in No. 1.

is no record that Lionel was given responsibility for looking after Edmund's properties, including Ludlow Castle, while there is evidence that others had that responsibility. Furthermore, Lionel was mainly in Ireland and Italy during the 1360s. It is possible that, when the coats of arms were placed in the Round Chapel two centuries later, this 'error' was made deliberately in order to emphasise the Tudor dynasty's royal descent from Edward III.

Ten years after their engagement as children, Edmund and Philippa married in 1368. Shortly afterwards, Lionel died aged only 30. He had spent much of his early career in Ireland where he was appointed Royal Lieutenant with a remit to repair the disordered state of the English colony by a demonstration of military might. Whilst in Ireland his wife, Elizabeth de Burgh, had died in 1363, and on his return to England in 1366 the king negotiated for Lionel to marry Violante Visconti, daughter of the Lord of Pavia. Lionel travelled to Italy in February 1368, celebrated the wedding at the end of May, but died in October.

## 5 Edmund Mortimer, 1352–81
### 3rd Earl of March

THE MARRIAGE OF Edmund Mortimer, 3rd Earl of March, to Philippa not only brought their children into the line of succession to the throne of England, but also greatly further enriched the Mortimer family. The death of Lionel soon after their marriage meant that in addition to the already significant Mortimer inheritance, the young couple inherited the earldom of Ulster and a large proportion of the Clare estates. Thus, Edmund, Earl of March and Earl of Ulster, became the largest landowner in Ireland, and the fourth largest in England after the Crown, the Black Prince and John of Gaunt, Duke of Lancaster.

Aged just 17, Edmund was appointed Marshal of England in 1369, and served in campaigns in France, as well as diplomatic missions to France and Scotland, benefiting from the support of his father's patron, the Black Prince. As Edward III grew older and more infirm, the last years of his

Edmund, 3rd Earl of March, in the west window of St Laurence's, Ludlow

reign saw increasingly bitter power struggles between the factions led by his eldest son, the Black Prince, and his next surviving brother, John of Gaunt, Duke of Lancaster. Edmund Mortimer became a leading member of the Black

---

THE COAT OF ARMS

*5 Edmund Mortimer, 3rd Earl of March & Philippa, 5th Countess of Ulster*
*Dexter: Mortimer / Sinister: the royal arms (Quarterly France Ancient & England)*
*with a label for difference – surmounted by an earl's coronet*

The arms of Mortimer on this shield are different from those of Roger Mortimer (3), as the *azure* and *or* have been switched. Many slight variations in the Mortimer arms exist and are often not significant. This switch of colours, however, may be intentional. Most of the early examples of Mortimer shields have the same colour pattern as that given to Roger Mortimer, including the early fourteenth century arms of Roger's sister in St Laurence's, Ludlow. The colour orientation shown in the 3rd Earl's shield here became the norm later.

Edmund's wife Philippa was Countess of Ulster in her own right and it is interesting that the de Burgh arms are not included here, the emphasis being given to her father's royal arms. However the arms of de Burgh (aka Ulster) reappear in subsequent generations.

Prince's faction, putting him in opposition to Gaunt, who was already wary of the ambitions of the Mortimers, as their descent from his elder brother, Lionel, was a threat to his own ambitions if the line of the Black Prince failed. This triggered the conflicts between the Mortimers and the House of Lancaster – a conflict inherited 50 years later by the House of York and which led to the Wars of the Roses.

In 1377 the aged Edward III finally died, leaving his 10-year-old grandson, the son of the Black Prince, to become Richard II. With a child on the throne, and thus no prospect of an heir for some time, the issue of the royal succession became even more prominent. Edmund was appointed a member of the regency council, leading missions to Scotland as a negotiator and to inspect border defences. In 1379 he was appointed as Lieutenant of Ireland, a prestigious role to which he was well suited as the Earl of Ulster and greatest landowner in Ireland, but one which, from Gaunt's perspective, removed him from affairs in England. Edmund travelled to Ireland in 1380 where he operated with moderate success, but before he could achieve much he was taken ill and died there in 1381.

Edmund was succeeded by his seven-year-old son, another Roger (d.1398), the fourth Earl of March. During his childhood, the issue of the possible Mortimer claim to the throne was raised again. A few years later, when Gaunt tried to have his own son named as heir, Roger Mortimer objected on the grounds that he himself was descended from the second son of Edward III. Aged 18, he was appointed King's Lieutenant in Ireland in 1392, consequently spending much of his short life out of England. As the tensions, turmoil and opposition to the rule of Richard II grew alongside the concerns over the lack of an heir, Roger was summonsed back to England to attend a Parliament called to meet in Shrewsbury in 1397. It is recorded that on his return he was greeted by a crowd of 20,000 demonstrating their support by wearing hoods in Roger's livery colours of red and white, and expecting him to lead the opposition to the arbitrary conduct of the king. At the Parliament, Roger was careful to give the king no grounds for action against himself, and managed to return to Ireland. However, he was killed in 1398 in a skirmish with the Irish, leaving as his heir the seven-year-old Edmund.

The death of Roger Mortimer in Ireland triggered a sequence of events that led to the deposition of Richard II and usurpation of the throne by the son of John of Gaunt, Henry Bolingbroke. Having himself usurped the throne, Henry IV was inevitably wary of other contenders, particularly the potential claim of the child Edmund Mortimer (d.1425), 5th Earl of March. Accordingly, he placed his potential rival, together with Edmund's younger brother, under strict supervision as a royal ward. This did not prevent others from rebelling against Henry iv, claiming that Edmund Mortimer was the rightful king. On one occasion Edmund and his brother were seized from their confinement, transported towards Wales, only to be recaptured near Cheltenham and returned to closer confinement.

When Henry v acceded to the throne in 1413, he released the 22-year-old Edmund from custody and knighted him. Two years later, in 1415, as the king prepared to invade France, Edmund found himself at the centre of the 'Southampton Plot' to depose Henry and proclaim him king. The leader of the plot was Edmund's brother-in-law, Richard, Earl of Cambridge (see below) and it is not clear whether Edmund had any involvement in it, or just became aware of the plan. Whichever, he informed the king, who accepted his pledges of loyalty and pardoned him. Although Henry v died young in 1422 leaving the nine-month-old baby Henry vi as his heir, there is no evidence that Edmund Mortimer tried to take advantage to pursue his own claims, despite the suspicions of others. Like his father and grandfather, he was appointed Lieutenant of Ireland – probably (like them) to get him away from Court. Within a few months, however, he fell ill with the plague and died at his castle of Trim in Ireland in January 1425. As Edmund was childless, the vast Mortimer inheritance passed through his sister Anne (who had died 13 years earlier) to her son, Richard, Duke of York.

After the fortunes of the Mortimer family had been won back by the 2nd Earl in the 1350s, and with the marriage of his son into the royal family, the Mortimers were at the height of their potential power and influence. The irony, however, is that the succession of early deaths and consequent child heirs meant that the family was never able to fully exploit the roles open to them by their wealth and status. This impacted also on Ludlow Castle. The long periods of minorities meant that the castle was often in the hands of governors appointed by the Council of the Mortimer family or by the Crown. Even when the heirs were old enough to take responsibility for their lands, their roles in national politics and time spent in Ireland meant that the third, fourth, and fifth Earls spent little time at Ludlow. This situation changed significantly in the following generation, but before moving onto that there is another anomaly on the Heraldic Roll to consider.

## 6  Richard of Conisburgh, 1375–1415
### 3rd Earl of Cambridge

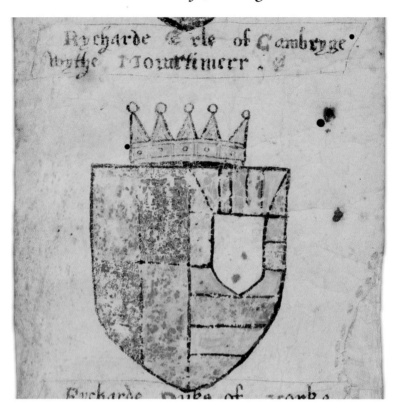

As with Lionel of Antwerp, it is a mystery why Richard of Conisburgh is included on the Roll, as he never owned Ludlow Castle. He was a grandson of Edward III by his fifth surviving son, Edmund of Langley, Duke of York, and married Anne Mortimer, sister of Edmund, fifth Earl of March. Since both Richard and his wife died before the fifth Earl, Richard could not have owned the castle. The only possibility is that, on marrying Anne in 1408, and with her brother still underage and in close confinement, Richard was given some responsibility for Ludlow. However, there is no evidence for this, and it is also highly unlikely as his hurried and possibly clandestine marriage to Anne took place without the king's permission. Furthermore, Richard does not appear to have been held in any esteem as he held no political or military office. His inclusion on the Roll is, therefore, most likely to be another mistake (this time, perhaps not deliberate) due to his being the father of Richard, Duke of York, who did inherit Ludlow, but from his maternal uncle.

Throughout his life Richard had no significant lands or income, and was not even provided for by his family. He was dependent on the Crown for an annuity, he won no patronage, and had no record of service to the Crown, leading to strong resentment on his part. This apparent neglect by his family led to speculation that he may have been born from his mother's liaison with John Holland, Earl of Huntingdon. Anne Mortimer died in 1411 soon after giving birth to their son, Richard. Although Henry v created Richard Earl of Cambridge in 1414, it was an empty title for it brought neither land nor money. If anything, it worsened his predicament for, as the poorest of the Earls, he lacked the resources to equip himself in a way befitting his rank.

The following year Richard's resentment surfaced when he tried to raise a rebellion against Henry v to place his brother-in-law, Edmund Mortimer onto the throne. Known as the Southampton Plot the whole scheme was impractical, and the planning was bungled. The plot was revealed and Richard of Conisburgh, Earl of Cambridge was executed.

Despite Richard being executed as a traitor, his son, also called Richard, was allowed to inherit his father's estates, which were of little value, but not his titles. A few months later, Conisburgh's elder brother, Edward, Duke of York was killed in 1415 at the Battle of Agincourt. As York died childless, his heir was Conisburgh's orphaned son. Thus, aged just four, the young child inherited the Duchy of York. Ten years later, when his maternal uncle, Edmund Mortimer, 5th Earl of March also died childless, Richard, Duke of York inherited the Mortimer lands – including Ludlow, titles and claim to the throne.

THE COAT OF ARMS
*6 Richard, 3rd Earl of Cambridge & Anne Mortimer*
*Dexter: the royal arms (Quarterly France Modern & England) with a label for*
*difference / Sinister: Mortimer – surmounted by an earl's coronet*

Richard never owned Ludlow castle. He was executed in 1415, ten years before the death of Edmund Mortimer, 5th Earl of March, who did own the castle. It is just possible to make out that the French arms are now *France Modern* with the number of fleurs-de-lys having been reduced to just three.

# 7  Richard of York, 1411–60
## 3rd Duke of York

R ICHARD'S MOTHER HAD died when he was still a baby; his father was executed for treason when he was only four years old; his paternal uncle was killed, childless, at Agincourt, and his maternal uncle died childless when he was 14. Consequently, from a very early age, Richard, Duke of York, Earl of March, Earl of Ulster (and potentially next in line to the throne while Henry VI remained childless), was the wealthiest and most important person after the King. Richard married Cecily Neville, daughter of Ralph Neville, 1st Earl of Westmorland in c.1426.

Henry VI had inherited the throne in 1422 when a baby less than one year old, resulting in an extremely long minority. As Henry grew into adulthood it became increasingly clear that he was unsuited to rule, and was prone to periods of passivity and mental breakdown. It seems that for nearly 20 years Richard took no steps to exploit this position, loyally serving in various positions at home and abroad, including Lieutenant-General and Governor of

France, and the King's Lieutenant in Ireland. In 1447 Richard, with Henry VI still childless, was named heir presumptive to the throne.

With his inherited lands and wealth spread across three countries, Richard did not have a strong local affinity anywhere. However, his Mortimer inheritance in the Welsh Marches contributed a large part of his landed wealth and many of his soldiers, so during this period Richard and Cecily came increasingly to use Ludlow Castle as one of their main bases, family home, and the administrative centre of their Marcher estates. They both joined the prestigious Ludlow Palmer's Guild and contributed to the extensive rebuilding of St Laurence's Church, which began in the 1430s. This generosity is reflected in the array of Yorkist symbolism throughout the church, including the misericords. Richard granted a charter to the town in 1449 and his sons, Edward (the future King Edward IV) and Edmund, were brought up at Ludlow Castle.

Misericords in St Laurence's, Ludlow, showing the falcon and fetterlock, symbol of Richard, Duke of York, and the White Rose of the House of York

From 1450 onwards, as conflict intensified between the factions around the king, Richard's association with Ludlow grew stronger: he lived there more often; he took refuge in the castle when events turned against him, and it was from Ludlow that many of his challenges to the advisers clustered around the king were issued. When the king suffered a complete mental collapse that

THE COAT OF ARMS
*7 Richard, 3rd Duke of York & Cecily Neville*
*Dexter: the royal arms (France Modern quartering England) with a label for difference / Sinister: Neville – surmounted by a ducal coronet*

It is much easier to see part of the royal differencing label on this shield, though no attempt has been made to show the three red balls that one would expect to see on the points of the label. The diagonal cross on the Neville arms is called a *saltire*.

lasted 18 months, Richard was officially appointed Protector. However, his position was weakened when the Queen, Margaret of Anjou, gave birth to a son and heir. When Henry recovered his wits, not only was there no need for a Protector, but Richard was now perceived as an even greater threat to the Lancastrian dynasty.

As the hostility between the factions moved into armed conflict and bloodshed, the queen, in order to protect her son's inheritance, began to take steps to exclude and crush Richard, his relatives and supporters. In 1459, the Yorkist forces met the king's army just to the south of Ludlow. However, when the king's own standard was raised, indicating his presence, the Yorkist army melted away, resulting in the Rout of Ludford Bridge. The victorious Lancastrians pillaged and looted the town of Ludlow. Richard and his elder sons fled into exile, leaving Cecily and the younger children to be captured by the Lancastrians. On their return the following year, it was in Ludlow that Richard first formally claimed the Crown based on his Mortimer inheritance. Receiving no support from his peers in London, a compromise was reached when he was officially named as the heir to Henry VI, effectively disinheriting the King's son. Inevitably, this was unacceptable to the queen, so armed conflict continued. In December 1461, after Richard's death at the Battle of Wakefield, the leadership of the Yorkist cause was inherited by his son, Edward, who was based at Ludlow.

# 8 King Edward IV, 1442–83

EDWARD WAS THE eldest son of Richard, Duke of York. He was brought up in Ludlow and, aged 18, was given his first independent command when his father gave him leadership of the Yorkist forces in the Welsh Marches. Edward was thus at Ludlow and Wigmore when he heard the news about the death of his father at the Battle of Wakefield. A few weeks later, Edward led his army to victory at the Battle of Mortimers Cross a few miles west of Ludlow, and marched on London to claim the crown. When he was crowned Edward IV in 1461, Ludlow Castle, along with the rest of the Mortimer inheritance, was brought into royal ownership (in which it remained until 1811 when the Castle was bought by the Earl of Powis). As King, Edward maintained his connection with Ludlow, spending a week there in September 1461, granting the town a new charter and making substantial contributions to the further rebuilding of St Laurence's. As stated in the charter, Edward was moved by, 'the laudable and gratuitous services

THE COAT OF ARMS
*8 King Edward IV & Elizabeth Woodville*
*Dexter: the royal arms (France Modern quartering England) / Sinister: quarterly of six; 1 Luxembourg; 2 Baux; 3 Lusignan of Cyprus; 4 Orsini; 5 St Pol; 6 Woodville – surmounted by a crown*

The most interesting aspect of this shield is the order of the six quarterings on the Queen's arms. Her mother was Jacquetta of Luxembourg, whose first marriage had been to John of Lancaster, Duke of Bedford, who was Henry V's brother. When he died, Jacquetta fell in love with the duke's chamberlain, Richard Woodville, and they married in secret. There was thus a huge disparity in rank between Elizabeth Woodville's father and mother, and this is reflected in her coat of arms. The normal practice is for the paternal arms to occupy the first quarter but here the humble Woodville arms are relegated to the final position, after five of her mother's much more impressive quarterings.

In Elizabeth's second quartering, the arms of Baux are quartered with those of *France Ancient*. However, the illustrator doesn't have room to indicate the correct pattern of fleurs-de-lys so settles for just showing three, one above the other.

which our beloved and faithful subjects the burgesses of the town of Ludlow had rendered unto us in the obtaining of our right to the crown of England (…) in great peril of their lives. And also the rapines, depredations, oppressions, losses of goods, and other grievances for us and our sake.'

Edward IV's connection with Ludlow continued when, in 1473, he sent his eldest son and heir, the Prince of Wales, Prince Edward, aged three, to be brought up and educated in Ludlow with his own household, away from the intrigues of London. As Edward was a young child, the rule of his household and lands, which included the Principality of Wales and later the Earldom of March, were entrusted to a Council. The 'Prince's Council' accompanied the three-year-old Prince to Ludlow, and in later years this Council developed into the Council in the Marches of Wales (see Chapter 5).

Having lived in Ludlow for ten years, the young Prince Edward was only thirteen when he heard of the unexpected death of his father, the King, in 1483. The Prince left Ludlow to travel to London for his coronation, but on the way was intercepted, confined in the Tower of London and, with his brother, subsequently disappeared – the 'Princes in the Tower', whose fate is hotly disputed. The young Prince's uncle, the brother of Edward IV, was crowned King Richard III.

Richard's reign lasted less than three years. In 1485 he was defeated at the Battle of Bosworth by the Lancastrian Henry Tudor, who was crowned Henry VII. It is interesting to note that Richard III and his arms are omitted from the Roll – perhaps not surprisingly given the Tudor campaign to blacken his name.

## 9 King Henry VII, 1457–1509

To bolster his claim to the throne, and to bring peace to the kingdom by uniting the opposing factions responsible for four decades of civil war, Henry Tudor married Elizabeth of York, daughter of Edward IV and niece of Richard III. Although Henry VII had no previous personal connection with Ludlow, the town was now the property of the Crown, and his wife was a descendant of the Mortimers through the Duke of York. This, combined with appreciation of Ludlow's strategic importance in securing his rule on the border and in Wales, ensured continued royal patronage of the town. Henry visited Ludlow on several occasions and, in 1493, continued the precedent established by Edward IV of granting the Castle, town and Lordship of Ludlow to the seven-year-old Prince Arthur. Henry also realised

the value of re-establishing the Prince's Council to govern the young Prince's lands. Arthur, Prince of Wales, was resident at Ludlow Castle with his wife Katherine of Aragon when he died there in 1502. His heart was buried in St Laurence's church, and his body in Worcester Cathedral where a chantry chapel, with a fine display of heraldry and badges of Arthur, marks his grave.

THE COAT OF ARMS
9 *King Henry VII & Elizabeth of York*
*Dexter: the royal arms of England (France Modern quartering England)*
*Sinister: Quarterly 1 the royal arms as above; 2 & 3 Burgh (Ulster); 4 Mortimer –
surmounted by a crown*

The royal arms in the first quarter in the queen's coat of arms show her status as Princess Elizabeth, the daughter of King Edward IV. The other quarters indicate her descent from the Mortimer Earls of March and the Earls of Ulster.

# 10 King Henry VIII, 1491–1547

O N THE ROLL, the arms of Henry VIII are quartered with those of his 2nd wife Anne Boleyn, 1501–36. Despite Anne being convicted of treason and beheaded in 1536, this version of Henry's arms was used during Elizabeth I's reign because Anne was Elizabeth's mother. Although Henry visited Ludlow as Prince of Wales, there is no record of him visiting after his coronation in 1509. However, Ludlow Castle was used as a royal residence once more when King Henry's eldest daughter, his only child with Katherine of Aragon, the Princess Mary (later Queen Mary I) lived in the castle with her court for three winters between 1525 and 1528.

During Henry's reign, the Prince's Council, still based in Ludlow, evolved into the Council in the Marches of Wales as a devolved form of administration and justice, when the powers of the Marcher Lordships and Principality of Wales were abolished. In their place, a system of county governance and sessions of court were established in Wales, and the administration of England and Wales was formally united by the Acts of Union of 1536 and 1543.

THE COAT OF ARMS
*10 King Henry VIII & Anne Boleyn*
*Dexter: the royal arms of England (France*
*Modern quartering England)*
*Sinister: quarterly of six, 1 Lancaster; 2 & 3*
*missing; 4 Butler quartered with Rochford; 5 & 6*
*missing – surmounted by a crown*

The full coat of arms for Henry VIII and Anne
Boleyn would have looked like this:

*Full list of the queen's quarterings: 1 Lancaster;*
*2 Angouleme; 3 Guinne; 4 Butler (Ormonde)*
*quartering Rochford; 5 Brotherton; 6 Warenne*

The queen's coat of arms has been 'beefed up' to make it as impressive as
possible. The first three quarterings were given to her by the king in 1532
when she was created Marchioness of Pembroke, before she became queen.
She had no familial or legal right to them otherwise. The Lancastrian coat
in quarter 1 of the queen's arms is the arms of England with a label charged
with fleurs-de-lys. The label is clear on the Roll but not the fleurs-de-lys.
    Quarter 4 represents Anne's father, Sir Thomas Boleyn, who had been
elevated to the titles of Earl of Ormonde and Viscount Rochford as well as to
the earldom of Wiltshire.

Arms of Henry VIII impaled with Anne Boleyn. *College of Arms MS Vincent 152 p. 59.*
© *Reproduced by permission of the Kings, Heralds and Pursuivants of Arms*

Henry VIII was succeeded by his only son, Edward VI, in 1547. When
Edward died at the young age of 16, he was succeeded by his older sisters,
first Mary in 1553, then Elizabeth in 1558.

## 11 Queen Elizabeth I, 1533–1603

AFTER THE SHORT reigns and religious turmoil and conflicts of her brother
and sister, Elizabeth's 44 years on the throne from 1558 to 1603 provided welcome stability for the kingdom and helped forge a sense of national
identity. Throughout most of her reign, there were only two Presidents of the
Council in the Marches of Wales: Sir Henry Sidney from 1560 to 1586 and his
son-in-law, Henry Herbert, Earl of Pembroke from 1586 to 1601. The stability
that resulted from two such long-lasting Presidencies enabled the Council
to flourish, and ensured that a grand household was maintained at Ludlow
Castle, although Queen Elizabeth never visited Ludlow.

Elyzabeth by the grace of god qneene of
France and Jerlande defender of the fayth

DIV : ET                 DROIT

MO · N

France

Southe Wailes

God save
her grace
amen

Ludlow Castle had been maintained in a suitable fashion for its ducal and
royal households throughout the later fourteenth and the fifteenth centuries,
but there is no record of any significant repairs or changes to the structures
for 200 years after the extensive building works of Roger Mortimer in the
first part of the fourteenth century. This was partly because the structure
of the castle was enough for the needs of successive households, but it also
reflected the owners' wider role in national affairs. However, the new requirements as the headquarters of the Council in the Marches of Wales in the
sixteenth century brought about another significant phase of development.

Thus, Ludlow's role as an important royal residence in the late fifteenth and early sixteenth centuries, and thereafter as the home of the Council in the Marches of Wales, ensured the active use, rebuilding and maintenance of Ludlow Castle into the seventeenth century, long after other castles had fallen into disuse, been abandoned to the elements or picked over by people keen to put the materials to other uses.

The use of the castle began to change as the role of the Council came under attack in the seventeenth century, leading to the abolition of its judicial powers in 1641, followed by the complete disruption of its activities during the Civil War and Cromwellian Commonwealth. At the start of the Civil War, Ludlow had been a Royalist stronghold but fell to the Parliamentarians when it was surrendered by its governor and commander, Sir Michael Woodhouse. Under both Royalist and Parliamentarian control Ludlow Castle was used as a garrison to billet soldiers.

After the Restoration of Charles II, the Council was formally re-established in 1661, but survived for only another 28 years. Although £2,000 was granted for the repair and furnishing of the castle, there were subsequent complaints that the Lord President had kept most of the funds for himself and had neglected repairs.

From 1689, when the Council was formally abolished by Act of Parliament, the decline of Ludlow Castle set in, with evident decay emerging quickly in

THE COAT OF ARMS
*11 Queen Elizabeth I*
*The royal arms are encircled by the Garter and the achievement includes a crowned helm, mantling, two supporters and the monarch's motto*

The supporters chosen by the queen are the lion of England and the red dragon of Wales. Below the main shield is an incomplete collection of smaller shields, presumably representing the countries of which Elizabeth was, or claimed to be, the monarch, including France. The shield labelled 'South Wales' is particularly interesting. It is identical to the arms used by successive native princes of Wales for many centuries. The colours have been reversed, though this was not uncommon. The Princes of Wales are linked historically with North Wales rather than South Wales, and the Welsh hero Owain Glyndwr used very similar arms. It is not clear why these arms have been associated here with South Wales. Mytton made a drawing of a very similar group of shields in the council chamber (see p. 74) and from that it can be seen that the two small coats of arms missing from the roll were probably the arms of Ireland and England.

SHREWSBURY
PUBLIC
LIBRARY.

Ludlow Castle
Sept. 21. 1789
132

Revd Edward Williams's watercolour of Ludlow Castle, 1789.
*6001/372/1/132 © Shropshire Archives*

subsequent decades. The castle was put in the hands of a series of Crown appointees – governors, low paid officials, who lived in fewer and fewer rooms, leaving the remainder to fall into disrepair. An inventory of 1708 shows that, after 20 years, only three rooms in the Hall range were in use, and only one in the Judge's Lodgings, with much of the furniture worn and broken. In 1714 the process of decay was accelerated when an order was given to unroof the buildings in order to strip them of their lead. Inevitably, this was quickly followed by the decay of the floors and other timbers, and the plunder of the furniture. By the early 1720s, Daniel Defoe described Ludlow castle as,

> The very perfection of decay, all the fine courts, the royal apartments, halls and rooms of state, lye open, abandoned and some of them falling down; for since the Courts of the President and Marches are taken away, here is nothing that requires the attendance of any publick people; so that time, the great devourer of the works of men, begins to eat into the very stone walls and spread the face of royal ruins over the whole fabric.

The decline continued into the 1760s when the Earl of Powis began to take an interest in Ludlow Castle, agreeing to lease the site from the Crown. It seems that the Earl had plans to build a residence for himself within the ruins of the inner bailey; however, his death in 1772 resulted in any plans being shelved. Despite this the Powis family did make some repairs to the buildings, and other improvements, including planting trees, laying out paths on the castle mound above the river, and opening the site to the townspeople.

During the Napoleonic wars there were plans to use the castle to house upwards of 4,000 prisoners of war, which fortunately came to nothing. In 1811, the Earl of Powis was allowed to purchase Ludlow Castle, and it has remained in the ownership of the Earls of Powis ever since. The castle was scheduled as an Ancient Monument in 1915. Gradually, the accumulation of undergrowth and the ivy that clad the walls was cut back, allowing the repair and stabilisation of the remaining structures.

During its 600 years of active use from the end of the eleventh century to the end of the seventeenth, Ludlow Castle developed from a frontier fortress to a royal castle, to be the centre of the Crown and government's administration and justice throughout Wales and the Marches. The physical development of the castle reflected not just new ideas and technology to improve the defences, but also the interests, needs and wealth of successive owners who desired a residence and castle that proclaimed their status to everyone.

# 12  Sir Henry Sidney, 1529–86

## Lord President of the Council in the Marches of Wales 1560–86

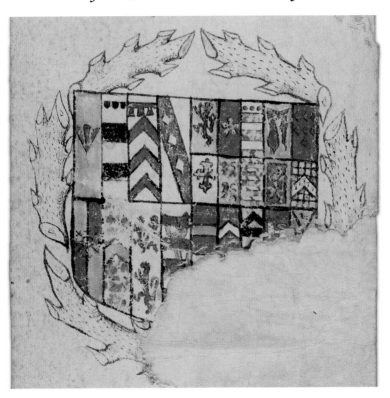

THE COAT OF ARMS

12 Sir Henry Sidney & Mary Dudley

Dexter: Quarterly of 8 – 1 Sidney; 2 Clowfield, Clunford etc.; 3 Barrington;
4 Merry or Mercy; 5 Mandeville; 6 Chetwynd; 7 ?Baard, Baare etc.; 8 Brandon
Sinister: Quarterly of 20 – 1 Dudley; 2 Beaumont; 3 Grey de Ruthyn; 4 Hastings;
5 Ferrers; 6 Lexington; 7 Somery; 8 Valence; 9 Talbot; 10 Newburgh;
11 Beauchamp; 12 Berkeley; 13 Lisle of Rougemont; 14 Lisle of Kingston Lisle;
15 Guildford; 16–20 missing. The shield is encircled by a design of six ragged
staffs, referring to his wife's Dudley ancestry from the Earls of Warwick

The main interest in this shield is the marked difference in status and
provenance of the quarterings on the dexter and sinister sides. The 15 visible
quarterings on Mary Dudley's arms represent many of the great families of
the Middle Ages, including Beauchamp, Beaumont, Berkeley, Ferrers, Grey,
Hastings, Lisle, Talbot & Valence. We can add to that list the illustrious name
of Mortimer which was in quarter 19. (*continued over*)

THE COAT OF ARMS (*CONT.*)
The rules of heraldry state that, when a man marries an heraldic heiress, their children may, on her death, quarter their mother's arms with their father's. Using this criterion, Mary Dudley was entitled to all of her 20 quarterings as it is possible to trace all the heiresses. By contrast, Sir Henry's arms on the dexter side are much less impressive. While he was certainly descended from the families of Clowfield, Barrington, Mercy and Brandon, there is no evidence that any of these grandmothers were heiresses. He may also have been obscurely descended from the families shown in the other quarters, but the overall impression is of a man who felt he 'needed' quarterings. He employed Robert Cooke, Clarenceux Herald, and was granted some more, whether he was strictly entitled to them or not.

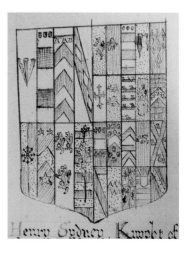

Arms of Sir Henry Sidney, showing the missing five quarters drawn by William Mytton, c.1735. MYT/3/573B © *Cadbury Research Library, Special Collections, University of Birmingham*

# 13 John Scory, ?–1585
## *Bishop of Hereford*
### *Councillor in the Marches of Wales 1559–85*

JOHN SCORY WAS one of the first bishops on the Council who had not followed the traditional pre-Reformation career pattern – in marked contrast to his episcopal predecessors. In 1530 he was a friar in a Dominican house in Cambridge, but by 1541 he was a chaplain to Archbishop Cranmer, suggesting he had swiftly converted to the Protestant religion. The Edwardian reformation furthered his career: he briefly held the see of Rochester in 1551 and then took Chichester in 1552 as part of the Protestant redistribution of sees. He was deprived by Mary but possibly saved his life by recantation, officiating quietly in London. If so, this was a brief period which he played down. In 1554, like many other Protestants, he went into exile, arriving in the expatriate community of Emden, Germany, where he quickly became the minister of the exile church. As one of the only two

John Scory lorde bisshope of

---

THE COAT OF ARMS

*13 John Scory, Bishop of Hereford*
*Dexter: the diocese of Hereford / Sinister: Scory*

The Hereford diocese adopted the arms of St Thomas Cantilupe who was
bishop from 1275–82. These include upside-down leopards' heads with a
fleur-de-lys issuing from them. The main tinctures on the Scory coat are
actually *or* and *sable*, though the gold has faded badly

   The arms of Scory include three 'pelicans in their piety'. This refers to the
legend in which, as the young pelicans grow, they begin to attack their parents.
Though the adult loves them, it strikes back and kills them. After three days,
the mother pierces her breast and the blood from the wound revives the
children. The 'pelican in its piety' is used as a symbol of Christ's sacrifice on the
Cross. Because of their religious significance, pelicans often occur in the arms
of clergymen (*see 15 Robinson*). The red splashes of blood from the pelican's
wounds are just visible on all three pelicans.

   There were Skories in Cornwall at the time of Edward I, whose coat of
arms was quite different. Bishop John Scory was granted the arms we see on
the Roll in ignorance of his possible descent from these earlier Skories. In 1588,
after his death, his son received a new grant of the original Skorie arms, so the
arms on the Roll do not appear to have been passed on to anyone else.

---

bishops to go into exile it was even suggested that he might take over the
more prestigious exile church at Frankfurt. He remained at Emden however, ministering in the best reformed style with elders and deacons, the

future Archbishop Young acting as his assistant. Scory was one of the first to return to England, arriving in December 1558, and the English church at Emden did not long survive his departure.

While in exile, Scory was noted for his protestant writings. He published translations of the church fathers Augustine and Cyprian, to demonstrate that the protestant church of Henry VIII and Edward VI was a true church, in doctrine and practice consistent with the early church. His 'Comfortable Epistle unto the Faithful that be in Prison' was intended to strengthen protestant resolve under persecution and does not even hint at any wavering of his own faith prior to exile. He was probably also involved in a new edition of Cranmer's *A Defence of the True and Catholic Doctrine of the Sacrament of the Body and Blood of Our Saviour Christ*. He was an ideal Protestant to take up a bishopric again on his return.

In fact, Scory turned out to be rather a disappointment, closer in spirit to the vacillation which preceded exile. He was originally intended for the diocese of Norwich, and took part in the disputation held with the Catholic bishops in March 1559. In June, however, he was appointed merely to Hereford, a remote and poor diocese. He found the diocese far from reformed. He reported that the cathedral was full of 'dissemblers and rank papists' and that 'priests and such like enemies of the Church find a safe asylum here and are maintained and feasted as if they were God's angels.' At first he encouraged radical Protestants in his diocese, and supported the 'prophesyings' favoured by zealous reformers. By 1576, however, he felt they had been hijacked by extremists and ended such 'prophesyings' in his diocese. He also found himself caught up in arguments over finances and the reduction of manors supporting the see. Scory's income was only £305, where his predecessors had enjoyed £519.

By 1580, most of the first generation of keen, returning exiles – like Grindal, Pilkington and Horne – were dead, and Scory seems to have lacked godly zeal in his later years and was not an effective bishop, though old age was probably a contributing factor.

As Bishop of Hereford, he was automatically a member of the Council in the Marches of Wales but he was opposed to Sidney, to the point of complaining to Cecil in 1582 that Sidney was bringing his name into disrepute. His main work for the Council was serving on commissions looking at offences against religious conformity.

# 14  Nicholas Bullingham, c.1511–76
## Bishop of Worcester
### Councillor in the Marches of Wales 1571–76

N ICHOLAS BULLINGHAM WAS another of the exiles at Emden who came to prominence in the Elizabethan church. He owed his favour to his close connection to Archbishop Parker, and like Scory was something of a disappointment as a diocesan.

---

THE COAT OF ARMS
*14 Nicholas Bullingham, Bishop of Worcester*
*The bishop's personal arms*

Usually a bishop's personal arms are impaled with those of their diocese, but the arms of Worcester are not included here. When they are present, it is normal for the arms of the diocese to be placed on the more important, *dexter* (left) side of the shield with the bishop's personal arms being placed on the *sinister* side. However, on his memorial in Worcester Cathedral (*see overleaf*), the Bullingham arms have, most unusually, been placed on the *dexter* side while the arms of the diocese have been relegated to the *sinister* side.

---

Like many pre-Reformation bishops, Bullingham had a legal rather than a theological background. A Fellow of All Souls in 1536, he too became a chaplain to Archbishop Cranmer, holding various posts at Lincoln: first a prebend in 1547, augmented by a rectory in 1552. Deprived by Mary because of his marriage, he was restored to his livings on return from exile, and became Bishop of Lincoln in 1560. Matthew Parker, the Archbishop of Canterbury, had been Dean of Lincoln in 1552, and became Bullingham's patron.

Monument of Bishop Bullingham, 'a painful preacher of the truth', Worcester Cathedral

Bullingham had displayed his credentials in Edward's reign, serving on commissions against the Anabaptists, and to enforce the new Protestant Prayer Book. In the 1560s, however, he showed himself a moderate like Parker, backing the drive for conformity in wearing the surplice, and only in 1565 starting to remove some of the more conservative elements from his cathedral. Until 1566 he was responsible for the custody of Bishop Bourne, and was active in the House of Lords. He was one of the translators of the *Bishops' Bible* in 1568, though his knowledge of Greek has been questioned.

In 1571 Bullingham was finally translated from Lincoln to Worcester, his home town, in a move probably intended to reduce his workload in old age. Here he proved a conservative diocesan, and not a particularly good administrator. He was conscientious to an extent, however, holding his last ordinations only a fortnight before his death.

## 15 Nicholas Robinson, c.1530–85
### *Bishop of Bangor*
### *Councillor in the Marches of Wales 1566–85*

NICHOLAS ROBINSON WAS a typical example of the clergy of the universities in the 1550s. He took his MA in 1551 in the reign of Edward VI, at Queens' Cambridge, of which he was bursar from 1551–53. He lost his post on Mary's accession but subscribed to a Catholic declaration of faith in 1555. As a result he was ordained in 1557, by special dispensation of Cardinal

Pole, by his old friend and patron Bishop Glyn, Bishop of Bangor. However he swiftly reverted to Protestantism in Elizabeth's reign, becoming vice-president of his college in 1561 and archdeacon of Merioneth in 1562. He was consecrated Bishop of Bangor in 1566, holding the diocese until his death in 1585. He was therefore automatically a member of the Council of Wales.

THE COAT OF ARMS
*15 Nicholas Robinson, Bishop of Bangor*
*Dexter: the diocese of Bangor / Sinister: Robinson quartered with Merbrook*

The arms of the diocese of Bangor include a good example of the use of droplets in heraldry. Black droplets, as in these arms, are said to be droplets of pitch and when a heraldic field or charge is covered in black droplets like this, it is said to be *goutée de poix*.

For one reason or another, the personal arms of Nicholas Robinson have caused considerable confusion over the years, and the version painted on the Roll is just one of three quite different ones that can be found around the country. More research needs to be done, but, for the purposes of this book, we'll assume that the arms on the Roll are the correct ones. Bishop Robinson's paternal ancestors were the family of Norreys (or Norris) of Speke Hall, Liverpool. It is said that, at some point, a John Norreys married an heiress called Millicent Ravenscroft. Although he kept the family name of Norreys, he adopted the Ravenscroft coat of arms, which features a chevron between three ravens heads – a pun on the name Ravenscroft (*continued overleaf*).

THE COAT OF ARMS (CONT.)

John Norreys's great-grandson was another John Norreys (c.1400–66). Keeper of the Wardrobe for Henry VI, he married the heiress Alice Merbrook, and their children quartered the Norreys (Ravenscroft) arms with Merbrook. The fact that these are the arms given to Bishop Robinson on the Roll implies, if they are correct, that he was a direct descendant of this John Norreys. The paternal great-grandfather of Nicholas Robinson was called Robin Norris. He had a son, Henry who was Henry Robin's son Norris and this eventually became Henry Robinson, so that's how the surname of this branch of the Norrises changed.

Research into their coat of arms is made more difficult by the fact that later members of the Norreys (Ravenscroft) branch decided to go back to the original coat of arms of Norreys of Speke, and in the nineteenth century these were incorrectly assigned to Bishop Robinson. The first two images below are from Knebworth House in Hertfordshire.

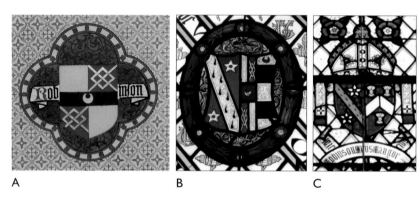

A                            B                            C

Image **A** shows the Arms of Norreys of Speke differenced with a crescent. Image **B** shows the back-dated arms of Bishop Robinson and his wife after his descendants had reverted to the old Norris coat.

Not content with two versions, there is another completely spurious one in existence (**C**). Here is Bishop Robinson's coat of arms in a window in Old Hall in Clare College, Cambridge. This version is the result of a mistake. The arms are actually those of his mother Elin Brickdale. It is thought that his own arms disappeared from his brass monument in Bangor Cathedral, but his mother's remained and were assumed to be his. This version also appears in Winchester College.

Robinson gave every impression of being a convinced Protestant. His 1566 report on his diocese declared his people to be loyal to the Queen but bound up in superstition – in other words, still Catholics. He complained that there were not 60 people in the three shires who could preach, and moreover the 'word of God was closed up in a foreign tongue' – not Latin, but English. He was known to be a fine scholar who wanted to see the translation of the Bible into Welsh.

Robinson's Protestantism fell foul of a number of obstinate Catholics within his diocese, especially Sir Richard Bulkeley, the most powerful of his gentry. Robinson objected to the stubborn survival of Catholic practices, and to Bulkeley's attendance at a 'papistical' funeral at Beaumaris. By 1577 he reportedly had only one feeble old priest in the diocese who still objected to reform, though some of the gentry – Bulkeley again – had been reprimanded for withdrawing themselves from church. It was remarkable that, having managed to quarrel with Bulkeley, the bishop was himself accused of having Catholic sympathies. Robinson continued to be troubled by the failure of Protestantism to make any headway. In 1582 he complained of being called a persecutor because he was watching out for missing priests and inquiring twice yearly which gentlemen withdrew themselves from services.

As a member of the Council in the Marches of Wales, Robinson, like Bishop Davies of St Asaph, headed a commission to inquire into uniformity of religion, which had been authorised by the Privy Council. In 1578 Robinson was ordered by the Privy Council to enquire particularly into the state of affairs among gentry in the Lleyn peninsula. One of the conspirators in the Ridolfi plot against Elizabeth had a brother living there and the bishop was to search various houses to find traces of other supporters. Despite information being leaked by one of the clerks to recusants being held in prison in Ludlow, the man sought was arrested and imprisoned after trial before the Council.

Robinson was keen on the execution of justice, praising the work of George Bromley, Justice of the Anglesey circuit and after 1580 chief justice of Chester. The bishop recalled that, 'in the three shires called Caernarvon, Anglesey and Merioneth (…) the people live in much obedience, freedom and quiet'. This he ascribed chiefly to Bromley's efforts. Robinson evidently took his judicial and administrative responsibilities towards Wales and the Council as seriously as his episcopal ones.

# 16  Richard Davies, c.1505–81
## *Bishop of St David's*
## *Councillor in the Marches of Wales 1559–81*

T HE CAREER OF Richard Davies runs parallel to that of other Elizabethan Welsh bishops. The offspring of a married cleric (a situation widely tolerated in pre-Reformation Wales), he was the Edwardian vicar of Burnham, Buckinghamshire in 1550. In Mary's reign he abandoned his Buckinghamshire parishes and fled to Frankfurt. In exile he struck up a friendship with Edmund Grindal, later Archbishop of Canterbury, with whom he long maintained contact, supporting him on the matter of 'prophesyings' in 1576. Returning on Elizabeth's accession, he was originally suggested for the Worcester diocese but appointed to St Asaph, some pressure being put on the canons to accept him. He was allowed to continue to hold his other livings as the Welsh dioceses were so poor, despite the undesirability of such practices, and was almost immediately translated to St David's in 1561, a diocese where he remained for the last 20 years of his life.

Davies was an adviser to Archbishop Parker and William Cecil on Welsh affairs, in which he took a deep interest. He collaborated with William Salesbury in translating the Bible into Welsh (a task first completed in

1567), and then revised part of the *Bishops' Bible* in 1568. With the Earl of Essex he co-founded Carmarthen Grammar School in 1576, and in 1578 he was on a commission for the suppression of Welsh piracy.

One of the most conscientious and hardworking of the Welsh bishops, he was keen that the church should support preachers and teachers. In 1561 he had ordered the clergy of his diocese to appoint three or four people in each church to keep order during services. Few ordinations were held before 1565 because, he claimed, of the lack of suitable candidates, though it is suggested that some from his diocese went to other bishops who were easier to reach, or more lenient in their expectations. In 1565 he begged for a replacement for Bishop Kitchen at Llandaff, whose see had been unoccupied for three years since his death: 'light was needed in the welsh darkness'. In 1570 his account of his own diocese claimed that there were no open recusants or opponents of the Queen; some however were 'careless of religion' or wished for Rome again. In 1577 he reckoned some of the diocese to be Catholic at heart, but only found one poor man in Radnorshire who stayed away from church.

---

THE COAT OF ARMS
*16 Richard Davies, Bishop of St Davids*
*Dexter: the diocese of St Davids / Sinister: the personal arms of Bishop Davies*

The most interesting thing about this shield is that the arms of the diocese of St Davids on the Roll are significantly different from the usual arms of the diocese. The design on the Roll is a rare variant which only occurs in a few other sixteenth-century manuscripts. There is an illustration of Bishop Davies' arms in the 1729 edition of Matthew Parker's *De Antiquitate Britannicae*, which shows the more usual version of the arms of the diocese.
   Bishop Davies' personal arms are very similar to Bishop Scory's (13) with pelicans in their piety.

---

Davies' sternest criticisms were usually reserved for the gentry and magistrates. In 1577 he complained that 200 persons in his diocese had been excommunicated for immorality, but the sheriff refused to execute the writs. By 1578 he had decided that to call a man before the Council in the Marches of Wales was more likely to lead to his correction than the use of episcopal courts. A special commission was sent by the Council into St David's diocese to try to deal with sexual immorality. This resulted in the bishop falling foul of important local laymen like Sir John Parrot, Richard Vaughan, and Fabian Phillips – the last a fellow member of Council from 1575. In 1580 he criticised inefficient and apathetic magistrates who failed to clamp down on recusancy. Meanwhile his duties as a member of Council included supervising ministers, investigating the bribing of sheriffs, recovering stolen cattle, and suppressing piracy.

Davies was probably not the easiest of colleagues to work with. Despite his keenness on Bible translation he parted company with Salesbury, his fellow translator, took on a younger assistant after 1575, and left an unfinished work which was taken up after his death by William Morgan. His literary interests included his friendship with Edmund Spenser who portrayed him, in *The Shephearde's Calendar*, as the character Diggon Davie, being opposed to the dogs [officials] who allowed wolves [papists] to attack the flock.

## 17 Thomas Davies, c.1511–73
### Bishop of St Asaph
### Councillor in the Marches of Wales 1561–73

T HOMAS DAVIES WAS a native of Caernarvon and a Cambridge graduate, becoming a Doctor of Law (LLD). In 1548, he was Chancellor
of Bangor Cathedral. However, by 1554 he was married with children,
and as such he was removed from office under the Catholic regime established by Queen Mary. He presumably accepted the Marian restoration of
Catholicism, and theoretically repudiated his wife and family because he
was appointed by Cardinal Pole as a caretaker for Bangor diocese on the
death of Bishop Glyn. His religious views were either elastic or politically
expedient since he is found again as an active reformer in Elizabeth's reign,
becoming Archdeacon of St Asaph before being raised to its bishop.

His diocesan career follows a familiar Elizabethan pattern. He too sought
to reform the diocese and establish a learned ministry. In November 1561 he
ordered that in church services the epistles, the gospel and the catechism were
to be read in English and then in Welsh to educate parishioners and children.
He argued that the stipends of former chaplains at the altars of the Virgin
Mary should instead be devoted to education to avoid youth being in idleness
but rather learning to be God-fearing and dutiful men.

---

THE COAT OF ARMS
*17 Thomas Davies, Bishop of St Asaph*
*Dexter: the see of St Asaph / Sinister: Quarterly: 1 & 4 his paternal arms,*
*descended from Sir Gruffudd Llwyd (d.1335); 2 his maternal arms, descended*
*from Iarddur ap Cynddelw; 3 unidentified*

This coat of arms is very special heraldically for two reasons. There appears
to be no other known example where the arms of the see of St Asaph have
a field *gules*. The usual arms now associated with St Asaph has two crossed
keys on a field *sable*. Earlier examples exist which display a key crossing a
bishop's crozier, as on the Ludlow Roll, but the field is then usually *azure*.

The third quartering on Bishop Davies' personal shield is very faded.
Nevertheless, it is possible to determine that the field is *or* and the charge is
a *lion rampant*. There is no remaining colour on the lion itself, except what
seems to be its red claws up near its head. Although it's tempting to say the
lion is *argent* this is highly unlikely as there is a strict convention in heraldry
that doesn't allow for the placing of one metal (silver) on top of another
(gold). This is an important quartering as it does not appear in any other
examples of the bishop's arms. Despite extensive research, it has not been
possible, so far, to link the bishop with any family bearing arms similar to
these. His ancestor, Sir Gruffudd Llwyd came from North Wales. A great
Anglophile, he faithfully served both Edward I and Edward II and is listed as
supporting the execution of Roger Mortimer, 1st Earl of March.

By 1570 Davies was more optimistic about his diocese: people were more obedient in religion, though the diocese still harboured too many of corrupt religion (in other words, Catholics), who could not be apprehended as both civil and ecclesiastical authorities were remiss. In his diocese Davies chiefly devoted himself to canon law and administration. As a member of the Council in the Marches of Wales he sat on a commission for the suppression of piracy on the Flintshire coast in 1566.

## 18  Sir James Croft, c.1518–90
### Councillor in the Marches of Wales 1570–90

J AMES CROFT WAS descended from an old Herefordshire family – the Crofts of Croft Castle – and several of his forebears served successive kings. Thus, Croft himself was well-placed to serve both at Court and in the Welsh marches. As a young man he warmly espoused the new Protestant religion. Yet, despite this his career was a complex one, with falls from royal favour followed by restoration into Court circles. He was often seen as being his own worst enemy as he had, 'not the readiest way to do good to himself as other courtiers have (...) and standeth in need of help more than, perhaps, his stomach will yield to make show to the world.'

Croft's career was initially that of an active soldier-administrator, serving in France under John Dudley, Earl of Warwick, and given commands in Scotland and Ireland.

His association with Dudley earned Croft rich rewards in the reign of Edward VI. He was knighted in 1547, followed in 1550 by his appointment to the Council in the Marches of Wales, becoming Vice-President the following year under William Herbert. In the same year he was appointed Lord Deputy of Ireland, with the near-impossible task of enforcing the Protestant religious reforms of Edward VI upon a strongly Catholic population, which, combined with military defeat and spiralling costs, resulted in his early recall. His next post, as Deputy Constable of the Tower of London, was also short-lived, as less than a year later his status had changed from prison keeper to prisoner, charged with treason for his part in the Protestant-led Wyatt rebellion against Queen Mary. Although sentenced to death, he was later fined and bound over – and eventually pardoned. By 1557, Mary seems to have forgiven Croft, trusting him enough to use his military talents in the Scottish war against Mary de Guise. On Elizabeth's accession he was given a prominent role in this war and in the negotiations with the Scottish Protestants. However, he was suspected of lack of commitment and double-dealing, and was dismissed.

Croft seems not to have learnt from his close shaves with Parliament and his royal employers. Accusations of playing a double-game for his private ends were to feature for the remainder of his life, and lost him the support of almost every influential person in the country, other than Queen Elizabeth. They had both been imprisoned in the Tower of London after the Wyatt

THE COAT OF ARMS
*18 Sir James Croft*
*Arms of Croft*

Mytton saw the original shield in the eighteenth century and correctly recorded the quarters as *azure* and *argent*, but mistakenly said the lion was also *argent*. Although not immediately clear on the Roll, microscopic pigment analysis has confirmed that the shield originally had the correct colours for the Croft arms, as seen here.

Croft arms. Havergal, F.T., *Fasti Herefordensis*, 1869, H.274.2446 p. 172 © Hereford Cathedral

rebellion of 1554, and Elizabeth never forgot the fact that Croft had refused to implicate her, even though, 'he was marvellously tossed and examined'.

Throughout the 1560s Croft was without royal office, so built up his power and influence in Herefordshire, acquiring large estates and making shrewd alliances with county families. He served as MP and Sheriff of the county several times and was a JP for Herefordshire, and later for Wales and the Marches. In 1570 he made a spectacular return to favour, being made Controller of the Queen's Household (a very senior post) and a Privy Councillor, which projected him into the inner circle at Court. He was again appointed to the Council in the Marches of Wales, but despite the proximity of Croft Castle to Ludlow he does not seem to have played an active role on the Council, being more occupied by his duties close to the Court and Elizabeth I.

Croft was, however, a vocal opponent of two successive Lord Presidents: Sir Henry Sidney and his son-in-law Henry Herbert, Earl of Pembroke. In about 1580, being under attack in his household role, Croft sent Elizabeth a lengthy defence of his conduct, which he turned into an attack on Sir Henry Sidney, accusing him of pocketing court fines and government allowances, and cooking the books accordingly. In addition his opposition to the powerful Court faction led by Sidney's brother-in-law and Elizabeth's favourite, Robert Dudley, Earl of Leicester, was perhaps less than wise.

Two incidents resulting from this rivalry had elements of farce. In 1584, on the death of her father, Barbara Gamage of Coity Castle, Glamorgan, became a very wealthy and highly sought-after heiress. From among several suitors, the Queen favoured James Croft's son, Herbert. Letters were sent from the Queen to Barbara's guardian forbidding any marriage without the Queen's consent. But these were evidently ignored, as meanwhile Pembroke and Leicester got to work and arranged Barbara's marriage to Sir Henry Sidney's son, Robert. This took place at her guardian's house in St Donats only 15 days after her father's death and just minutes before the dramatic – and probably staged – arrival of a letter from the Queen summoning the heiress to Court, but now too late to change the outcome.

The second incident occurred in 1588 at a time when Croft, under accusation of double-dealing in his conduct of treaty negotiations with the Spanish, had once again spent time in prison and was out of favour. Robert Dudley had died suddenly and unexpectedly in September, causing suspicion to fall on Croft's son, Edward, who had blamed Dudley for his father's disgrace. It was alleged that Edward had contrived Dudley's death through witchcraft by the employment of a London conjuror. Fortunately, charges weren't pressed and

Elizabeth restored James once again to the Privy Council in 1589. He died the following year and was buried in St John's Chapel, Westminster Abbey, 'his Prince's favourite and in fair esteem of all who knew him.'

## 19 Sir John Throckmorton, 1524–80
### *Councillor in the Marches of Wales 1558–80*

THE COAT OF ARMS
*19 Sir John Throckmorton*
*Quarterly: 1 Throckmorton; 2 two versions of the Olney arms impaled; 3 Spynnye; 4 Bossan or Buzon. In the centre of the shield a small annulet or ring used to indicate John's position in the family*

This shield has several interesting features. The small ring in the centre of the shield is a cadency mark, there to indicate that Sir John was his father's fifth son. It appears, however, that John was actually the seventh son. The first four sons grew to adulthood, so we can assume that, by the time John was born, the fifth and sixth sons were already dead, and John was given the ring as the fifth surviving son. The second quarter contains two different versions of the Olney arms side by side. Pigment analysis has shown that the field of the one on the right was originally *azure*. In the third quarter, the chevron is *argent* but analysis has confirmed that the crescents were *or*. The charges in the fourth quarter are bird-bolts: missiles with blunt points used for killing birds without piercing them.

JOHN THROCKMORTON WAS the son of Sir George Throckmorton, who owned Coughton Court in Warwickshire (a house now in the care of the National Trust, but still owned by descendants of the family).

A seventh son in a family of 19 children, John Throckmorton had little in the way of material wealth but much in terms of patronage. An education at the Middle Temple, together with having Catherine Parr as a great-aunt by marriage, started off his career (he might well have had a position with her at Court). However, it was during Edward VI's short reign (1550–53), when John Dudley, Duke of Northumberland led the government, that Throckmorton really began to rise in status and power. A man of no deep political or religious conviction at a time when both politics and religion were rapidly shifting sands, he was an opportunist. He quickly lost faith in Northumberland and changed both his allegiance and religion. He joined Mary Tudor, the queen-in-waiting, at Framlingham Castle, and changed his religious coat back to Catholicism.

When Elizabeth I became queen in 1558, he managed to survive another change of ruler and religion. At the start of Elizabeth's reign, she confirmed him as Justice of Chester, an appointment made by Mary before her death. Appointed to the Council in the Marches of Wales, he soon became a prominent member. Elizabeth was so well pleased with Throckmorton's good counsel there, that in 1559 he was granted an annuity of £100.

Despite the fact that many of his family were recusants and Throckmorton himself had changed religious sides in Mary's reign, he seems to have accepted the Elizabethan settlement. In 1562 his loyalty and conformity resulted in him being appointed one of the commissioners to enforce the new religious settlement in the diocese of Chester. His loyalty was further rewarded when, in 1565, as recorder for Coventry, he received the queen and was knighted by her. He had continued to thrive in his role as a member of the Council in the Marches, becoming one of the trusted lieutenants of Sir Henry Sidney. He also had the Earl of Leicester as a patron and when Sidney became Lord Deputy of Ireland in 1565, these two patrons secured Throckmorton's appointment as Vice-President of the Council. As this was in the same year as his knighthood, he must have felt he had reached the pinnacle of his career.

In 1576, when Sidney's administration of the Council in the Marches was under attack, Throckmorton also came into the firing line. He was accused of corruption when he diverted to his own use fines imposed by the Council. The charges were not proved, but it was another step in his downfall. Additionally, the recusancy of Throckmorton's wife and son meant his own loyalty was suspect and he finally lost Leicester's favour.

Throckmorton then brought an unsuccessful lawsuit against his tenants at Feckenham, who had destroyed his enclosures. This resulted in him being suspended as Justice of Chester. Religious problems reared their head again when he was accused of partiality towards his Catholic brother-in-law John Edwards of Chirk, at whose home Throckmorton's wife and son used to hear Mass. The final straw was when he gave judgement in favour of a relation, Edward Grey, concerning the disputed barony of Powys. He was fined heavily by the Star Chamber and imprisoned in the Fleet. Although the place of his death is not known, it is possible that he died in prison, for William Herle (one of Elizabeth's spies) wrote from prison to the Earl of Leicester on 24 May 1580 that, 'God has visited me here with a hectic fever, as he did Sir John Throckmorton.'

Throckmorton died on 22 May 1580. His problems seem to have pursued him beyond the grave, for his will reveals heavy indebtedness which made his hoped-for provision for his daughter and younger sons doubtful. Four years later came an even worse disaster. His son and heir, Francis, was the main conspirator in what is known as the Throckmorton plot of 1583 – an attempt by English Catholics to murder Queen Elizabeth and to replace her on the throne with Mary Queen of Scots. Francis was accused of high treason and executed.

## 20 Sir Hugh Cholmondeley, c.1513–97
### Councillor in the Marches of Wales 1560–97

S IR HUGH CHOLMONDELEY, a soldier, was the second of three sons of Richard Cholmondeley and his wife, Elizabeth. The family had been established at Cholmondeley, Cheshire, since the late eleventh century, and on 9 February 1539, aged 26, Hugh inherited the estates from his elder brother, Richard. Also, as a soldier, Hugh served with distinction in the Scottish wars. Apart from his work for the Council in the Marches, he was a devoted local government servant in Cheshire and Lancashire, holding a wide variety of posts during his long and uneventful career. Little is known of his personality. In religious matters he conformed passively. In 1579 his religious leanings aroused the comment: 'No man knoweth, but obedient.'

In about 1550 he married his first wife, Amy (or Anne), the daughter of Sir George Dorman of Malpas, Cheshire; they had three sons and a daughter.

sir Hughe Chomondley knyght

In 1569 Sir Hugh raised 130 men, led by his eldest son, another Hugh, to help suppress the northern uprising. After his wife's death in 1571, he married Mary, daughter of Sir William Griffiths of Penrhyn, Caernarvonshire, the widow of Sir Randall Brereton of Malpas; they had no children.

Sir Hugh was appointed to the Council in the Marches by Elizabeth I in 1560, but apparently he did not appear at any meetings of the Council until he was appointed its Vice-President in 1569, during the absence in Ireland of Sir Henry Sidney. The role of the Vice-President was to act in the place of the President. Under Sir Hugh's Vice-Presidency, there was a properly-established examiner's office, and new instructions were issued for the Queen's attorney and the lawyers practising at the court there. Although discharged from the Council in 1571, Sir Hugh was reinstated

THE COAT OF ARMS
*20 Sir Hugh Cholmondeley*
*Arms of Cholmondeley*

On the Roll, the colour of the helmets and sheaf of corn both appear to be *argent*. In most representations of the Cholmondeley arms the corn is coloured *or*, but the pigment analysis failed to find any trace of that colour, so the corn on the Roll was presumably always intended to be *argent*.

Effigies of Sir Hugh and Mary Cholmondeley, Malpas Church, Cheshire

in 1575 for Sir Henry Sidney's second period as Lord Deputy of Ireland, although it was Sir Andrew Corbet who became Vice-President.

Sir Hugh the elder died at his home on 16 January 1597. He and his second wife, Mary, are buried in the Cholmondeley chapel in Malpas parish church, Cheshire, and commemorated by an impressive alabaster tomb, which, on its west end, has a finely-carved shield of his arms with many quarterings.

## 21 Sir Andrew Corbet, c.1522–78
### *Councillor in the Marches of Wales 1553–78*

SIR ANDREW CORBET came from an important landholding family in the Welsh marches, and succeeded his father Roger Corbet. Andrew was not a common given name in Tudor England. Andrew Corbet was named after Sir Andrew Windsor, his maternal grandfather, whose given name was derived from the surname of his mother, Elizabeth Andrews. The Windsors remained important and useful contacts for the Corbets. Andrew Windsor had made a vast fortune from his post as Keeper of the Great Wardrobe for Henry VII.

Sir Andrew Corbet remained a member of the Council in the Marches from 1553 until his death. He had served with distinction in the Scottish

Sir Andrewe Corbet

campaigns of Edward VI, and was knighted for his military services in 1547 by John Dudley, Earl of Warwick. Corbet remained a member of the Council after the fall of his patron Dudley, and continued to progress and prosper throughout Mary's reign, although his Protestant sympathies must have been apparent.

Sir Andrew had married Jane Needham, the daughter of Sir Robert Needham of Shavington Hall, Shropshire by 1542. When Dudley became Lord President of the Council in the Marches of Wales, he arranged for Corbet to be excused further service in Scotland in order to help him in the Welsh Marches. Sir Andrew was a considerable landowner, with estates in both Shropshire and Buckinghamshire; he was Sheriff of Shropshire in 1553, and MP for Shropshire in 1555 and 1559.

In 1560 he served at Berwick against the French, and this experience led to a renewed interest in military affairs. He was appointed Commissioner for Musters (an officer or gentleman tasked with raising men for military service when required) for Shropshire in 1562, and prepared a detailed account of the forces available and the state of armour in the county. His report proposing a small standing force was noted in the State Papers.

Sir Andrew Corbet served as a reliable Protestant agent for the Privy Council, ensuring careful vetting of parliamentary candidates. He used his influence to secure the nomination of George Bromley as MP in 1571 and 1572. Bromley and Corbet were seen together in public on numerous occasions, and in 1573 the pair feasted together at a cost of £2 1s 6d to Shrewsbury Council.

Sir Andrew lived mainly at Moreton Corbet Castle to the north-east of Shrewsbury, which he improved from a medieval fortress into a manor house. He altered the gatehouse, adding his badge of a castled elephant. He probably planned and began the fine new Renaissance building to the south, which was continued by his son, Richard Corbet (d.1583), and is also decorated with Corbet badges.

In 1575, when Sidney left to become Lord Deputy of Ireland, Sir Andrew Corbet was appointed Vice-President of the Council. The appointment was denounced by William Gerard, a conscientious justice in Wales and a former Vice-President, on the grounds that Andrew was, 'a very sickly man, not able to take the toil of that service.' Although ill, Sir Andrew proved competent and energetic, however, making a determined effort to stamp out corruption. When famine followed plague in Shrewsbury, he took steps to increase food supplies.

---

THE COAT OF ARMS
*21 Sir Andrew Corbet*
*Quarterly of seven: 1 Corbet, 2 Leybourne, 3 Hopton, 4 Lucy, 5 Archdeacon,*
*6 ?Burley, 7 Burley*

In the first quarter are the original arms of Corbet showing a single crow. They are an example of 'canting' arms which make a punning reference to the holder's name: the French for crow is *corbeau* and in Scotland crows are sometimes called 'corbies'. The Corbet family had many branches and they differenced their arms by increasing the number of crows, by adding borders and by changing the colours. Despite these alterations, the crows make them instantly recognisable as Corbet arms.

The Lucy coat in quarter 4 is also an example of canting arms. A *luce* is another name for a pike. As a young man, Shakespeare is said to have had a run-in with Sir Thomas Lucy of Charlecote near Stratford while out poaching. He apparently got his own back by depicting Lucy as Justice Shallow in *The Merry Wives of Windsor*. In the play, Shallow and his kinsman Slender describe their coat of arms as having *luces* which are then described as louses.

The family arms in quarter 5 are those of Arcedekne, pronounced 'Archdeacon'. Quarter 7 contains the most frequently seen arms of Burley, but the 6th quarter appears to represent another branch of the same family.

---

Sir Andrew wrote to the town bailiffs in August 1576, offering to buy food from other markets in the marches for the beleaguered town, 'daily as you shall warn or send me word.' Jane, his wife, died around 7 January 1577, and Sir Andrew resigned from the vice-presidency later that year. Queen Elizabeth commented, 'we could be well content to have used you longer in our service', and asked him to report to her soon on the state of the Marches. He died in August 1578, greatly mourned in the county, it being declared that he was, 'such a jewel to all Shropshire there has never been the like before.'

## 22 Sir Nicholas Arnold, c.1509–80
### Councillor in the Marches of Wales c.1551–54, 1560–80

S IR NICHOLAS ARNOLD was a lawyer and soldier, who profited from the dissolution of the monasteries, by acquiring Llanthony Abbey in Monmouthshire. He was the second, but eldest surviving, son of John Arnold of Churcham, Gloucestershire, and his wife, Isabel Hawkins. He attended Lincoln's Inn and became a gentleman pensioner of Henry VIII in 1540. He married Margaret, daughter of Sir William Denys of Dyrham, Gloucestershire. He fought with Edward Seymour at Boulogne in France, and until Boulogne was returned to France in 1550 he remained a member of the Town Council. His knighthood probably dates from 1550.

Sir Nicholas was first appointed to the Council in the Marches from about 1551 to 1554, in the reign of Edward VI, but lost his position under Mary. Protestant by faith, he maintained relations with various conspirators against her, and in January 1556 was implicated in Henry Dudley's and Richard Uvedale's plot against Mary, and was sent to the Tower.

On Elizabeth I's accession Sir Nicholas was restored to favour, reappointed to the Council by Elizabeth in 1560, and served until 1580. He was Sheriff of Gloucestershire from 1559 to 1560, and was one of the visitors who administered the Oath of Supremacy to the Welsh clergy. In 1562 he was chosen to go to Ireland to report on complaints against the Lord Lieutenant, Thomas Radcliffe, 3rd Earl of Sussex. Arnold was described as 'a man of resolution and industry, who cared little for popularity, and might be trusted to carry out his orders.'

Elizabeth accepted Sussex's resignation in April 1563, and on 24 May 1564 Arnold was appointed Lord Justice of Ireland. Sussex's achievements were swept away and it seemed that the government might lose its last foothold in Ireland. Sir William Cecil himself was shocked by a letter from Arnold in January 1565, stating that he treated the wild Irish like 'bears and bandogs. So that I see them fight earnestly, and tug each other well, I care not who has the worse.' Cecil replied reprovingly that as a Christian man he 'could not without perplexity contemplate' this policy. Arnold wanted to be appointed Lord Lieutenant. This was refused and on 22 June 1565 he was recalled from Ireland. It was then that Sir Henry Sidney was selected to succeed Sussex.

Thereafter, Sir Nicholas confined himself to local affairs. He was an active member of four parliaments, and was involved in matters concerning Bristol.

THE COAT OF ARMS
22 Sir Nicholas Arnold
Arnold quartering Rhun ap Gronwy

Arnold sounds quite an English name, but Sir Nicholas's paternal great-great-grandparents were actually called Arnallt ap Arnallt Fychan and Joan ferch Madog. Arnallt's arms, in quarters 1 & 4, are descended from Gwilym ap Meurig (b. c.1350) and they have been associated by the Welsh with the fifth-century King Ynyr of Gwent. Arnallt's wife, Joan was an heiress and it is her ancestral arms that appear in quarters 2 & 3, going back to Rhun, Lord of Llys Talybont near Cardiff. The charges on Joan's quarterings are called 'hawk's lures'. Made by tying two wings together and attaching a string, the lure is swung in the air by a falconer to recall his bird.

On 8 May 1572 Arnold was returned as MP for Gloucestershire. He maintained his wide interests, speaking on Wales, the vagabonds' Bill, and the water supply of the city of Worcester among other matters.

William Harrison wrote that, 'Sir Nicholas Arnold of late hath bred the best horses in England, and written of the manner of their production,' (Arnold's writings have not survived). Arnold was buried in Churcham parish church, 'withowte any greate funerall/ pompe and common dole to beggers', and apparently without any monument. Arnold made his will on 10 April 1580. He granted generous legacies, especially to family and servants, and his most notable bequests were horses. He gave and bequeathed, 'to Sir Thomas Lurie, knight, my baye ambling mare that I rode on.'

## 23  George Bromley, c.1526–89
### Councillor in the Marches of Wales 1560–89

GEORGE BROMLEY CAME from an important Shropshire legal family, the most eminent member of which was his brother, Thomas, who became Lord Chancellor in 1579. George was the eldest son of George Bromley of Hodnet, and, like his father, he trained as a lawyer in the Inner Temple, where he had a long and successful career, becoming a bencher and treasurer of the Inn.

THE COAT OF ARMS
*23 George Bromley*
*Arms of Bromley*

The most interesting thing about the Bromley arms is their similarity to those of Leighton, also on this Roll (28 Edward Leighton, 33 William Leighton). The only difference is that the colours are transposed. It has been suggested that the coats of both Bromley and Leighton are variants of the twelfth-century arms of Fulk FitzWarin which are identical to Leighton except that they are *argent* and *gules* rather than *or* and *gules*.

The hole in the fourth quarter of these arms is a natural flaw in the parchment. During the manufacture of parchment the animal skin is stretched on a frame and any cut or insect bite will result in a hole in the parchment. These were very common and a scribe would simply write around the hole or, as in this case, incorporate it into the painting.

In the reign of Elizabeth, he was appointed to a series of important judicial and civic posts. He served as MP several times, for Much Wenlock, Liskeard or Shropshire and was a member of the 1572 parliamentary committee which called for the execution of Mary Queen of Scots.

As a Justice of the Peace in the counties of Denbighshire, Shropshire, Cheshire and Warwickshire, Bromley was appointed to the Council in the Marches of Wales in or before 1560. When Sir Henry Sidney complained

that the balance in the Council was tipping towards lawyers and against the bench of judges, George Bromley was a name that he singled out as not being sufficiently present. However, Bromley does seem to have served the Council well as a justice of Anglesey circuit, becoming Chief Justice of Chester in 1580, the most senior post in the Council next to the President and Vice-President. In this capacity he acted as President of the Council after Sir Henry Sidney's death until the appointment of his successor.

In 1564 a report was commissioned by the Privy Council to investigate the suitability and religious reliability of the

Alabaster tomb of Sir George Bromley (d.1588), Worfield, Shropshire, erected in 1622

local magistrates in Wales, Bromley was noted to have, 'good standing as a Protestant'. This sentiment is endorsed on the epitaph on his elaborate tomb in the church of St Peter the Apostle, Worfield, Shropshire, which describes him as, 'a just man and a great professor of the Religion now established.' The tomb was erected in 1622 and shows the Bromley arms together with those of his wife.

## 24 William Gerard, 1518–81
### *Councillor in the Marches of Wales 1560–81*

W ILLIAM GERARD WAS an Elizabethan statesman who held many offices during his career. He was born at Ince in Lancashire, the son of Gilbert Gerard and Elizabeth Davison. The Gerards were wealthy and distinguished, and several members of the family had notable careers in public service. Gerard was no exception. He entered Gray's Inn in 1543 and was called to the Bar in 1546. He was made Attorney General for Wales in 1554 and Recorder of Chester in 1555, a role he kept for 20 years. Starting in 1555 he sat in six consecutive parliaments as a Member for Chester.

He was appointed to the Council in the Marches of Wales in 1560, and was made Vice-President of the Council in 1562. He served on the council for 16

THE COAT OF ARMS
*24 William Gerard*
*Gerard quartering Ince. A mullet in the centre for difference*

The Gerard family acquired the manor of Ince in Lancashire, together with the arms of Ince, when William's great-great-great-great-grandfather, John Gerard, married the heiress Ellen de Ince in Wigan around 1399, so the Ince arms had been quartered with those of Gerard for nearly 200 years.

Comparison with the arms on William Gerard's monument in Chester Cathedral shows that the arms on the Roll are incorrect; not only do the arms of Ince in quarters 2 & 3 on the Roll lack the black *bendlets* on either side of the red roundels, but the cadency mark is different too. On the Roll, a *mullet* has been added (suggesting that he was the third son) but a crescent has been added to the arms on his monument, stating that he was the second son.

The arms of William Gerard on his monument in Chester

years, and together with Sir Henry Sidney, the Lord President, and Sir John Throckmorton, Justice of Chester, they formed a dominant group within the Council. Gerard gained the reputation of being an energetic and efficient administrator and a man of integrity. In reply to an attack on the Council's governance of Wales in 1576, Gerard sent the Secretary of State, Sir Francis Walsingham, 'A discourse on the estate of the country and people of Wales', which contained a careful analysis of the history of Welsh government and its current weaknesses. It contained suggestions as to how they might be remedied, which were in part adopted in new instructions issued to the Council. His membership of the Council ended in 1576 when, on the recommendation of Sir Henry Sidney, he was appointed Lord Chancellor of Ireland.

Sidney, who was serving his second term as Lord Deputy of Ireland, was delighted with his appointment, writing, 'I have had long experience of him, having had his assistance in Wales now 16 years, and know him to be very honest and diligent and of great dexterity.' In Ireland, Gerard showed the same qualities. He endeavoured to raise the standards of justice and administration, and attacked the system of taxation, which kept the Irish peasantry poor, encouraged lawlessness, and angered the settlers within the Pale. On the subject of taxation reform he differed in approach to Sidney. In a report to the Privy Council on the state of Ireland he effectively undermined Sidney's whole Irish policy, resulting in a violent quarrel with his former patron who felt betrayed. Sidney was recalled while Gerard remained in post.

Gerard had often been in ill health during his years in Wales, and was no better in Ireland where he complained about the effect on his constitution of the damp Irish climate. By 1579 he complained he was suffering from dysentery, shortness of breath, severe pains in his legs, and a skin disease. In 1580 the queen granted him permission to retire to Chester as he had become too ill for active service in Ireland. It soon became clear that he could not live long. He wrote a loyal letter to Elizabeth I, saying that he hoped to see her one more time even if he had to crawl to London, but by then he was too ill to leave Chester, where he died in early May 1581. He was buried close to his grandfather in Chester Cathedral, as specified in his will.

## 25 John Rastall (or Rastell), c.1511–74
### *Councillor in the Marches of Wales 1570–74*

L ITTLE IS KNOWN about John Rastall. Although his father, John Rastall senior, and his elder brother, William, are both well documented, John junior is relatively elusive. He was born in Coventry, the second son of John Rastall senior, a printer and lawyer, and his wife, Elizabeth, a sister of Sir Thomas More. Although the family initially thrived under More's political influence, when John Rastall senior rejected Catholicism, he and Thomas More, once close friends, became estranged. More was executed in 1535, and John's father died in poverty in the Tower of London a year later, having been committed there by Thomas Cranmer, Archbishop of Canterbury, due to his vocal opposition to the payment of tithes to support clergy income.

John Rastall junior was admitted to Grays Inn in 1533, from where he was also called to the Bar. However, in 1536, the year of his father's death, he joined a number of other gentleman adventurers on an expedition to Newfoundland led by Richard Hore. In this he was following in his father's footsteps, as John Rastall senior had joined a similar expedition in 1517 (albeit one that was abortive, as he only reached Ireland). In Hakluyt's account of this 1536 expedition, after a crossing of two months, they succeeded in reaching Newfoundland where they encountered a now extinct aboriginal tribe, the Beothuk people, who fled on sight. One of their ships became unseaworthy, and they ran out

John Rastall esquier Justice of the thre Shiers in North Walles & ... dyed the xiii day of July 1574 +

of food and faced starvation. Some allegedly resorted to cannibalism before the arrival of a well-victualled French ship which they stole and returned in it safely to Gravesend six months after first setting out.

The remainder of John Rastall's life was quietly respectable. He was made JP for Pembrokeshire in the 1540s, and settled in Tenby where he was elected mayor on six occasions between 1552 and 1571. When he was appointed Chief Justice of South Wales in 1570, he became a Member of the Council in the Marches of Wales, a post he held until his death four years later. He seems

THE COAT OF ARMS
*25 John Rastall*
*Arms of Rastall*

The tinctures of heraldry include two metals (*or* and *argent*) several colours (*azure*, *gules*, *vert* etc.) and various furs. In winter the stoat turns completely white, apart from its black tail, and it is then called an ermine. Ermine furs were sewn together to make rich warm garments worn, particularly, on ceremonial occasions. Heraldically, ermine is shown as a white background with a pattern of little black shapes representing the tails of the individual animals. John Rastall's attractive coat of arms is a nice example of the use of ermine in heraldry. It also includes good illustrations of *pheons* which are arrowheads with barbed inner edges.

to have been well-regarded during his long service as a justice in Wales, being described in George Owen's *The Dialogue of the Government of Wales* (1594) as, 'a learned and just man and one well-acquainted with the people and affairs of the country for he dwelled here among us.'

## 26 Charles Fox, c.1516–90
### Councillor in the Marches of Wales 1560–90

CHARLES FOX (OR FOXE) came from a family that rose to prominence in Ludlow in the sixteenth century. William Fox, Charles' father (d.1554), built his fortune through acquiring monastic property, notably the Hospital of St John in Lower Broad Street, Ludlow, near the bridge to Ludford. He leased all its lands and buildings, both in the town and in Herefordshire and Staffordshire, before acquiring the freehold from John Dudley, Earl of Warwick in 1547 for the price of £161. In 1540 William Fox also gained monastic property at Snitton near Ludlow. William died in 1554 and was buried in Ludford church, with a brass that records that he founded the north aisle and re-edified the almshouse of St Giles, Ludford, which was decayed.

Charles was the second of William's six sons and, since the estate went to his elder brother, Edmund, made his career in the law, becoming a very successful lawyer at the Temple in London. He acquired Bromfield Priory (a former Benedictine monastery) by lease in 1541, and by purchase in 1558.

Eighteenth-century watercolour by Revd Edward Williams of the heraldic corbels in the crossing of Bromfield Church, Shropshire put up by Charles Fox in 1577.
*Add MS 21237 © The British Library Board*

He converted the monastic buildings of the Priory into a private house, and some of the ruined walls of Fox's house can be seen still attached to the south side of the church. The nave of the church continued in parish use, and the west end has eight corbels with the arms of Fox and associated families (Stoke, Leighton, Stevinton, Swynnerton and Crosby) incised on their shields. Each bears the date 1577.

In 1537, at the age of 21, Charles apparently procured for himself and his elder brother the opportunity to acquire, upon the death of the present office-holders, two lucrative offices in the Council in the Marches: the Clerkship and the Clerkship of the Signet. He also tried to obtain the post of Secretary and this led to a dispute with Rowland Lee, then President, which Charles lost, resulting in him being confined in the Tower of London for a short period. He made good his position later on the death of the clerk, and was a member of the Council in the Marches of Wales from 1560, holding the two most powerful and lucrative offices of the Council: Secretary and Clerk of the Signet.

THE COAT OF ARMS
*26 Charles Fox*
*Quarterly: 1 & 4 Fox, 2 Stoke, 3 Stevinton. A crescent for difference to indicate that Charles was a second son*

The arms of Fox are an example of canting or punning as the heads represent foxes. The charges on the bend in the second quarter are dolphins which are frequently shown bowed as here. The Stevinton arms in the third quarter are quite difficult to blazon. The black spikes coming from the left are called *piles*, but it is not at all clear what the black shape on the right-hand side is meant to be. It has been described as 'a rectangle with a point at the bottom' but that is not a really adequate description.

As Secretary, Charles was required to be in continual attendance on the Council, and not to depart at any time without the licence of the President or Vice-President. He was also Recorder of Shrewsbury and of Ludlow. He succeeded his father, William, as MP for Ludlow in 1539, and sat for Ludlow in four out of the next five Parliaments.

Fox's land at Prior's Halton supplied the spring which supplied the castle and town with water from 1566, for which he received an annual fee of two deer from the royal forest of Bringewood (Sir Henry Sidney subsequently created a fountain for the spring which supplied the castle – see p. 49). He also had a major town house in Ludlow. Quality Square, near the Market Square, preserves the courtyard plan of this house, which was some 100 feet wide and built of brick, a rarity in Ludlow at the time.

Charles married twice, first to Elizabeth Crosby, an heiress from Bury St Edmunds. This must have taken place well before 1542, for between 1544 and 1547 he sued his mother-in-law's executors for the jewels and two dozen silver spoons bequeathed to his three daughters. After Elizabeth's death in 1575, he married Catherine Leighton, daughter of Edward Leighton of Wattlesborough, Shropshire, with whom he had three sons (in addition to an illegitimate son by an unknown mother).

The Leighton marriage explains the impaling of the Fox arms with those of Leighton on the shield on the almshouses in Corve Street, which were in the course of erection on his death in December 1590, and for which he left provision in his will. They were to be financed by the rent from four houses in Worcester, and the inhabitants were to attend services in St Leonard's chapel. His will, made in 1590, extends to some 20 pages and shows an intention to control even after death. The will disperses his lands among his surviving sons and leaves instructions for the completion of the almshouses. In this will he also states that his Secretary of Council fee (some £20) has not been paid for several years and his executors are to petition Lord President Pembroke for payment. He also leaves money to build a new church at Gwernogoe Hay. This was a former grange of the Cistercian Abbey of Abbey Cwmhir (Radnorshire) at Llanfihangel, in the parish of Kerry, Montgomeryshire, which the Fox family had acquired at the Dissolution (the church was never built). In his will, he also leaves his son, Edmund, 'one chair of needlework with his grandfather's arms and mine together wrought thereupon.' This would represent the arms of William, his father, and Charles. Charles was a great family estate builder, and a highly successful and hardworking (if, perhaps, grasping) official of the Council.

# 27 Ellis Price, c.1512–94

## *Councillor in the Marches of Wales 1560–94*

NICKNAMED 'THE RED DOCTOR', Ellis Price mainly served the Council in the Marches of Wales as a Justice of the Peace throughout Wales. He earned considerable notoriety as a tough and ruthless agent for the Welsh estates of Robert Dudley, Earl of Leicester. He was vilified by his opponents and described by Thomas Pennant in his *Tour of Wales* of 1781, as, 'the greatest of our knaves in the period and the most dreaded oppressor in his neighbourhood'. On the other hand he was praised by leading Welsh

---

THE COAT OF ARMS
*27 Ellis Price*
*Quarterly Marchweithian and the Lordship of Rhos & Rhufeiniog*

Rhos and Rhufeiniog were adjacent sub-kingdoms in the Dark Ages, with most of the latter now being in Denbighshire. Marchweithian was an eleventh-century leader of one of the '15 noble tribes of North Wales', based in Denbighshire. But Marweithian would never have seen these arms, because heraldry as we know it didn't exist until the twelfth century. So these are both later creations which have been used very widely by the descendants of Marweithian.

---

bards for his learning in Hebrew and Classical languages and his promotion of the rule of law.

Ellis Price came from a family of royal supporters. His grandfather was reputed to have been a standard bearer for Henry Tudor at the battle of Bosworth in 1485, where Richard III was killed and Henry took the crown. His father, Robert ap Rhys was a chaplain to Cardinal Wolsey and his principal agent in North Wales.

In 1535, shortly after completing his legal education, Price was appointed by Thomas Cromwell to the commission inspecting Welsh monasteries prior to their dissolution. However, his lewd and arrogant behaviour caused complaint from his fellow commissioners, and despite the support of Bishop Rowland Lee, Lord President of the Council in the Marches, he was swiftly dismissed. He didn't have to wait long for his reinstatement, though, becoming Chancellor of the Diocese of St Asaph, where he enthusiastically continued work there on the suppression of Catholic images and practices.

Following the Acts of Union of Wales with England in the 1540s, Price began his career in the new civil administration serving as a Justice of the Peace throughout the Principality, Keeper of the Records (*custos rotulorum*) and Member of Parliament for Merioneth, and additionally was appointed sheriff 17 times to several Welsh counties.

At the beginning of Elizabeth's reign in 1560 there was a step change in Price's fortunes, when the queen awarded him both Plas Iolyn and Isbyty Ifan in Denbighshire, and appointed him to the Council in the Marches of Wales. Shortly after this he attracted the patronage of Robert Dudley, Earl of Leicester, who made him the agent for his Lordship of Denbighshire. His years of devoted service in carrying out his patron's instructions fuelled Price's unpopularity.

In 1566 there was a surprising attempt to increase Leicester's influence in North Wales by the nomination of Ellis Price as Bishop of Bangor. Despite his dubious moral reputation and having no religious qualification whatsoever, Price's appointment was only narrowly averted and the cleric Nicholas Robinson was chosen instead.

The following year a royal commission was set up by the Council in the Marches to tackle the 'intolerable multitude and shameless disorders of vagrant and idle persons naming themselves minstrels, rythmers and bards' in North Wales, who were hindering the livelihood of 'expert minstrells and musicians in tonge'. This was to be achieved by organising an Eisteddfod at Cearwys to showcase the experts, while the idlers would be dealt with through the harsh vagrancy laws of the time. Ellis Price, who was recognised for his knowledge in this field, was appointed one of the principal commissioners. Price was well regarded by the bards who wrote verses in his praise, while his eldest son, Thomas, became a notable bard combining his literary career with that of a privateer using Bardsey Island as his base.

Ellis Price died in 1594 and may have been buried in Ysbty Ifan where his father and brother are interred, though no monument survives.

## 28 Edward Leighton, c.1525–93
### *Councillor in the Marches of Wales 1570–93*

THE LEIGHTONS WERE among the richest and most influential landowners in Shropshire in the late sixteenth century, and several of Edward's forbears had been knights of the shire. Edward was the eldest son of John Leighton of Wattlesborough Castle in Shropshire, and Joyce, daughter of

THE COAT OF ARMS
*28 Edward Leighton of Wattlesborough*
*Arms of Leighton*

Edward Leighton was second cousin to William Leighton of Plaish (33) who has the same arms. See 23 Bromley for a comparison and a reference to their possible joint ancestry.

Edward Sutton, 2nd Baron Dudley and Cecily Willoughby. Thus, through his mother he was a kinsman of both the Sutton and Devereux families.

Edward succeeded to his father's estates in 1532 at the tender age of seven. A few years later his mother married Richard Lee, MP for Much Wenlock, who became his guardian. Edward married twice: firstly Elizabeth (née Edwards), the widow of Mr Meverell, and secondly Anne, the daughter of Paul Dayrell of Lillingstone Dayrell, Buckinghamshire, with whom he had four sons and three daughters.

In 1541 Edward was admitted to Gray's Inn to study law. Although he was a member of Queen Mary's first parliament, he stood for what he saw as the 'true religion' against Mary's attempts to restore the Catholic faith. As a result he was excluded from public affairs during her reign. However, it seems unlikely that he actively supported the opposition to Mary's accession in 1553, as his name did not appear on the pardon roll at her accession. Edward's lack of public office under Mary was in marked contrast to his activity under Elizabeth, when he became one of the leading political figures in Shropshire in the late sixteenth century.

Edward was twice appointed High Sheriff of both Montgomeryshire and Shropshire, and similarly was twice MP for Shropshire in 1553 and 1563. He was a member of the Council in the Marches by 1570, and was actively employed in the business of the Council. He played a dominant part in organising the county musters, an important role at times of political unrest – such as 1588 when the Spanish Armada threatened British security. He was often employed by the Privy Council, and in 1584 when Robert Dudley, the Earl of Leicester and Robert Devereux, the Earl of Essex visited Shrewsbury as part of their northern progress, he arranged a lavish banquet at the Council House for them with, as entertainment, long orations by scholars of Shrewsbury School where Sir Henry Sidney's youngest son, Thomas, was then a pupil. Edward was appointed Keeper of the Rolls, the most senior public post in the county, in 1587, and although described as 'old and feeble' was knighted in 1591. He died three years later, on 10 September 1593, 'bearing great fame and countenance throughout the shire.' He was buried at St Michael's and All Angels at Alberbury, but no tomb survives there.

# 29 Richard Seborne, 1524–84
## *Councillor in the Marches of Wales 1560–?1577*

Richarde Seborne efquier

UNLIKE MANY OF his fellow Councillors, Richard Seborne seems to have led a quiet and modest life on the Herefordshire borders, fitting into the changing times rather as a chameleon changes colour to fit its surroundings. He was born at Sutton St Nicholas and was of 'gentle birth but modest patrimony.' He had to earn a living, rather than relying on inherited wealth, and to this end he studied law. Early in his career he seems to have developed a successful local practice in Herefordshire and the Borders. When he was called to the Bar in 1555, he was already so well launched on his career that he preferred to pay a fine of £40 in order to avoid the obligation of holding office at his Inn.

---

THE COAT OF ARMS
*29 Richard Seborne*
*Arms of Seborne*

In this coat of arms we can clearly see that the lion's tongue and claws are red. In heraldic terms the lion is said to be *armed and langued gules*. However, as red is the default colour for the tongue and claws, it is only necessary to mention the colour in the blazon if it is not red.

---

Seborne became a JP in Herefordshire in 1547 and, in 1554, was elected as a 'first knight of the shire' (MP). He had a very short-lived parliamentary career, representing Herefordshire in the 1555 Parliament only. His election seems to have been irregular and there might have been a degree of official intervention from either Bishop Heath, the President of the Council, or from John Price, its secretary, as his name was inserted over erasures in the election return.

Despite his family being noted Catholics, Seborne was made a Member of the Council in the Marches of Wales by Elizabeth I in 1560, and by 1564 he was serving the council as a JP for all of Wales and the English border counties. In the same year, when Hereford's Bishop Scory complained about the 'dissemblers and rank papists' he found in the cathedral, he included Seborne who was judged as 'unfavourable' (and, by implication, Catholic). Nevertheless, Seborne was, in addition to his judicial duties, an active member of the Council until the early 1570s. However, all his official appointments seem to have come to an end in 1577, several years before his death. Quite why this was is not clear, but he might still have been under suspicion of recusancy. In giving evidence to the Privy Council in 1576 William Gerard described Seborne as learned and sober and a good councillor, but he also confirmed that he was, 'suspected of papistry yet observes the orders in repairing to the Church and receiving (communion).' So, whatever his religious sympathies might have been in his younger days, Seborne's career suggests that he at least appeared to conform to the Protestant faith. In his will of 1584 he made sure that his widow was well provided for, either in the family home or at Sugwas with her sister, Anne Willison. As well as bequests for his son and daughters, he left money to various servants, including John Spencer for his 'good service and attendance done unto me especially in my time of sickness.' He also left 100 marks for the poor of Sutton, and asked to be buried alongside his parents in the church there.

## 30 Richard Pate, 1516–88
### Councillor in the Marches of Wales 1560–88

RICHARD PATE WAS born in Cheltenham on 24 September 1516, and was probably the son of Walter Pate, a prosperous tradesman, being a baker, butcher and innkeeper. Richard was admitted to Corpus Christi College, Oxford but seems to have left without a degree in 1536. Five years later, he was admitted to Lincoln's Inn.

Although there were Catholic allegiances in the family, Pate himself was a zealous Protestant. Employed first as an agent for evaluating former ecclesiastical property in Gloucestershire for appropriation by the State, and then as a leading commissioner for the dissolution of chantries, he took the opportunity to acquire ex-monastic land and property for himself, making him a very wealthy man.

In 1547 he made an advantageous marriage to the twice-widowed Matilda, daughter of John Rastell, Mayor of Gloucester. In the same year he was appointed a Justice of the Peace, and within a few years was Recorder of Gloucestershire, the highest legal officer in the county. He was appointed to the Council in the Marches of Wales in 1560, and was a diligent member, attending its meetings regularly.

---

THE COAT OF ARMS
*30 Richard Pates*
*Arms of Pates*

In heraldry, discs are called *roundels*, and *roundels* of different colours are given special names. The black *roundels* on this shield are called *pellets*, while the red *roundels* on the Gerard arms (24) are called *torteaux*. Yellow *roundels* are *bezants* and white ones are *plates*. As the crosses on the chief have spikes at the bottom instead of a fourth arm, they are said to be *fitchy*.

Pate had a chequered parliamentary career, first representing Gloucester in 1558. However, despite his standing in the county, he was defeated in successive elections in the 1570s by Thomas Atkyns, the town clerk whom Pate claimed won, 'by gathering together of a multitude by great labour, and by some threatening words, contrary to the law.' Pate was returned again in 1586, by then an elderly man, and was appointed to the committee tasked with persuading Elizabeth I to agree to the execution of Mary Queen of Scots in the aftermath of the Babington Plot.

Pate's name lives on today in the name of the Richard Pate School, formerly Cheltenham Grammar School, whose foundation dates back to the early sixteenth century. Pate seems to have been involved with its new foundation in Elizabeth's reign, when both the grammar school and an almshouse were set up on former ecclesiastical property and eventually endowed by Pate in 1586. The school's endowment included clear regulations about the high standard of teaching and pupil attainment required. Residents of the almshouse were similarly vetted, being required to be able to recite from memory the Lord's Prayer, the Articles of our Belief, and the Ten Commandments of God.

Richard Pate died on 29 October 1588 and was buried in the south transept of Gloucester Cathedral, where a monument, arrayed with coats of arms, includes a now-faded painting of the lawyer, his wife and four children.

## 31  Ralph Barton, 1523–92
### Councillor in the Marches of Wales 1570–92

RALPH BARTON WAS born at Smithills Hall near Bolton in Lancashire. In 1485 this ancient Hall passed into the hands of the Bartons, wealthy sheep farmers who lived there for nearly 200 years, well beyond Ralph Barton's lifetime.

However, Ralph suffered from being a second son and thus needed to make his own way in the world. He received none of the considerable estate of his family, but merely an annuity of £10 a year 'towards his exhibition and learning'. He was educated at Gray's Inn, and was called to the Bar in 1545. He nevertheless made a 'good living' through his work for the Crown, particularly during Elizabeth's reign. In 1563 he became Queen's attorney for much of north Wales, Lancashire and Cheshire. He was appointed to the Council in the Marches of Wales in 1570 and seems to have been an active Member of Council until the early 1580s. As a Council Member he also served as a JP for Herefordshire and Shropshire.

He represented Nottingham as an MP but neglected his duties, resigning in 1582 after complaints by his constituents. Shortly before, he had inherited the family estate on the death of his brother, but was involved in a lengthy legal dispute with his sister-in-law. This dispute seems to have diverted his attention from Council and parliamentary duties. He remained a JP for Lancashire and died a wealthy man with estates in Nottingham and Lancashire.

THE COAT OF ARMS

*31 Ralph Barton*

*Quarterly: 1 Barton, 2 Radcliffe, 3 Ashton, 4 Norley. A crescent for difference to indicate that Ralph was a second son*

The deer in the Barton arms have big flat antlers and therefore are blazoned as *bucks*. When an animal's head is depicted full-face but no neck is shown, it is said to be *caboshed*. So, on these arms we have three *bucks' heads caboshed or*.

The various branches of the Radcliffe family varied their arms, but they were always recognisable. Thomas Radcliffe, 3rd Earl of Sussex, married Frances, a sister of Sir Henry Sidney, who left money in her will for the creation of Sidney Sussex College in Cambridge.

On the right are two other versions of the arms of Radcliffe (**A** and **B**), together with the arms of Sidney Sussex College, Cambridge (**C**).

## 32 George Fettiplace (or Phetiplace), c.1531–77

### Councillor in the Marches of Wales 1570–77

Geore phetiplace esquier

G EORGE FETTIPLACE WAS the third son of Edmund Fettiplace and his wife Margaret Mordaunt, both from Berkshire. The family was an ancient one, dating back to the late twelfth century. Members of the family often served the Crown: Sir Thomas Fettiplace accompanied Henry VIII to the Cloth of Gold meeting in 1520, while another Fettiplace accompanied Ann of Cleves, Henry VIII's fourth wife, to England.

George Fettiplace was still just a boy when his father died. In 1546 he went to Corpus Christi College, Oxford, leaving there in 1550, the year in which he married Cecily, the daughter of Henry Poole of Poole Keynes, Gloucestershire. There is a tenuous link to Hereford, as George's stepfather was Thomas Denton, whose son Alexander married an Anne Willison of Ledbury. Anne died young in childbirth and there is a very fine monument in Hereford Cathedral to her and Alexander. In his will, Alexander Denton left various properties to his, 'well beloved brother George Fettiplace', and also requested that he, 'shall have the duration and bringing up of my sonne, Thomas Denton, until he shall accomplish his full years.'

George Fettiplace was admitted to the Middle Temple in 1552 and sat twice as an MP for Buckingham, but his career was more fully realised by steady progression in the law outside Parliament. His membership of the Council in the Marches was a brief one. He was appointed in 1574 as a Justice of the Carmarthen circuit, but died only three years later when he contracted gaol fever (typhus) during an outbreak of the disease at the assizes in Oxford. They became known as the Black Assizes because about 300 people died during the outbreak, including the Lord Chief Baron of the Exchequer and the Lord High Sheriff. Fettiplace was able to make his will three days before he died. He was a wealthy man, having property in three counties and leaving generous bequests to friends and a long list of servants including a butler and under-butler.

---

THE COAT OF ARMS
*32 George Phetiplace (or Fettiplace)*
*Arms of Phetiplace with a mullet for difference showing that George was a 3rd son.*

The chevron is one of the most common 'ordinaries' found in heraldry and it has been in use since the earliest times. If the chevron is quite narrow, or there are several of them, it is called a *chevronel*. On George Phetiplace's shield the chevrons are borderline in width so one might reasonably blazon the coat of arms as either *gules two chevrons argent* or as *gules two chevronels argent*.

The *mullet*, or *molet*, used here to indicate the third son, is not a star. It is a representation of a spur-rowel (*shown right*) and, by default, it has five points. In heraldry a star is represented by wavy lines and is called an *estoile*.

---

## 33 William Leighton, 1533–1607
### *Councillor in the Marches of Wales 1570–1607*

WILLIAM LEIGHTON WAS the son of William Leighton who was the second son of John Leighton of Wattlesborough. He entered the Inner Temple in 1553, and was called to the Bar and elected a Bencher in 1569. He had a long judicial career, and held many posts in Wales, becoming Justice of the Anglesey circuit in 1570, and Chief Justice of North Wales in 1580. He was appointed to the Council in the Marches of Wales in 1570 and was initially a very active Member, but by 1590 was recorded as being reluctant to attend.

Leighton prospered in his career and rebuilt Plaish Hall in contemporary style in brick (one of the earliest uses of the material in the county).

Its chimneys are especially tall and elaborate, made of moulded bricks, and there is a tradition attached to their building. It is said that when Leighton was presiding over the trial of prisoners during the building of the house he asked the High Sheriff whether he knew of a workman capable of building brick chimneys. The Sheriff replied that the prisoner his lordship had just sentenced to be hanged was the best workman he knew. 'Then he shall build my chimneys first', said the Judge, and gave the man a reprieve until the chimneys were finished, after which the man's sentence was carried out.

William Leighton was married twice. By his first wife, Isabella, he had six children, and by his second wife, Ann, daughter of Reginald Corbet of Stoke, two. These children are shown on the base of his fine alabaster monument in Cardington church. William lies recumbent on the tomb, under a canopy decorated with the arms of Leighton and Corbet, the arms of his wife. William left £50 for this monument which includes the fulsome epitaph:

Here lieth the body of William Leighton of Plaish, Esq., chief Justice of North Wales and of ye Council in the Marches which place he exercised by the space of above fortie years with great sincerity and without complaint. He was humble in prosperitie, in hospitalitie liberal, to the poore bountiful, loving to his familie, and to his friends, tenants and neighbours comfortable to all conditions and affable, contented with competencye, wherewith God blessed him sufficientlye for his calling.

It would be interesting to know whether some of the poor wretches who stood before him in court would have agreed with these sentiments.

Tomb of William Leighton of Plaish, Cardington church, Shropshire, dated 1607

THE COAT OF ARMS
33 William Leighton of Plaish
*Arms of Leighton differenced with a crescent to indicate that he was a 2nd son*

William Leighton was second cousin to Edward Leighton of Wattlesborough (28) who has the same arms. See 23 Bromley for a comparison of their arms and a reference to their possible joint ancestry.

## 34 Miles Sandys, ?–1601

*Councillor in the Marches of Wales 1570–1601*

BORN IN FLADBURY, Worcestershire, Miles Sandys was one of several brothers of Edwin Sandys, the eminent cleric who was successively Bishop of Worcester, Bishop of London and Archbishop of York. As Bishop of Worcester, Edwin would have been a member of the Council in the Marches of Wales and was probably responsible for the appointment of his brother, Miles, to the Council in 1570. However, Miles seems to have had little to no role in the Council and was not reappointed in 1574.

He was a career parliamentarian and Crown official. He sat in every Parliament from 1563 to 1597, although he never represented the same constituency twice. Through marriage to Hester Clifton of Barrington he acquired land in Somerset, and later moved to Buckinghamshire having bought an estate in Latimer. He was a staunch Protestant throughout his life and his Puritan sympathies recommended him to several influential patrons, who advanced his parliamentary career. For example, through the patronage of Sir Francis Knollys Sandys acquired his first seat, representing Taunton in 1563, while Robert Dudley, the Earl of Leicester, was probably instrumental in his election for Abingdon in 1586.

He completed his legal training in Middle Temple and was appointed a JP for several counties including Buckinghamshire and Worcestershire. He was also an influential Crown official, working in the Court of Queen's Bench and becoming Clerk of the Crown.

By the time of his death Sandys had property in eight counties and was a very wealthy man. However, in tune with his religious leanings he directed that he be buried without 'vain pomp, ostentation and chargeable funeral.' He left generous gifts to many friends and the poor of several parishes. To his trusty servant Robert Heton he left an allowance for life because 'he has been a loving careful and faithful servant to me.'

---

## THE COAT OF ARMS

*34 Miles Sandys*
*An incorrect version of the arms of Sandys differenced with a crescent, which usually indicates a 2nd son*

The arms of Miles Sandys on our Roll present a series of interesting heraldic questions. Firstly, Miles is normally listed as the fifth son of his parents, not the second. However, as was explained in the case of Sir John Throckmorton (19), a son may be 'upgraded' if an older brother has died before he was born. But this doesn't seem to be the case here, as Miles appears to have had two older brothers alive when he was a member of the Council in the Marches. It seems that the only way the crescent representing the second son can be right is if the assumed date of birth of one or more of his brothers is not correct. Otherwise it's a strange mistake to make.

This inaccuracy with the cadency mark is not the only enigmatic thing about these arms, however: the two colours on the shield are also wrong. The coat of arms for this branch of the Sandys family looks identical to that on the Roll, but it has the field *argent* and the charges *gules*, unlike here where they are respectively *gules* and *or*. The correct arms can be clearly seen on the tomb of his brother Edwin Sandys, Archbishop of York, in Southwell Minster, and you would expect Miles to have arms identical to those of his brother. As a younger son, of course, he may have chosen to difference the arms in this way; but, if so, he surely wouldn't have included a cadency mark for difference. Convincing proof that the wrong colours have been used on the Roll is supplied by Mytton in the eighteenth century. He recorded the original shield in the castle as having its correct colours of *argent* and *gules*. Surprisingly, however, he also includes the crescent for difference, indicating a second son!

## 35 John Alcock, c.1430–1500
### Bishop of Worcester
### Lord President of the Council in the Marches of Wales 1473–83

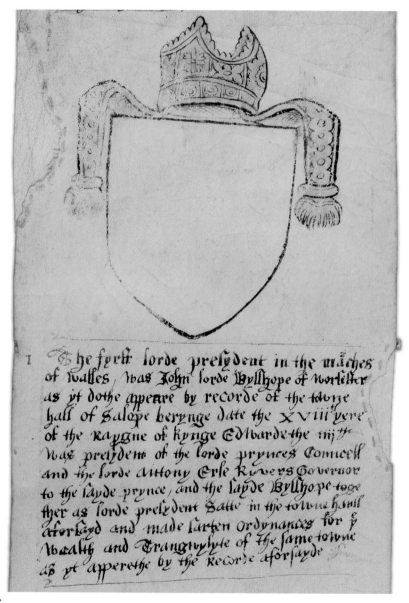

JOHN ALCOCK, BISHOP successively of Rochester (1472), Worcester (1476), and Ely (1486), and the founder of Jesus College, Cambridge, started his career as a leading figure in the administration of the Yorkist kings before successfully transferring to similar roles for the Tudor regime. A Yorkshireman, he was a protégé of Bishop Stillington and an able chancery clerk. By the time that Edward IV regained his throne in 1470–71, he was Dean of St Stephen's Westminster and a Privy Councillor. In 1471 Edward IV made him Lord Chancellor, and the following year Alcock was appointed to the bishopric of Rochester. A year later, in 1473, he was appointed President

THE COAT OF ARMS
*35 John Alcock, Bishop of Worcester*
*A blank shield surmounted by a bishop's mitre, as they 'coulde not come by' his coat of arms at the time*

It is a little surprising that the painters of the shields in the castle and of the Roll could not discover the arms of Bishop Alcock. Mytton records seeing the arms of Presidents of the Council in the Bull Inn in Ludlow. He noted that Bishop Alcock's shield included no personal arms; just the arms of the see of Worcester. Bishop Alcock went on to greater things, becoming Bishop of Ely where there is an Alcock chantry chapel. His arms can be seen in a window there, impaled with those of the diocese. Unsurprisingly, given his name, his shield features three cockerels.

He was the founder of Jesus College in Cambridge, and his arms are incorporated into the college's arms. At some point he added a bishop's mitre to the *fess* on his shield to indicate his status. This was omitted from the official arms granted to Jesus College.

| Alcock arms, Ely Cathedral | Arms of Jesus College, Cambridge © 123RF.com |

of the Council that had been created to administer the lands of the child, Edward, Prince of Wales. Alcock was also tutor to the young prince, while the prince's maternal uncle, Lord Rivers, was governor of the household established at Ludlow.

Alcock remained President throughout Prince Edward's time at Ludlow, and during his tenure the Council was given additional responsibilities beyond the administration of the Prince's lands. When the death of Edward IV was followed by the accession of Richard III and the disappearance of Prince Edward, the Council ceased to exist.

During his presidency, Alcock was transferred from the bishopric of Rochester to Worcester. The stained glass windows in Malvern Priory, celebrating the Yorkist royal family, date from this period. Despite his prominence under the Yorkist regime, Alcock was able to continue his career under the Tudors. For a short period from October 1485 to March 1486 he once again acted as Chancellor of England, opening Parliament for the declaration of the title of the new king, Henry VII. Thereafter the chancellorship passed to Morton, Archbishop of Canterbury, and Alcock was rewarded for his passive acceptance of this with Morton's old bishopric of Ely. Although Alcock baptised Arthur, the new Prince of Wales, he took no part in his education or the Prince's Council when it was reconstituted, but rather focused on his diocese where he was remembered as a saintly bishop. He was the author of several devotional works and was unusual for a bishop of the early sixteenth century for publishing his sermons, such as on the need for clergy to observe their vows and set a good example. In 1497 he suppressed the dilapidated and dissolute nunnery of St Radegund's in Cambridge to found Jesus College in its stead. He died in 1500, and his very fine tomb remains at Ely.

## 36 William Smyth, c.1460–1514
### Bishop of Lincoln
### Lord President of the Council in the Marches of Wales
#### c.1490s–1512

UNLIKE THE YORKIST Alcock, William Smyth had impeccably Lancastrian origins. He had been educated in the household of Margaret Beaufort and has been described as a typical, hardworking but unspectacular Tudor administrator. Through his Beaufort connections, in 1486 he became Henry VII's Clerk of the Hanaper (an official who was paid fees and other monies

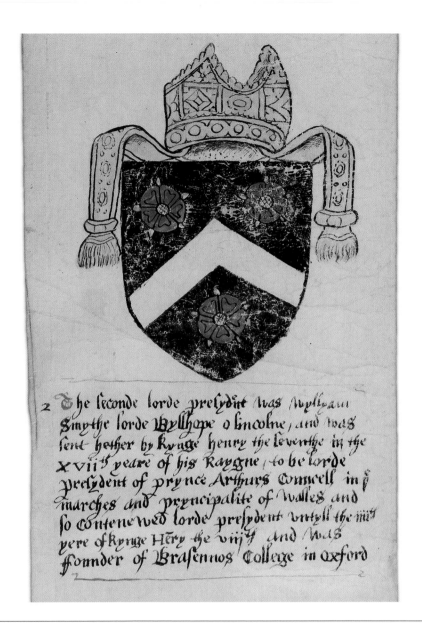

2 The seconde lorde presydent was William
Smythe lorde Byllhope o Lincolne, and was
sent hether by Kynge henry the seventhe in the
xviith yeare of his Rayggne, to be lorde
presydent of prynce Arthurs Councell in ye
marches and prynicpalite of Walles and
so contenewed lorde presydent untyll the iiid
yere of Kynge Hery the viijth and was
ffounder of Brasennos College in oxford

THE COAT OF ARMS

*36 William Smyth, Bishop of Lincoln*

*An incorrect version of the Bishop's personal arms, surmounted by a bishop's mitre.*

The most interesting thing about this coat of arms is that the painter made a big mistake. William Smyth's correct coat of arms has a black chevron on a white field, but the painter of the Roll switched these colours in error. (*continued overleaf*)

THE COAT OF ARMS (*CONT.*)
We can be sure it was the painter
of the Roll's fault because we have a
description of the original shield made
by Mytton and this describes the Smyth
coat accurately. In 1509, Bishop Smyth
was one of the founders of Brasenose
College in Oxford and his arms appear
in his portrait at the college and in the
arms of Brasenose College itself.

When recording or copying arms
it was often the practice to just 'trick'
them. 'Tricking' involved making a
sketch of the arms and then indicating
the colours by labelling the drawing
with abbreviations – including, for
example: 'g', 'ar', 'az' etc. It is quite
possible that the person copying Bishop
Smyth's arms was working from a less-than-perfect trick and accidentally
switched the black and white, leading to the arms as they appear on the Roll.

Modern arms of Brasenose College,
Oxford, with Bishop Smyth's arms
on the left

for the sealing of charters, patents, writs, etc., and who issued certain writs
under the Great Seal) and was Bishop of Coventry and Lichfield in 1493,
before being translated to the wealthier bishopric of Lincoln. It is likely that
Smyth was President of the Council during the 1490s when the Council was
re-established by Henry VII for his eldest son, Prince Arthur; however, the
records are not clear. There is a record of Smyth's appointment in 1501, but it
is thought that this was a re-appointment to the position. The main recorded
item that survives of his period is as an arbitrator over the lordship of Usk and
Gwent in 1494.

Smyth, though a keen patron of education and promoter of a reformed
clergy, spent most of his episcopal career in royal service. Margaret Beaufort
remained a close friend, interested in his finances and remembering him
in her will. He is thought to have exercised some influence over Prince
Arthur's education as well as Council administration – much as Alcock did
for Prince Edward. He certainly liaised with both the king and the king's
mother, whose council he also headed, about the conduct of the Council.

As Chancellor of Oxford University from 1500 Smyth was closely linked
to a number of other bishop administrators. As diocesan bishop he was
largely an absentee, though there is some record of his involvement in

heresy inquiries in 1506. Smyth took the humane and generous view that most Lollards were faithful but misguided Christians, preferring to send them home rather than to the stake.

As both a bishop and President of the Prince's Council, Smyth played a major part in the obsequies for Prince Arthur in 1502. At Ludlow he sang the vespers of the dead on the first day, and the third requiem mass on the following day. At Worcester, he blessed the body again and sang masses as he had done at Ludlow. At the actual inhumation he was barely able to pray for tears, and was the first to cast earth and holy water on the coffin. He remained President of the Council, despite the change of prince, until 1512, in which year he too became co-founder of a college: Brasenose in Oxford.

## 37 Geoffrey Blyth, c.1470–1530,
### Bishop of Coventry and Lichfield
### Lord President of the Council in the Marches of Wales 1512–24

B LYTH WAS THE nephew of Archbishop Rotherham and became well provided for as a pluralist (a holder of several church offices all at the same time). He was a Prebendary of York in 1493, Treasurer of Sarum in 1494, Prebendary of St Paul's c.1496, Dean of York in 1496, Archdeacon of Sarum in 1499, Warden of Kings Hall 1499–1528, Bishop of Lichfield in 1503 and Lord President of the Council in the Marches of Wales 1512–24.

Like most serial pluralists, who held a number of ecclesiastical posts simultaneously, Blyth regarded these posts simply as a source of income whilst he pursued a career as an active councillor of the king in the early years of Henry VIII. Previously, he had been involved in several diplomatic missions for Henry VII, to which he probably owed the promotion to a bishopric.

He was an ideal choice for the Presidency of the Council, but there is little evidence for the years of his presidency. His role – and, indeed, the extent of the powers of the Council itself – remain vague. Some positive facts do, however, emerge. For example, he led the commission of 1512 to investigate 'insurrection, rebellions and Lollardy' in south Wales – but the outcome of the investigation remains unknown. Records of heresy trials in his diocese are formulaic and standardised, so it is unlikely that much was achieved. However, he did take, in person, 40 abjurations of heresy within his diocese, and was involved in the notorious heresy trail of Richard Hunne, being one of the examiners of Hunne's 'book'.

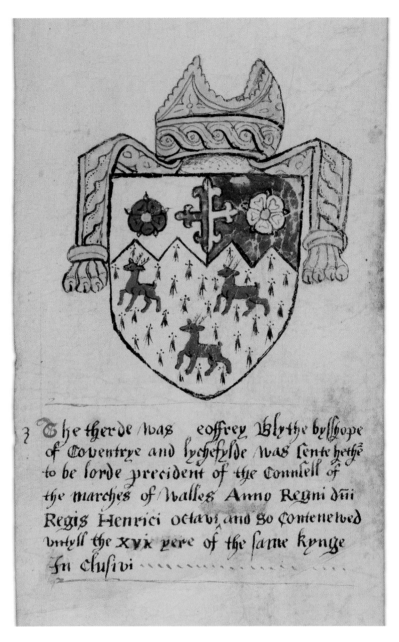

3  The therde was  eoffrey Blythe byſſhope
of Coventrye and lychefylde was ſente hethe
to be lorde preſident of the Connſell of
the marches of Walles Anno Regni dñi
Regis Henrici octaui, and so contenewed
vntyll the xvi yere of the ſame kynge
ſn clusivi ~~~~~~~~~~~~~

For reasons that remain unclear, Blyth came under suspicion of heresy himself, and also faced a charge of treason in 1523, brought by an unknown Welshman. It is assumed that he had annoyed either the Council in the Marches of Wales or possibly his cathedral dean and chapter. He left the Council and devoted himself thereafter to Lichfield diocese. In 1530, along with 13 other bishops, he was found guilty of *praemunire* (the offence of asserting or maintaining papal jurisdiction in England). Soon after Wolsey's downfall, Blyth died in London. He was buried in his cathedral before the image of St Chad. Legacies included one to St Chad's in Shrewsbury, suggesting a special devotion to the missionary saint. His cathedral also benefited, as did Norton in Derbyshire, his birthplace, where he established a chantry.

---

THE COAT OF ARMS
*37 Geoffrey Blyth, Bishop of Coventry & Lichfield*
*The Bishop's personal arms*

Geoffrey's father, William Blyth is said to have been married to a half-sister of Thomas Rotherham, Archbishop of York. William was granted a coat of arms by Henry VII in February 1486, shortly after he won the Crown at the Battle of Bosworth. The Rotherham arms have three white stags on a green field, and it seems likely that William chose three stags himself because of his family closeness to the Archbishop. Geoffrey's older brother, John Blyth, became Bishop of Salisbury, and he retained his father's coat of arms which were *ermine* with three red stags or roebucks. Geoffrey Blyth appears to have differenced the arms by adding a *chief* at the top.

There are several examples of this coat of arms in different places. The description of the arms varies a little from one example to another, but not in any significant way. Sometimes the deer are called stags and sometimes roebucks or bucks. Sometimes they are said to be standing (*statant*) and sometimes walking (*trippant*). The shape of the cross is sometimes called *patonce* and sometimes *paty* or *formy*. The cross on the Ludlow Roll is correctly described as *flory*.

---

# 38 John Veysey (or Voysey), c.1464–1554

## Bishop of Exeter
## Lord President of the Council in the Marches of Wales 1525–34

ORIGINALLY KNOWN AS John Harman, he adopted the surname of Veysey in 1488, possibly as a compliment to the Oxford graduate and London rector John Veysey (d.1492) who made bequests to Harman and his brother. A fellow of Magdalen College Oxford in 1486–87, he was chaplain to Queen Elizabeth [of York] in 1489. By 1512 he was Dean of the Chapel Royal; hence, he supported the Crown as the ultimate authority when the question of *praemunire* arose. He was a notable pluralist: Chancellor of Lichfield Cathedral 1498–1502; Archdeacon of Chester 1499–1515; Canon of Exeter

4 The fourthe was iohn vesye lorde
Byſſhope of Exeter and was ſente
hether to be lorde preſydent of thys
Counſell in the tyme of the lady mary
prinses of walles in the xviij yere of
kynge Henry the viijᵗ her ffather and
contineωed vntill the xxvᵗ yere of the ſaim
kyng In Chriſti

1503–09, and then Dean 1509–19; Dean of Windsor 1515–19; finally, he was
Bishop of Exeter 1519–51, in reward for his earlier support for the Crown.

He was not a very active Bishop of Exeter: he performed fewer than 400
of the 1,338 institutions of clergy throughout his long episcopate, but nevertheless lamented to Cromwell in 1539 that he had few promotions he could
bestow on his chaplains who were learned and virtuous preachers. In 1523

he had complained that the majority of the parishioners of Crediton only attended Sunday Mass four times in the year, and in the 1520s he also took over parishes where monasteries had failed to put in a vicar. He ordered his clergy to learn part of the New Testament by heart each day. However, after 1542 he ceased to live in his diocese and returned to Sutton Coldfield, where he restored the market, rebuilt houses and endowed the grammar school.

Under Edward VI, Veysey's brand of spirituality was seen as unacceptable. He was first obliged to alienate the property of the See, and then in 1551 he was deprived of it altogether, being replaced by the reformer and bible translator Miles Coverdale. On Edward's death he was restored to his see, dying a year later in extreme old age.

Veysey's record as President of the Council was undistinguished. He was appointed in 1525 when Princess Mary took up residence in Ludlow castle for three years, but he appears to have lacked either perseverance or energy to deal with the problem of lawlessness in Wales and the Marches. Complaints

---

THE COAT OF ARMS
*38 John Veysey, Bishop of Exeter*
*The Bishop's personal arms*

This coat of arms appears to have been newly-granted to John Veysey. His name at birth was Harman but there don't appear to be any records of a Veysey or a Harman using these arms at an earlier date. While all the other available examples of the bishop's arms differ in some way from that on the Roll, the basics are the same in each case. All the shields have a black cross on a white field and then have another cross in the centre of a blue chief. But then the variations start. Sometimes the deer is called a stag and sometimes a buck and sometimes it has gold antlers, as here. The four white birds are sometimes called doves and sometimes *martlets*, which are swift-like birds shown with no feet (as they were thought never to land, so they didn't need them). The examples on the Ludlow Roll appear fairly nondescript so have been referred to simply as birds.

The most significant variations that occur in the Veysey arms concern the *chief*. On the Ludlow Roll there are red roses to either side of the central cross; but, in records of about 1520, just after John Veysey had been appointed as Bishop of Exeter, the roses are said to be yellow. Another early source has one of the yellow roses replaced by a leopard's head.

In one way the Veysey coat on the Ludlow Roll differs from all the others. The black cross does not extend to the edges of the shield. Because this unusual variation occurs elsewhere on the Roll (see *16 Davies*) it may be a particular idiosyncrasy of the painter.

---

were raised in 1532 that he was often absent (as he seems, at this stage, to have been a responsible diocesan these seem well-founded). Moreover, as a cleric he felt unable to impose the death penalty, and by implication was unwilling to take the strong line required to manage the area. His weakness drove Cromwell to reform the Council, as a result of which the elderly bishop was replaced by the inimitable Rowland Lee.

## 39  Rowland Lee, c.1487–1543
### Bishop of Coventry and Lichfield
#### Lord President of the Council in the Marches of Wales, 1534–43

B Y BIRTH, Lee was a Northumbrian, a native of Morpeth. His father
was Receiver-General of Berwick upon Tweed in 1509. In 1512 Lee was
ordained by Bishop Smyth after a legal training. He came to the attention
of Bishop Blyth, and presided over his consistory court at Lichfield, 1525–27.
He was briefly chancellor of the diocese and Bishop's Commissioner in 1529,
administering the vacancy in 1531–33, before becoming the Bishop. A servant of Wolsey (and, through him, a friend of Cromwell) his contact with
the diocese in this period was limited. His correspondence with Cromwell,
however, means that his activities as Bishop and President of the Council
are far better documented than those of his episcopal predecessors.

Lee took an active part in supporting the king's case in the divorce proceedings against Katherine of Aragon, persuading the Northern Convocation
to support the king. After 1534, now Bishop, he promoted with energy the
cause of the Royal Supremacy. Within weeks of his consecration he was also
President of the Council, a role which he approached with his customary
energy and enthusiasm. Administration of his diocese was henceforth the
responsibility of his officers, and it was in his time that the shrine of St Chad
at Lichfield, so dear to Bishop Blyth, was dismantled (1538), and the monastic community of Coventry Cathedral dissolved. In 1541 the archdeaconry of
Chester was lost to the diocese, a new bishopric of Chester in the province of
York being created instead. None of this, however, compared with his activity
in Wales and the Marches.

THE COAT OF ARMS
*39 Rowland Lee, Bishop of Coventry & Lichfield*
*Dexter: the arms of the see of Lichfield / Sinister: Quarterly Lee and Trollope*

The arms of the diocese of Lichfield are a good example of colours being
counterchanged. The basic shield is split down the middle into two colours,
*gules* and *argent*, then the charges placed on top take the opposite colour.
The main cross in the middle is an unusual shape. Because of the crossbars at
each end, it is called a *cross potent*, and because of the square at its centre it
is said to be *quadrate*, so this is a *cross potent quadrate*.

The bishop's personal coat of arms shows his father's arms quartered with
his mother's. The coat of arms of Lee or Legh in the first and fourth quarters
is interesting for the *checky* pattern on the *bend*. Although it is not clear on
the Roll, the colour of the field of his mother's Trollope arms in quarters 2
and 3 is actually *vert*, and this has been confirmed by pigment analysis.

It has been said of Lee that, unlike his episcopal predecessor, he 'never allowed his spiritual functions to interfere with his tasks as President'; tasks which he tackled with great energy and which resulted in some restoration of law and order. He regarded the main problems on the borders as murder and theft, to which he saw the solution as being fear, induced by some notable hangings, preferably in Ludlow for publicity. Thus, notorious offenders like Lewis Gethyn (executed in August 1535) and, shortly afterwards, David Lloyd and Richard Hokulton were swiftly dealt with. He was not afraid to punish criminal gentry either, with four gentlemen 'of the best lineage' being executed in Shropshire in 1538. Lee held that hanging one gentleman was more effective in deterrence than the deaths of one hundred 'petty wretches'. On the other hand, the judicious pardoning of offenders who were prepared to turn informer built him up a useful intelligence network.

Lee was adamant that his physical presence was necessary in the Marches, and in 1534–37, with the backing of Thomas Cromwell, he toured the area thoroughly. His pugnacious energy dealt with problems ranging from sheep stealing to church discipline: in 1535 the Abbot of Shrewsbury was admonished for having no inventory of monastic property and keeping no accounts, whereas the Prior of Leominster was praised as of good reputation.

Lee was not in favour of the reforms that were brought about by the Acts of Union, which integrated Wales and the Marcher Lordships into the English judicial system (including the appointment of JPs in the new shires). He was not keen on these innovations, objecting strenuously but in vain that the Welsh gentry were incapable of exercising proper authority in their new shires. He was, in his own view, the only one capable of this, and he was not afraid to execute justice alone in the absence of other Members of the Council. He complained of underfunding for his task and had his household income increased in 1534 and again in 1542. He argued that the border castles must be kept in good order for security, focusing particularly on Ludlow, Wigmore, Radnor, Montgomery, Brecon and Monmouth.

Cromwell's fall in 1540 reduced the support he received for his ruthless approach to law and order in Wales and the Marches (an incidental consequence was that it also reduced the survival of records for this period). Lee has been accused of dealing with the symptoms not the causes of disorder, but the energy with which he tackled his responsibilities as President of the Council is undeniable. He died in post in January 1543, and was buried at St Chad's, Shrewsbury.

# 40 Richard Sampson, ?–1554

## Bishop of Coventry and Lichfield
### Lord President of the Council in the Marches of Wales, 1543–49

6 The sixte lorde preysident was Rychardes Sampson lorde Byshope of coventre and lycheffylde was sent hether lorde preysident in the marches of Walles Anno Regni Regis Henrici Octabi the xxxv.º and conttenewed vntyll the seconde yere of the Ragne of kynge Edwarde the Syxte in Clusivi

---

**THE COAT OF ARMS**
*40 Richard Sampson, Bishop of Lichfield & Coventry*
*The arms of Sampson with a mullet for difference*

On the Roll, Richard Sampson is described as the Bishop of Coventry and Lichfield. However, the cathedral at Coventry was demolished in 1539,

THE COAT OF ARMS (*CONT.*)
as part of the suppression of the monasteries, and the title of the see
changed officially to Lichfield and Coventry.

The Sampsons were a wealthy Suffolk family. There are several variants of
their coat of arms, but the version on the Roll is associated with the Sampsons
of Sampson's Hall in Kersey, Suffolk. The small mullet in the centre tells us
that Richard was the third son in his family. In earlier records, the cross on
his shield has been described as either a cross *patonce* or a cross *flory*. As the
cross has three leafs springing separately from the knob at the end of each
arm, however, it is more correctly blazoned today as a cross *floretty*. The four
black rather frilly-looking objects are meant to be scallop shells.

R ICHARD SAMPSON SUCCEEDED Lee both in his diocese and as President
of the Council. Like so many other senior clergy, he was a professional
diplomat and administrator whose church livings were chiefly a source of
income. He qualified in law in 1513, became chaplain to Wolsey and, in 1516,
to Henry VIII. He served the king as Dean of the Chapel Royal and, by
1523, Dean of Windsor; his successful career was now assured. He received
the Archdeaconry of Cornwall in 1519, the Prebend of Newbold in 1519, the
Prebends of St Paul's and Lincoln in 1526 and 1527 respectively, and the
Archdeaconry of Suffolk in 1529. His support for the king's divorce from
Katherine probably helped him to the Prebend and Deanery of Lichfield
in 1533 and the Treasurership of Salisbury in 1534. His first bishopric was
Chichester in 1536, which he held until promotion to Lichfield in 1543.

Sampson was ambassador to the Holy Roman Emperor in 1522–25 and
was well-placed therefore to advise on Charles v's attitude to the attempted
divorce of his aunt, Katherine of Aragon. Sampson, though a royal supporter,
seems to have had conservative religious leanings; he was briefly imprisoned
as a 'papalist' just before the downfall of Cromwell, whose fall from grace
probably saved Sampson's career. He had shown some interest in the state of
his diocese of Chichester by wishing in 1538 that all ministers were learned
enough to understand the Latin of the offices and the prayers they repeated.
Little is known of his direction of his second diocese of Lichfield.

Equally little is known of his presidency, which was presumably less active
than Lee's and certainly less well-recorded. His term of office was curtailed
by the death of Henry VIII and the sudden regime change at the accession of
Edward VI. His religious conservatism was no longer seen as acceptable, and
he was replaced on the Council by the first lay President, the Earl of Warwick.

# 41 John Dudley, 1504–53, Earl of Warwick
## Lord President in the Marches of Wales 1549–50

JOHN DUDLEY, 1ST Duke of Northumberland, was a royal servant and admiral who led the government of King Edward VI from 1550 until 1553, and unsuccessfully tried to install Lady Jane Grey on the English throne after Edward's death. He was the son of Edmund Dudley, a minister of Henry VII, who was executed after the accession of Henry VIII. He became a ward of Sir Edward Guildford and married Guildford's daughter Jane in 1525, by whom he had many children. Their eight sons included John Dudley (1527–54), Earl of Warwick, Ambrose Dudley (c.1530–90), Earl of Warwick,

John Dudley, Duke of Northumberland. © *National Trust Images*

Henry Dudley (*c*.1531–57), Robert Dudley (*c*.1532–88), Earl of Leicester, and Guildford Dudley (*c*.1535–54). Their daughters were Mary Sidney (1530–86) and Katherine Hastings, later Countess of Huntingdon (*c*.1538–1620).

THE COAT OF ARMS

*41 John Dudley, Earl of Warwick*

*Quarterly of 15: 1 Dudley; 2 Beaumont; 3 Grey de Ruthyn; 4 Hastings;*
*5 Lexington; 6 Somery; 7 Ferrers; 8 Valence; 9 Montgomery; 10 Talbot;*
*11 Newburgh; 12 Beauchamp; 13 Berkeley; 14 Lisle of Rougemont;*
*15 Lisle of Kingston Lisle. In pretence: Guildford quartering Haldon.*

## THE COAT OF ARMS (*CONT.*)
*The arms are encircled by the Order of the Garter with an earl's coronet on top*

There is much of heraldic interest in this complicated shield. It is easy to miss the small shield, or escutcheon, that has been placed in the centre of this coat of arms. John Dudley's wife was an heraldic heiress as she was the only surviving child of Sir Edward Guildford. So John Dudley is allowed to place the Guildford arms 'in pretence' in the centre of his own shield.

John Dudley inherited only four of his 15 quarterings from his father, Edmund Dudley, namely Dudley, Somery, Beaumont and Lexington. He inherited the other 11 quarterings from his mother Elizabeth Grey, Baroness Lisle, and these quarterings include many of the most powerful families in medieval England. There are very few rules about the display of quarterings on a shield, so it is very common for different versions to be found. Often a man will choose not to include all the quarterings to which he is entitled.

There are a number of unusual features about the quarterings displayed on John Dudley's shield on the Roll. He was related to the Earls of Shrewsbury who were Talbots, and quarter 10 shows the arms of Talbot with a lion *rampant* on a red field. In 1066 Roger of Montgomery came to England with William the Conqueror and was created Earl of Shrewsbury. This first earldom died out early in the twelfth century, well before heraldry became established, but the coat of arms in quarter 9, with the lion *rampant* on a blue field, is always used to represent it. By including quarter 9 in his coat of arms, John Dudley is claiming a direct link to the three early Earls of Shrewsbury. No such family link seems to exist, however, so the inclusion of quarter 9 appears to be quite fanciful.

John's wife Jane Guildford was entitled to several important quarterings. Although four of these could have been displayed on the small escutcheon in the centre of John's arms, he has chosen to include only two. However, several of Jane's other family quarterings appear in the arms of their children, including Mortimer of Chirk.

The coat of arms of Ferrers in quarter 7 is unusual. Their normal coat has seven diamonds – three at the top, another row of three and an odd one below – with all the diamonds joining each other. Because of the inescutcheon in the middle of the shield it is not clear whether the diamonds on this coat are arranged 3, 2 & 1 or 3, 2 & 2 (probably the latter, to make a total of seven like the normal Ferrers coat).

The Dudleys used to be called Sutton, and the arms of Lexington in quarter 5 are interesting for the fact that they came into the family as many as 12 generations before, when Rowland Sutton (who died in 1284) married Alice Lexington.

One significant coat of arms that is not found here is Stafford, which is commonly included in other versions of John Dudley's shield.

Dudley served as Vice-Admiral and Lord Admiral from 1537 until 1547, during which time he set novel standards of naval organisation and was an innovative commander at sea. He also developed a strong interest in overseas exploration. In 1553 his patronage of Sebastian Cabot, and the cosmographer, John Dee, promoted England's first officially sponsored voyage of discovery to attempt to find the north-east passage under the command of Sir John Willoughby. Dudley took part in the 1544 campaigns in Scotland and France and was one of Henry VIII's intimates in the last years of the reign. For his military services to the king he gained substantial former ecclesiastical and Crown property, and lucrative government offices. He was also a leader of the religious reform party at Court, which Henry finally espoused in his last years, leaving him on the king's death one of the richest (as well as one of the most important) subjects of the Crown.

Dudley was able to consolidate his position when Edward VI came to the throne in 1547. He was created Earl of Warwick and, since the new king was a minor, England's Lord Protector, jointly with the Duke of Somerset. Dudley distinguished himself in the renewed Scottish war at the Battle of Pinkie Cleugh. In 1549, he put down Kett's rebellion in Norfolk, and was raised to the Dukedom of Northumberland in October 1551, the highest title possible for a subject. By this time the Duke of Somerset had become the object of a Privy Council-led conspiracy and had been deposed, leaving Dudley, as Lord President of the Privy Council, effectively heading the king's government.

Edward VI fell ill in early 1553 and excluded his half-sisters, Mary and Elizabeth, whom he regarded as illegitimate, from the succession. Edward changed his will so that his Protestant cousin Jane Grey, Northumberland's daughter-in-law, could inherit the Crown. On the king's death, Dudley, with the backing of the Privy Council, quickly promoted Jane's claim to the throne, while that of Mary was rejected. The Duke marched to East Anglia to crush the growing force gathering around Mary, but in his absence the Privy Council changed sides and proclaimed Mary as queen. Dudley was forced to surrender, and was imprisoned and executed for treason.

In 1549 Dudley was appointed Lord President of the Council in the Marches of Wales. He was the first lay President of the Council, but was only in post for a few months, since his responsibilities at Court prevented him from coming to Wales, and he quickly handed over the Presidency to William Herbert (42). Sir Henry Sidney was presumably very conscious of the fact that his father-in-law had been the first lay President of the Council, and this, together with Sir Henry's marriage to Mary Dudley, the daughter of John Dudley, 1st Duke of Northumberland, may explain Sir Henry's enthusiasm for showing his family relationships and political connections through heraldry.

## 42 (44) William Herbert, 1506–70
### *Earl of Pembroke*
### *Lord President of the Council in the Marches of Wales*
### *1550–53 and 1555–58*

WILLIAM HERBERT HAD good Welsh and border credentials. He was born in Monmouthshire, the son of Sir Richard Herbert of Ewyas Harold and Margaret Cradock of Swansea. William was described by John Aubrey as, 'strong sett, but bon(e)y, reddish favoured, of a sharp eye, stern look', and as, 'a mad fighting fellow'. It was said that he could neither read nor

William Herbert, 1st Earl of Pembroke by Steven van der Meulen.
© *Amgueddfa Cymru – National Museum Wales*

write, and that the only language he knew well was Welsh. This strong Welsh background gave him a closer connection with Wales and the Marches than most of the Presidents, and he served the sovereign well in this, as in many other of his myriad royal appointments. He began his career as a gentleman-servant to the Earl of Worcester, but after killing a Welshman in an affray he fled to France. His hot-headed nature was better able to serve him in the

8 The eyghte lorde prefident was
Sir Wyllyam harbert knyght of the
noble order was fent hether prefident
of thys Counsell Anno quarto Regni
Regis Edwardi Sexti and Conteneived
vntyll mychellmas in the ffirfte yere
of the Raygne of Queene marye
in clufivi

army of King Francis I, and he quickly earned a reputation for courage and skill on the battlefield. Francis recommended him to King Henry VIII who also came to value him. He became a man of means when, for his service to the king, he was granted the estates of Wilton Abbey and Remesbury in Wiltshire, and Cardiff Castle in south Wales.

Herbert rose further in the King's favour when, in 1543, Henry married Catherine Parr, the sister of Herbert's first wife. This marital connection led to a knighthood for Herbert and a position close to the centre of power – so much so that he was an executor of Henry's will and, when Henry died in 1547, one of the Council of Regency for the young King Edward VI. This led to further honours: he was made a Knight of the Garter in 1549 and in 1550 was appointed Lord President of the Council in the Marches of Wales. Throughout his life he bought up land in several counties in both England (particularly Wiltshire) and Wales, many of them being former monastic properties. Rents and other sources resulted in an income of between

---

### THE COAT OF ARMS

*42 (44) William Herbert, 1st Earl of Pembroke of the 10th creation*
*Quarterly of 7: 1 Herbert; 2 Morgan; 3 Gam; 4 Morley; 5 Craddock; 6 Horton; 7 Cantilupe – all encircled by the Order of the Garter*

When Sir William Herbert was appointed as Lord President in 1550 he was not yet a peer, and it was not until the following year that he was created Earl of Pembroke. There is little sign on the Roll of the earl's coronet one might expect to see above the arms. There were several examples of these arms in the castle, and Mytton includes a coronet in some of his drawings but not in others. These may refer to his second presidency.

The Herbert arms in the first quarter are very interesting. William Herbert's father was an illegitimate son of William Herbert, 1st Earl of Pembroke of the 8th creation. The red and white border has been added to the usual Herbert arms to signify bastardy. The border is really red and yellow, but the gold has almost completely faded on this part of the shield.

Quarter 2 contains spearheads tipped with blood; the heraldic term is spearheads *imbrued*. This coat of arms is generally ascribed to Morgan, though sometimes to Vaughan or Gam. In quarter 5 it is possible to make out a white cross near the base, and this is one of several variants of the Craddock arms. Mytton records a black crescent in the gold rectangle in quarter 6, but there is no remaining evidence of it here. The Cantilupe arms in quarter 7 are identical to the arms of the diocese of Hereford in 13 Scory. Hereford adopted the arms of Cantilupe in honour of St Thomas Cantilupe, bishop in the thirteenth century.

---

£4,000 and £5,000 per annum, an income which would make him a millionaire today. He spent a fortune on houses to match his ever increasing status, pulling down the abbey on the Wilton estate and building the first Wilton House there, and making significant alterations to Cardiff Castle. Not a man to hide his light under a bushel, he had a fondness for ostentatious display, whether it be in entertaining the young Edward vi or in the funeral ceremony for his first wife.

He was also a fearless fighter and in 1549, when the 'Prayer Book' rebellion broke out in various parts of England, he acted so vigorously against the insurgents in the west that Edward vi recorded that, 'Sir William Herbert did put them down overrun them and slay them'. Allied to John Dudley, Earl of Warwick, his rise to power continued, with ever increasing financial rewards and, in Wales, becoming Lord President of the Council in the Marches of Wales. On Mary's accession in 1553 he was replaced by Bishop Nicholas Heath. When Heath became Archbishop of York, Herbert was reappointed to the presidency in which he remained until 1558.

Nor was he a man to let family loyalty interfere with his political ambitions. Shortly before Edward vi died, Herbert married his eldest son to Catherine, a sister of Lady Jane Grey, whose claim to the throne he supported. However, when it became clear that Mary Tudor, rather than Jane Grey, would become queen, he cast his daughter-in-law out of his house and had the marriage annulled. He obtained the new queen's favour by crushing the Wyatt rebellion. Although his power, wealth and experience (especially as a fighting man) made him indispensable to Mary, after her death he was equally important to Elizabeth.

He was at Hatfield, at the first Privy Council of Elizabeth's reign, and had her respect as well as that of Sir William Cecil, the queen's secretary. Although his health deteriorated in the 1560s, this did not stop his relentless pursuit of wealth or his involvement in Court politics. He was willing to take risks with his money, investing in expeditions to find the north-east passage to China; in slaving expeditions and others for the discovery of lands unknown. Closer to home, he was a shareholder in mining and other like ventures. He was briefly out of royal favour when he backed a scheme for the Catholic Mary Queen of Scots to marry Thomas Howard, the fourth Duke of Norfolk; however, having successfully pleaded his innocence, he was allowed to retire to Wilton.

He died on 17 March 1570 at Hampton Court and was buried with his first wife in the old St Paul's Cathedral.

*The following Presidents do not appear on the Roll which seems to have lost a final section. However, their arms were displayed in the Chapel of St Mary Magdalene in Ludlow Castle and are included in order to complete the record of Sir Henry Sidney's heraldic decoration of the Round Chapel.*

## (43) Nicholas Heath, c.1501–78,
### Bishop of Worcester
### Lord President of the Council in the Marches of Wales, 1553–55

N ICHOLAS HEATH WAS another traditional clerical administrator and diplomat, passing from Cambridge fellowships to the Archdeaconry of Stafford in 1534, and becoming King's Almoner in 1539 (a post once held by Wolsey). Heath worked closely with Archbishop Cranmer over the translation of the Bible into English, resulting in the publication of the Great Bible in 1539. Bishoprics naturally followed: Rochester in 1539 and Worcester in 1543. As a traditional conservative he fell foul of the Protestant regime of Edward VI and was deprived of Worcester, which passed to the evangelical Hooper in 1551. He was sent to the Fleet prison but, shortly after, was released into the custody of Nicholas Ridley, Bishop of London.

Mary's accession in 1553 led to a reversal of policy. Heath was reinstated to his diocese and made Lord President of the Council in 1553, replacing William Herbert, 1st Earl of Pembroke. In 1555, however, he was promoted

THE COAT OF ARMS
*(43) Nicholas Heath,*
*Bishop of Worcester*
*The arms of Heath*

The black birds in the three roundels on this shield are heathcocks, each one bearing a piece of heather in its bill, and thereby referring to the name Heath. Heathcock and moorcock were both folk names for the black grouse.

Arms of Bishop Heath drawn by William Mytton, c.1735
*MYT/3/672 © Cadbury Research Library, Special Collections, University of Birmingham*

Archbishop of York and resigned his presidency of the Council, becoming also Mary's Lord Chancellor in 1556.

Heath is noted as a non-persecuting bishop and a scholar. He proclaimed Elizabeth on her accession but, like most Marian bishops, was deprived and imprisoned for refusal to accept the Elizabethan settlement. He was released from the Tower on his promise to abstain from public affairs, and retired to Chobham in Surrey, where he lived in comparative obscurity. However, he was questioned twice by the Privy Council about Mass being celebrated regularly in his house – though escaped prosecution. When he died in 1578 he was buried in Chobham church without objection, despite his undoubted recusancy.

## (45) Gilbert Bourne, ?–1569
### Bishop of Bath and Wells
### Lord President of the Council in the Marches of Wales, 1558–59

BOURNE'S CAREER AS Lord President of the Council was even shorter than Heath's. On 31 October 1558 he was rewarded with the presidency; 17 days later, Queen Mary was dead. He remained in post until February 1559 when, together with the other bishops who had refused to take the Oath of Supremacy (which declared the monarch supreme head of the church in England), he was deprived of his bishopric. From the presidency

THE COAT OF ARMS
(45) Gilbert Bourne, Bishop of Bath and Wells
The arms of Bourne with a crescent for difference

This pen sketch gives all the necessary information about the arms of Gilbert Bourne. The field is *argent* and the shading shows that the chevron is *gules* and the lions *sable*. The chief has been drawn as *ermine*, but the note written underneath ('tails inverted') tells us that the pattern should really be *sable* with the tails *argent* rather than the other way round. When *ermine* is inverted like this is it is called *ermines*.

Arms of Bishop Bourne drawn by William Mytton, c.1735
MYT/3/537A © Cadbury Research Library, Special Collections, University of Birmingham

he was politely dismissed with thanks. Originally imprisoned in the Tower, he was later detained under house arrest and died in 1569. He was the last bishop to hold the presidency of the Council, and it is unlikely that he ever actually exercised his presidency.

Bourne's career during the reign of Henry VIII had followed a familiar pattern of clerical promotions, from Fellow of All Souls in 1531 to a prebend at Worcester (1541), and St Paul's (1545) where he became proctor for the clergy of London diocese and chaplain to the notoriously persecuting Bishop Bonner. He probably received Bath and Wells in 1554 as a reward for Catholic fidelity to his bishop. He had conformed without enthusiasm in Edward's reign and preached at St Paul's Cross commending Bonner's restoration. Under Mary, Bourne took an active part in the disputation of 1554 with the Oxford Martyrs, and later sat on several heresy commissions, where he was usually moderate, though a zealous promoter of traditional Catholic worship.

After Elizabeth I's accession, Bourne was imprisoned in the Tower of London for three years for Nonconformity, but in 1561 he was released into the custody of Nicholas Bullingham, Bishop of Lincoln. He was later handed over to George Carew, Archdeacon of Exeter, and probably remained in Carew's keeping until his death at Silverton, Devon, on 10 September 1569.

# (46) John, Lord Williams of Thame, c.1500–59
## Lord President of the Council in the Marches of Wales, 1559

ON HIS FATHER'S side, John Williams had some Welsh blood in him as his father, also John Williams, was a kinsman of Morgan Williams, who married Thomas Cromwell's eldest sister, Katherine. As such the family had access to royal circles and, by 1526, Williams was a rising, minor official around the Court. He was also beginning to accumulate profitable minor county offices and leases of lands and lordships. In 1530 he was appointed Clerk (later, Master) of the King's Jewels. He continued to move steadily up the ladder of royal financial offices and, by 1535, he was one of Thomas Cromwell's trusted inner circle.

Although one of his sisters was prioress of Studley, Williams seems to have been a willing reformer, being assiduous in receiving the surrender of monasteries and confiscating their treasures. In 1538 he wrote to Cromwell that, 'we intend both at Hyde and St Mary's [Winchester] to sweep away all the rotten bones that be called relics (...) lest it should be thought we came

## THE COAT OF ARMS
*(46) John Williams, Baron Williams de Thame*
*Arms of Williams*

The two crossed items here are organ pipes. This coat of arms had certainly been used by Lord Williams' family since the time of Henry VII, but no explanation has been found for the use of the organ pipes. The four crosses of this design are described as *formy* or *paty*. The crest is a fish weir used to trap fish.

Arms of John Williams, Lord Thame. *Soc Ant MS 68.* © *Society of Antiquaries*

more for the treasure than for avoiding of the abomination of idolatry.' By June 1539 he had been knighted and by 1540 he was making a considerable profit from the purchase and resale of monastic lands, continuing to expand his estates until his death. He was steward to a number of royal manors and, last but not least, was appointed Master of Cygnets on the Thames in 1542.

He survived Cromwell's fall from grace in 1540, remaining Master of the Jewels. In March 1544 he was appointed Treasurer of Augmentations responsible for a lot of government expenditure, a position he retained through Edward's reign until its dissolution in January 1554. There was speculation that he was not altogether efficient or honest in this office, and he spent a short time confined to the Fleet prison for making unauthorised payments (though was later pardoned). After he left office the final accounts showed he owed the Crown £28,000; however, this debt was waived on account of his services to the Queen.

Williams was a staunch supporter of the Catholic Queen Mary who had good reason to reward him; for, even before her accession on 13 July 1553, he had proclaimed her Queen in Oxfordshire and raised troops on her behalf. His loyalty led to his appointment for the third time as Sheriff of Oxfordshire and Berkshire, which in the year 1553–54 gave him a key role in maintaining Mary's hold on the Home Counties.

In 1554, Williams became chamberlain to King Philip, and was also made responsible for the safe-keeping of Princess Elizabeth, escorting her from the Tower to Woodstock, and establishing a good relationship with her

Sir John Williams supervises the burning as a Protestant martyr of Thomas Cranmer, former Archbishop of Canterbury, at Oxford during Queen Mary's reign, 21 March 1556. *Foxe's Book of Martyrs, D.4.14 p1713. © Hereford Cathedral Library*

in the process. He was involved in the custody and execution of Cranmer, Latimer and Ridley, and was present at their burnings in 1555 and 1556.

Yet, despite this loyalty to Mary, Williams's religious attitude was unclear. There were rumours that he was favourable to Protestants, a report that was later found to be untrue. In November 1558 he was one of those who accompanied Elizabeth, when she became Queen, from Hatfield to London.

In February 1559, the Queen replaced Gilbert Bourne, Bishop of Bath and Wells, with Lord Williams as President. On appointment he was too ill to take up the post, and it was not until June that he was able to enter the role. However, his tenure was very brief as he died at Ludlow Castle on 14 October 1559.

Williams married twice, first in 1524 to Elizabeth, a widow by whom he had three sons and two daughters. Following her death in 1556 he married Margaret, the daughter of the first Lord Wentworth, by whom he had one daughter. He was buried with great pomp at Thame where his tomb still remains.

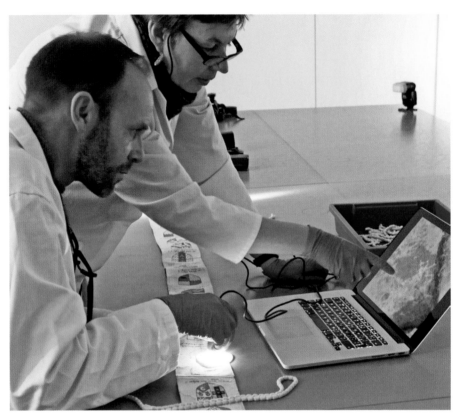

Stephen Rickerby and Lisa Shekede examining the arms of Thomas Davis, Bishop of St Asaph in ultraviolet light using portable microscopy

# Investigations into the Painting Technology of the Ludlow Castle Heraldic Roll
*by Stephen Rickerby and Lisa Shekede*

## METHODOLOGY

Each of the arms on the Roll was imaged at different light wavelengths to provide information not visible to the naked eye: shorter, ultraviolet wavelengths are particularly useful for detecting organic materials such as binding media and colours composed of vegetable dyes, while the longer ones in the infrared range can help investigate under-drawing and compositional changes. Examination under magnification was also conducted using portable microscopy at up to x200 to help identify individual pigments based on particle size and shape, and to characterize the components of paint layers made up of pigment mixes. These in-situ investigations helped identify suitable sample locations, following which ten samples were obtained for lab-based analysis to provide confirmatory information. This consisted of polarised light microscopy of dispersed samples and micro-chemical testing.

Interpretation of the results was assisted by research drawing not only on technical references but also on contemporary treatises on drawing and painting, including an anonymous publication of 1573 and early seventeenth-century works by Henry Peacham and Edward Norgate.

## ANALYTICAL FINDINGS

The results of analysis demonstrated an exceedingly rich and varied palette of up to 12 different pigments, reflecting the prestigious nature of the commission. It contained up to two blacks (charcoal black and a finely divided carbon black such as lamp black); up to two whites (lead white and probably also chalk); three blues (azurite, natural ultramarine, and an organic blue); three yellows (yellow iron oxide, lead tin yellow, and orpiment) and two reds (vermilion, and an organic red). Whether singly or in combination, these materials were used skilfully, and with a clear intent to achieve subtle variations in hue, shade and texture.

**Black:** neither the black letter text nor the outlines and fine details of the escutcheons were sampled as this could not be safely done without unacceptable disruption. However portable microscopy revealed that they were composed of uniformly minute dense black particles suggestive of one of the fine blacks described in contemporary treatises, which itemise a number of such pigments, including **lamp black**, and blacks derived from burning ivory, date stones, walnut shells, hartshorn and bread. Particles of a coarser black derived from **charcoal** were also used in the dark green paint layers, identified in dispersion by their distinctive plant fibre structure.

**White:** in contemporary treatises, whites are limited to either lead white in different grades of purity, or chalk. Both seem to have been used for the Ludlow Roll. Where a dense, opaque bright white impasto paint was wanted, this was achieved using **lead white**, as demonstrated by characteristic fluorescence in ultraviolet light, and confirmed through dispersion analysis and microchemical testing. Other effects were also sought, however: a mark of the subtlety of the painting technique lies in the way the cadence bars in escutcheons of Lionel of Antwerp and Richard of York are painted: these impasto white layers are semi-translucent so as not to obscure the charges beneath, achieved by altering the pigment volume ratio and/ or by adding **chalk**. Chalk also seems to have been used as a substrate for red organic dye.

**Blue:** portable microscopy revealed that the blue paint passages were composed of large individual crystals of two distinct types. The first type was composed of semi-transparent bright blue-green crystals of slightly varying hue, while the second was composed of angular particles of an intense dark rich blue. Dispersion analysis and microchemical tests identified the first type as **azurite**. This pigment was the second most expensive pigment available to artists of the time, and while it was listed as an artist's pigment in contemporary accounts, azurite was commonly substituted with cheaper options, including the artificial copper and cobalt blues, verditer and smalt, and a range of organic blues.

The use of azurite here, therefore, provides telling evidence of the high status of the Ludlow Roll, evidence which is firmly reinforced by the identification of the second blue. The deeper, truer blue particles were found to be **natural ultramarine**. Derived from lapis lazuli, this rare and highly prized pigment from Afghanistan's Kokcha valley was imported into Europe by Venetian traders. Demand for natural ultramarine has always exceeded supply and was the most expensive of all pigments, at this period costing eleven pounds and ten shillings per ounce. Astonishingly, this was equivalent

**Fig 1**: detail of the arms of Sir Andrew Corbett, showing a quartering of white lions rampant on a blue field

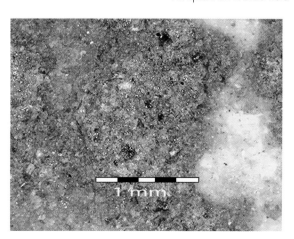

**Fig 2**: portable microscope image of the blue paint layer at ×200 showing its heterogeneous nature. Deep blue particles of natural ultramarine are distributed within a matrix of lighter blue azurite crystals, varying in colour from a pale sky blue to green-blue

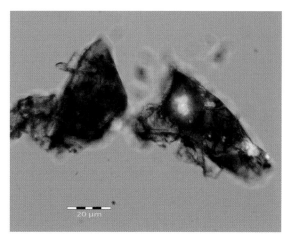

**Fig 3**: two large, deep blue, high-relief crystals of natural ultramarine in dispersion at ×400 using polarized light microscopy, imaged in crossed-polars

to about a year's wages for a skilled labourer in Elizabethan England (figures obtained from Mass Historia http://walternelson.com/dr/node/8920). Although Norgate provides a detailed description of its preparation for use as a pigment, it is only mentioned by Peacham in relation to its application in a parchment glue binder rather than in his list of blue pigments, presumably because by this date the prohibitive cost of the pigment meant that it was rarely used. An added subtlety was the addition of small quantities of an **organic red**, presumably to enhance the highly prized purplish-blue hue of the ultramarine (*see below*) [**FIGS** 1–3, *p. 209*].

**Green**: a number of mineral green pigments and a few organic greens were available to artists of the time. However, green was also often made by combining yellow and blue pigments. Individual particles in the Ludlow Roll's dark green paint passages were difficult to discern even using portable microscopy, but in dispersion the heterogeneity of the green layers was apparent. Four particle types were observed: a blue quite unlike the mineral blue particles used for the blue paint passages, which suffused the other particles with a distinct deep blue-green stain. The second formed masses of small, uniform, pale yellow particles. Some larger brownish-yellow particles, and opaque black particles were also present.

These four particle types displayed characteristics consistent with identifications, respectively, of **organic blue**, **lead tin yellow (type 1)**, a **yellow iron oxide**, and **charcoal black**. At this time artists obtained organic blue from a number of different plants all yielding the blue colorant, indigotin, including 'indebaudias' (bagdad indigo), 'florey' blue (woad), and lichen-derived blues such as cork, litmus & orchill. These were relatively inexpensive but had two drawbacks: the blue colour they yielded was rather dull, and it was prone to fading in the presence of light. Expense probably had little to do with its choice as a pigment in this context, however: while bright, brilliant mineral pigments were always used to create the blue paint passages, organic blues were perfect for producing a serviceable dark green. Fading, also, is hardly a problem when the roll would have been exposed to light only occasionally – indeed, the green colour remains perfectly preserved. The use of lead tin yellow and yellow ochre is similarly confined to the green paint passages where they function well in combination with the organic blue, while a more brilliant yellow pigment was reserved for representing yellow and gold paint passages on the escutcheons (*see below*).

Yellow: pigments listed in contemporary treatises to produce a yellow colour are orpiment, lead tin yellow, and various organic and iron oxide pigments. While the Ludlow Roll painter used lead tin yellow and yellow iron oxides with organic blue to make green, only the most expensive yellow available at the time – the naturally occurring mineral pigment, **orpiment** – was used when a brilliant yellow or gold colour was required. It was a problematic pigment to use, not only on account of its poisonous nature and offensive smell (it is a sulphide of arsenic), but because it is difficult to grind and is a poor drier in oil. Added to these drawbacks, it readily oxidises, causing it to lose its colour, and is unstable in alkaline environments and in contact with lead- and copper-based pigments. Norgate was so put off by these negative qualities that he refused to list it among the pigments suitable for 'limming'. The painter of the Ludlow Roll had no such reservations, however: offsetting these many disadvantages were its unrivalled bright yellow colour, its intense lustre, and its micaceous sparkle, for which reasons it was known as 'king's yellow', and often referred to in early sources as suitable for heraldic blazonry in the imitation of gold [**FIGS** 4–6, *p.* 212].

Red: many reds were available to late-sixteenth-century artists, including vermilion, red lead, a wide range of iron oxide pigments, and an even wider range of pigments derived from red organic dyes. For representing the bold red needed for blazoning arms, however, only the truest, and most brilliant red – the mercuric sulphide pigment, **vermilion** – was used. Vermilion was produced either from the naturally occurring mineral cinnabar, or was synthesized, at this time using the 'dry process' which produced a pigment which was chemically and structurally identical to that derived from the natural mineral. While it was common for vermilion to be adulterated by cheaper red pigments (either by the colour merchants or by the artists themselves), the purity of the Ludlow Roll vermilion provides a further testament to its high quality. For peripheral decorative elements of the more elaborate heraldic achievements such as those of Elizabeth I and Sir William Herbert, an entirely different red was used, the translucency, and delicate, pinkish coloration of which indicates an **organic red**.

A whole range of reds ranging from warm rose to cool purple could be obtained using organic colorants processed in different ways. Of the traditional European sources, madder (a not very light-fast organic red derived from *rubiaceae sp.*) had fallen out of favour by this period and is mentioned by none of the sources consulted. The only locally produced organic red still

**Fig 4**: detail of the arms of Henry VIII, showing the use of a bright yellow pigment to represent gold in areas such as the crown, and the lion and fleur-de-lys charges

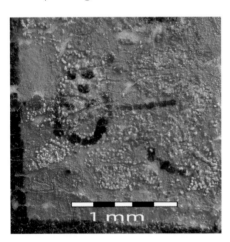

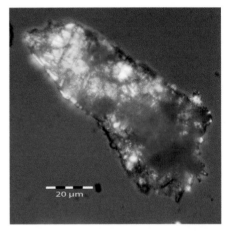

**Fig 5**: portable microscope image of one of the lion charges at x50 displaying brilliant yellow, coarsely ground particles of orpiment. Note the propensity of the orpiment particles to alter to a white form in contact with the background red colour, composed of vermilion

**Fig 6**: a large particle of orpiment in dispersion at x400, imaged using polarized light microscopy. Its crystal structure is elongated and cross-grained, displaying typical birefringence in crossed-polars

**Fig 7**: detail of the two-sided mantling (or lambrequin) of the arms of Elizabeth I, which is composed of a fabric of pink and gold stripes lined with ermine

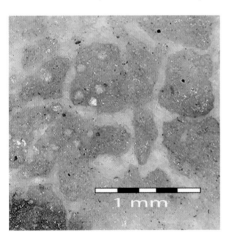

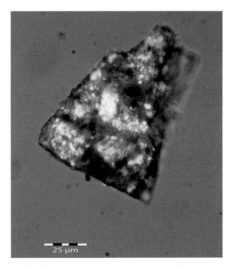

**Fig 8**: portable microscope image of one of the pink stripes at ×200. At this magnification it is possible to see tiny amorphous fragments of the organic colorant within the glossy, translucent pink matrix. Chunky particles of yellow orpiment from the gold stripe can be seen in the upper left-hand corner

**Fig 9**: fragment of organic red in dispersion at ×400 using polarized light microscopy. The chalk base is composed of the tiny shells of marine micro-organisms (coccoliths), which can be discerned in crossed-polars as bright, rounded particles

in use was turnsole (a violet colour obtained from linen cloth dyed with the berries and tops of *croton tinctorium*). However, by the end of the sixteenth century the artist's palette was expanding to incorporate exotic organic reds from Asia and the New World. These included logwood, a red dye extracted from the Mexican tree *Haematoxylum campechianum*; brazilwood, a red dye extracted from the heartwood of east Asian or south American species of *caesalpinia sp.* known as 'roset'; and lac, an extract of the scale insect *laccifer lacca* from southern and southeast Asia known as 'sinaper lake' or 'indian lake'. Through a complicated process of extraction and precipitation onto a base such as aluminium hydroxide, dyestuffs could be transformed into organic pigments known as 'lakes'. Some could simply be mordanted onto chalk or alum for use as paint materials, and these were known collectively as 'pinks', (even though those made from yellow dyes were actually yellow). The popularity of brazilwood in the sixteenth and seventeenth centuries seems to have been partly due to the relative ease with which it could be prepared as a 'pink' by the artists themselves. The Ludlow Roll pigment is certainly derived from a red organic dye, and there is evidence from examination using polarised light microscopy that it was mordanted onto a chalk base. It therefore seems to be a '**pink**', possibly derived from brazilwood. What appears to be the same organic 'pink' was also added to blue paint passages to produce a purplish effect, and combined with orpiment on the yellow charges and crests (never with the yellow backgrounds and ordinaries) to produce a warm gold effect [**FIGS** 7–9, *p. 213*].

# Blazons of the Arms on the Roll

This section describes the component coats of arms of the individual families, which contribute to each shield on the Roll. They are listed in alphabetical order. Individual family coats of arms may appear on more than one shield, and the number of the shield on which each coat of arms can be found is given in brackets after the name. In the blazon a question mark (?) indicates that what follows it is either conjectural or possibly incorrect.

As a general rule, the arms are blazoned as they appear on the Roll, even where they are known to be incorrect. Because of fading and damage to the Roll, some of the finer points of the coats of arms cannot be seen. A family's coat of arms may, for instance, normally display a crowned lion, or a voided mullet, but if the crowning or voiding is not clear on the Roll, these features are not usually mentioned in the blazon. The exception is where Mytton has recorded these features as being visible on the original shields themselves, or where there is clear evidence from the pigment analysis. However, the absence of these features from the blazon should not be taken to imply that they were not there originally.

For the sake of ease of understanding, the expressions 'of the first' or 'of the second' have been dispensed with, and we have chosen to repeat the colour concerned. A glossary of heraldic terms follows this section.

Archdeacon, Arkedekne (21)
*Argent three chevrons sable*
Arnold (22)
*Gules a chevron between three pheons or*
Ashton (31)
*Argent a mullet sable*

Baard (12)
*Argent three lions rampant gules*
Bangor diocese (15)
*Gules a bend gouttée de poix between two mullets pierced argent*

Barrington (12)
*Argent three chevronels gules, in chief a label of three points azure*
Barton (31)
*Azure a fess between three bucks' heads caboshed or*
Baux (8)
*Gules an estoile argent quartered with a simplified version of 'France Ancient'*
Beauchamp (12, 41)
*Gules a fess between six crosses crosslet or*

Beaumont (12, 41)
*Gules a cinquefoil pierced ermine*
Berkeley (12, 41)
*Gules a chevron between 10*
*crosses split 6 and 4*
Blyth (37)
*Ermine three bucks trippant gules*
*attired or, on a chief indented*
*party per pale argent and azure a*
*cross flory counterchanged between*
*two roses, dexter gules sinister*
*argent both barbed and*
*seeded ?proper*
Bosun, Bossan, Buzon (19)
*Gules three bird-bolts palewise*
*pointing downwards in fess argent*
Brandon (12)
*Barry of ?10 argent and gules a*
*lion rampant or*
Bromley (23)
*Quarterly per fess indented gules*
*and or*
Bullingham (14)
*Azure an eagle displayed argent*
*armed gules carrying in its beak*
*a sprig vert, on a chief or a rose*
*gules barbed and seeded proper*
*between two crosses botonny gules*
Burgh (4)
*Or a cross gules*
Burley 1 (21)
*Sable two bars argent and a chief*
*?paly of four argent and sable,*
*overall an escutcheon barry of*
*six ermine and gules*
?Burley 2 (21)
*Gules two bars ?compony azure*
*and argent*

Butler (10)
*Or a chief indented azure*

Cantilupe (42)
see also Hereford diocese (13)
*Gules three leopards' heads*
*reversed jessant-de-lys or*
Chetwynd (12)
*Azure a chevron between three*
*mullets or*
Cholmondeley (20)
*Gules two helmets in profile in*
*chief and a garb in base argent*
Clowfield (12)
*Argent two bars and in chief three*
*escutcheons sable*
Corbet (21)
*Or a crow (or raven) proper*
Craddock (42)
*Azure three boars heads couped*
*close and ?several crosses argent*
Croft (18)
*Quarterly per fess indented azure*
*and argent and in dexter chief a*
*lion passant guardant or*
Cynddelw (17)
*Gules a chevron between three*
*bucks' heads couped argent*

Davies, Richard (16)
*Party per chevron argent and*
*gules, three pelicans in their piety*
*counterchanged, on a chief azure a*
*fleur-de-lys or*

Davies, Thomas (17)
Quarterly 1 & 4 gules a chevron
or and a chief ermine (Dafydd ap
Robert of Caerhun, descended
from Sir Gruffudd Llwyd); 2 gules
a chevron between three bucks'
heads caboshed argent (his
maternal coat descending from
Iarddur ap Cynddelw);
3 unidentified
Dudley (12, 41)
Or a lion rampant double-queued
vert armed and langued gules

England (4–11)
Gules three lions passant guardant
in pale or

Ferrers (12, 41)
(12) Gules seven mascles or
arranged 3, 3, 1
(41) Either Gules six mascles
or arranged 3, 2 and 1 or
possibly Gules seven mascles or
arranged 3, 2 and 2, one
mascle may be hidden under
the escutcheon
Fox (26)
Argent a chevron between three
foxes heads erased gules
France Ancient (4, 5)
Azure semy-de-lys or
France Modern (6–11)
Azure three fleurs-de-lys or

Gam (42)
Argent three chickens gules
beaked, crested and legged or

Geneville (2, 3)
Azure three horse barnacles in pale
or, on a chief ermine a
demi-lion gules
Gerard (24)
Azure a lion rampant ermine
armed gules and crowned or
Grey of Ruthyn (12, 41)
Barry of six argent and azure, in
chief three torteaux
Guildford (12, 41)
Or a saltire between four
martlets sable

Halden (41)
Argent a chief sable, over all a
bend engrailed gules
Hastings (12, 41)
Or a maunch gules
Herbert (42)
Per pale azure and gules three
lions rampant argent, a bordure
compony or and gules
Hereford diocese (13)
see also Cantilupe (42)
Gules three leopards' heads
reversed jessant-de-lys or
Hopton (21)
Gules crusily a lion rampant or
Horton (42)
Argent three bendlets engrailed
gules, a canton or

Iarddur ap Cynddelw – see Cynddelw
Ince (24) – incorrect
Argent three torteaux in bend

Lacy (1, 2)
  Or a fess gules
Lancaster (10)
  England differenced with a label
Lee (39)
  Argent two bars azure, overall a
  bend checky or & gules
Leighton (28, 33)
  Quarterly per fess indented or
  and gules
Lexington (12, 41)
  Argent a cross flory azure
Leybourne (21)
  Azure six lions rampant 3, 2, 1
  argent and a bordure engrailed or
Lichfield & Coventry diocese (39)
  Party per pale gules and argent,
  a cross potent quadrate between
  four crosses paty all
  counterchanged
Lisle of Kingston Lisle (12, 41)
  Gules a lion passant guardant
  argent, langued gules and
  crowned or
Lisle of Rougemont (12, 41)
  Or a fess between two
  chevrons sable
Llwyd (17)
  Gules a chevron or and a
  chief ermine
Lucy (21)
  Gules three luces haurient or
Lusignan of Cyprus (8)
  Barry argent and azure a lion
  rampant gules
Luxembourg (8)
  Argent a lion rampant gules

Madog (22)
  Sable a chevron ermine between
  three stringed lures argent
Mandeville (12)
  Quarterly or and gules, overall a
  carbuncle sable
Marweithian (27)
  Gules a lion rampant argent
Merbrook (15)
  Argent five bendlets gules
Mercy (12)
  Argent on a bend gules three
  lozenges argent
?Montgomery (41)
  Azure a lion rampant, a bordure
  engrailed or
Morgan (42)
  Sable a chevron between three
  spearheads imbrued argent
Morley (42)
  Argent lion rampant sable
  crowned or
Mortimer-A (3)
  Barry of six azure and or, on a
  chief azure two pallets between
  two gyrons or, overall an
  escutcheon argent
Mortimer-B (5, 6)
  Barry of six or and azure, on a
  chief or two pallets between two
  gyrons azure, overall an
  escutcheon argent

Neville (7)
  Gules a saltire argent
Newburgh (12, 41)
  Checky azure and or a
  chevron ermine

Norley (31)
*Gules a cross engrailed argent*
Norris – *see Robinson*

Olney-A (19)
*Argent a fess embattled between six crosses paty fitchy gules*
Olney-B (19)
*Azure a fess?*
Orsini (8)
*Gules two bendlets argent, on a chief argent a rose gules*

Pates (30)
*Argent a chevron sable between three pellets, on a chief sable three crosses paty fitchy argent*
Phetiplace (32)
*Gules two chevronels argent*
Price (27) – *see Marweithian*

Radcliffe (31)
*Argent two bendlets engrailed sable*
Rastall (25)
*Ermine on a pale gules three pheons or*
Ravenscroft – *see Robinson*
Rhos & Rhufeiniog
*Argent a rose gules seeded ?or barbed vert*
Rhun ap Gronwy (22)
*Sable a chevron ermine between three stringed lures argent*
Robinson (15) – derived from Norris & Ravenscroft
*Argent a chevron between three ravens heads erased sable*

Rochford (10)
*Argent a lion rampant sable crowned or*

St Asaph diocese (17) – unique variant?
*Gules a key in bend crossed by a bishop's crozier in bend-sinister argent*
St Davids diocese (16) – alternative arms
*Or on a cross couped sable five roses or*
St Pol (8)
*Gules three pallets argent, on a chief or a label of five points gules*
Sampson (40)
*Argent a cross floretty gules between four escallops sable, a six-pointed mullet or for difference*
Sandys (34) – incorrect arms
*Gules a chevron dancetty between three crosses crosslet fitchy or*
Scory (13)
*Party per chevron embattled or and sable, three pelicans in their piety counterchanged, vulning proper; on a chief azure a fleur-de-lys between two estoiles or*
Seborne (29)
*Barry wavy of 10 argent and azure a lion rampant or*
Sidney (12)
*Or a pheon azure*
Smyth (36) – incorrect arms
*Sable a chevron argent between three roses gules*

Somery (12, 41)
*Or two lions passant in pale azure
armed and langued gules*
Spynnye (19)
*Sable a chevron argent between
three crescents or*
Stevinton (26)
*Argent 5 piles issuant from the
dexter, in sinister a billet urdé sable*
Stoke (26)
*Argent on a bend sable three
dolphins embowed or*

Talbot (12, 41)
*Gules a lion rampant within a
bordure engrailed or*
Throckmorton (19)
*Gules on a chevron argent three
bars gemelles sable*
Trollope (39)
*Vert three bucks argent attired or*

Unidentified (17)
*?Or a lion rampant*

Valence (12, 41)
*Barry argent and azure, an orle of
martlets gules*
Veysey (38)
*Argent on a cross couped sable a
buck's head couped argent attired
or, between 4 birds argent, on a
chief azure a cross flory or between
two roses ?proper*

Woodville (8)
*Argent a fess and a canton
conjoined gules*

# Glossary of Terms found in the Blazons

**armed** – when applied to a lion it refers to its claws; for an eagle its beak also
**attired** – refers to the colours of the antlers of a stag

**barbed and seeded** – refers most commonly to roses. 'Barbed' refers to the
  tips of the sepals seen outside and between the petals. 'Seeds' refers
  to the central area. Roses that are *'barbed vert and seeded or'* are said to
  be *'barbed and seeded proper'*
**barnacle** – a hinged implement placed around the top lip for calming horses
**barry** – a coat of arms is *barry* if split into an even number of horizontal
  strips. The colour at the top is given first and often the number of bars
  (e.g. *barry of six azure and argent*). A coat divided into an odd number
  of horizontal strips that might be described as *'barry of seven azure and
  argent'* is instead usually blazoned *'azure three bars argent'*. Sometimes,
  if a coat of arms is split into many narrow horizontal strips, no attempt
  is made to count them, or decide whether there is an odd or even
  number. It would just be described as *'barry'*
**bars** – the term used for more than one horizontal strip across a shield
**base** – refers to the bottom area of a shield
**bend** – a diagonal strip starting in dexter chief (see **ordinaries**)
**bendlets** – narrow bends in combination
**bend sinister** – a diagonal strip starting in sinister chief (see **ordinaries**)
**billet** – an upright rectangle
**bordure** – border
**botonny** – see **crosses**
**bray** – a hinged implement placed around the top lip for calming horses
**bucks** – stags or roebucks with broad antlers

**caboshed** – a head is caboshed if looking outwards and no neck is shown
**cadency mark** – a small charge added to a coat of arms to indicate a son's
  position in the family. A label is used for the eldest son, a crescent for
  the second, a mullet for the third, etc.
**canting arms** – arms which make a punning reference to the person's
  name (for example, using 'ravens' for 'Ravenscroft')
**canton** – a square or rectangular charge placed right in the dexter
  chief corner

**carbuncle** or **escarbuncle** – a charge of eight radiating spokes emanating from a central hub and each usually ending in a fleur-de-lys or similar

**charge** – something placed on a shield

**checky** or **chequy** – decorated in a checkered pattern

**chevron** – see **ordinaries**

**chevronels** – narrow chevrons in combination

**chief** – refers to the top area of a shield (also see **ordinaries**)

**cinquefoil** – a stylised plant or flower head with five petals or 'lobes'

**cinquefoil pierced** – a cinquefoil with a hole in the middle through which the field can be seen

**compony** – a single row of chequers

**counterchanged** – this can occur where the field or part of a field is split into two parts of different colours, say *argent* and *gules*. Charges placed on the shield are said to be counterchanged if those on the *argent* part of the field are coloured *gules* while those on the *gules* part are coloured *argent*

**couped close** – a head cut off with no neck showing

**cross** – a simple cross which may extend to the edges of the shield (throughout) or be couped (see **ordinaries**)

**crosses** (various):

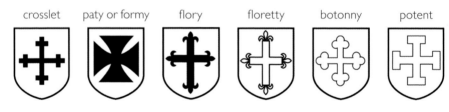

crosslet    paty or formy    flory    floretty    botonny    potent

**cross couped** – a cross whose limbs don't reach to the edge of the shield and are cut off square

**crosslet** – see **crosses**

**crusily** – covered with a pattern of crosses

**dancetty** – in a large zig-zag pattern

**demi-lion** – the top half of a lion *rampant*

**dexter** – the left side of a shield as we look at it

**double-queued** – with a double tail

**embattled** – use of an edge shaped like a battlement

**embowed** – curved like a bow

**engrailed** – a scalloped edge made up of semicircles with the points outwards

**erased** – used to describe the way a head is cut off at the neck. When heads are erased they are torn off leaving ragged edges

**escallop** – a scallop shell

**escutcheon** – a term usually used to describe a charge in the shape of a small shield

**estoile** – a star with wavy rays

**fess** – the name for a single horizontal strip across a shield (see **ordinaries**)

**fess embattled** – a fess with the top edge battlemented

**field** – the basic tincture of the arms or a section of them

**fitchy** – in a cross fitchy the lower arm of the cross is replaced by a spike

**fleur-de-lys** – a stylised lily as seen on the arms of France

**floretty** – see **crosses**

**flory** – see **crosses**

**garb** – a sheaf of corn

**goutée de poix** – powdered with droplets of black pitch

**guardant** – looking straight out of the shield

**gyrons** – triangular charges or parts of the field

**haurient** – erect, head upwards; used of a fish

**imbrued** – stained with blood

**impalement** – the placing of two coats of arms side by side on a shield

**in fess** – side by side

**in pale** – one above the other

**in pretence** – this usually describes the practice of a man displaying, on an escutcheon placed in the centre of his shield, the arms of his wife if she is an heraldic heiress

**indented** – a zig-zig line or edge

**jessant-de-lys** – this indicates a fleur-de-lys issuing forth from something, notably seen in leopards

**label** – a horizontal strap with three or more 'points' hanging from it that is placed over an existing coat of arms as a mark of cadency to indicate the eldest son. It can be of any colour. While cadency labels are temporary, some coats of arms have incorporated labels into their design, and these are permanent

**langued** – refers to the tongue

**leopard** – the terms leopard and lion were initially used interchangeably for some situations. Leopard is still used to describe an outward-facing lion's or leopard's head without a neck, even if it has no spots

**lion passant** – a lion with three feet on the ground and one raised

**lion rampant** – a lion rearing up with one foot on the ground

**lozenges** – diamond shapes

**luce** – a pike (fish)

**lure** – two bird's wings joined together, used as a decoy for hawks

**martlets** – small birds like swallows or swifts shown without feet but usually with shaggy 'trousers'

**mascle** – a diamond shape with a diamond-shaped hole where the field shows through

**maunch** – a long detachable lady's sleeve

**mullet** – a straight-sided star shape usually with five points

**mullet pierced** – a mullet with a central circular hole through which the field or charge below can be seen

**ordinaries:**

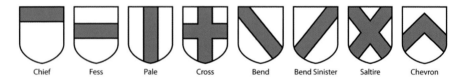

Chief   Fess   Pale   Cross   Bend   Bend Sinister   Saltire   Chevron

**orle** – a thin band, or set of charges, following the outline of a shield but situated just inside the edge

**pale** – the name for a single vertical strip down the centre of a shield (see **ordinaries**)

**palewise** – oriented vertically

**pallets** – small pales – vertical strips

**party** – indicates that the field or charge of a coat of arms has been split into separate parts (eg. *party per chevron* means that it has been split into upper and lower parts using the shape of a chevron as the boundary; *party per pale* indicates that it has been split into left and right halves by a vertical line down the middle

**paty** – see **crosses**

**pelican in its piety** – a long-necked bird bending down and piercing its breast from which blood flows

**pellets** – black balls

**per fess indented** – the coat is split in two by a horizontal zigzag line

**pheon** – an arrowhead, point-down, with barbs on the inner edges

**pile** – usually a long thin triangle issuing from the top edge of the shield
with its point at or near the base. Sometimes several are grouped
together and piles may be 'reversed' if coming from the base, or 'issuant'
from any other part of the shield

**potent** – see **crosses**

**proper** – refers to colours on a shield. If a charge is coloured naturally,
the way you would expect it to be, then it is 'proper'. For instance, 'a
raven sable' might be described as 'a raven proper'

**saltire** – a cross set diagonally (see **ordinaries**)

**semy-de-lys** – means covered with a pattern of fleurs-de-lys

**sinister** – the right side of a shield as we look at it

**torteaux** – red balls

**trippant** – walking

**urdé** – pointed, or having a point

# Mortimer and de Lacy Family Trees

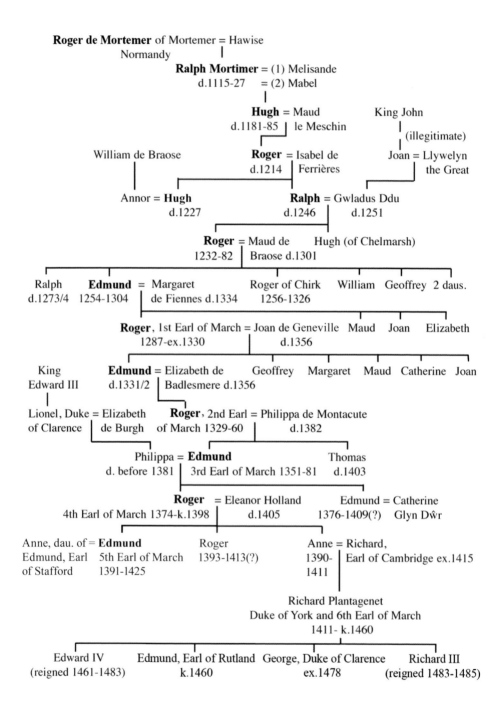

Roger de Mortemer of Mortemer = Hawise
Normandy

Ralph Mortimer = (1) Melisande
d.1115-27 = (2) Mabel

Hugh = Maud          King John
d.1181-85 le Meschin
                              (illegitimate)

William de Braose          Roger = Isabel de          Joan = Llywelyn
d.1214 Ferrières          the Great

Annor = Hugh          Ralph = Gwladus Ddu
d.1227          d.1246 d.1251

Roger = Maud de          Hugh (of Chelmarsh)
1232-82 Braose d.1301

Ralph          Edmund = Margaret          Roger of Chirk          William          Geoffrey          2 daus.
d.1273/4          1254-1304 de Fiennes d.1334          1256-1326

Roger, 1st Earl of March = Joan de Geneville          Maud          Joan          Elizabeth
1287-ex.1330          d.1356

King          Edmund = Elizabeth de          Geoffrey          Margaret          Maud          Catherine          Joan
Edward III          d.1331/2 Badlesmere d.1356

Lionel, Duke = Elizabeth          Roger, 2nd Earl = Philippa de Montacute
of Clarence de Burgh          of March 1329-60          d.1382

Philippa = Edmund          Thomas
d. before 1381 3rd Earl of March 1351-81          d.1403

Roger = Eleanor Holland          Edmund = Catherine
4th Earl of March 1374-k.1398          d.1405          1376-1409(?) Glyn Dŵr

Anne, dau. of = Edmund          Roger          Anne = Richard,
Edmund, Earl 5th Earl of March 1393-1413(?)          1390- Earl of Cambridge ex.1415
of Stafford 1391-1425          1411

Richard Plantagenet
Duke of York and 6th Earl of March
1411- k.1460

Edward IV          Edmund, Earl of Rutland          George, Duke of Clarence          Richard III
(reigned 1461-1483)          k.1460          ex.1478          (reigned 1483-1485)

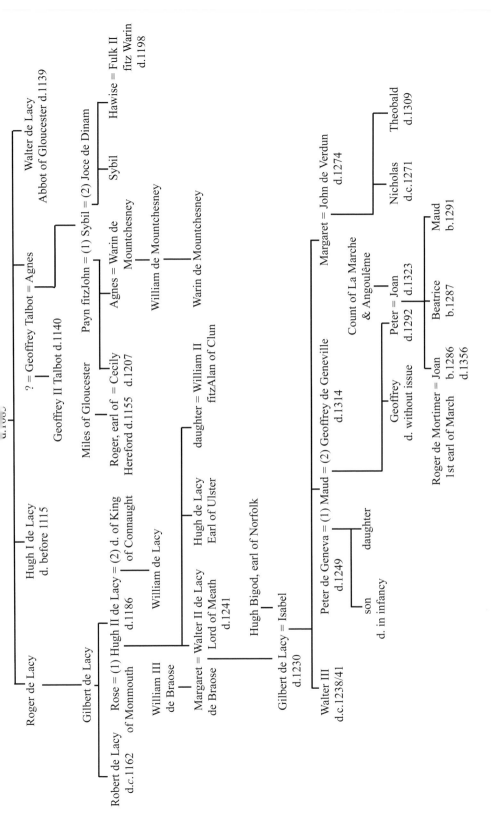

227

# Endnotes

## 1. What is the Roll?

i    Chetham's Library, MunE.8.22, fol. 29

ii    The National Archives, Greenwood's will Prob 11/68, fol. 372r, Kent Archives, U1475/A4/4, A5/7, A57

iii    London Metropolitan Archives, DL/C/B/007/MS09172/030 v

iv    Siddons, M.P., *Welsh Pedigree Rolls*, Aberystwyth, (1996), 7,11,21,41; Morgan, P., 'Pedigree of John Watkins, Dean of Hereford, 1590, with some account of its Compiler, Thomas Jones of Tregaron, and its painter, Richard Adams of Ludlow', *Transactions of the Woolhope Field Naturalists' Club*, (1947) 32, 114–121; The National Archives, SP 46/164 fols. 50–84; Shropshire Archives, LB8/1/139, fol 17; Powell, D., *The Love of Wales To Their Sovereign Prince*, (1616)

## 2. Ludlow Castle Chapel and its Heraldic Decoration

i    Gilbert de Lacy subsequently joined and held office in the Knights Templar. There are other examples of round nave churches in Herefordshire at Garway and St Giles, Hereford (not extant)

ii    Faraday, M., *Ludlow 1085–1660*, Phillimore (1991), 56; Calendar of Patent Rolls, 1327–30, 343; Calendar of Patent Rolls 1354–58, 87; The National Archives, C143/316/4

iii    Bannister, A.T., *The register of John Stanbury, Bishop of Hereford (1453–1474)*, Cantilupe Society (1918), 47; The National Archives, Evidence of Edward Croft to the Court of Augmentations, 1542, E315/130

iv    Coppack Glyn, 'The Round Chapel of St Mary Magdalene' in Shoesmith, R. and Johnson, A. (eds) *Ludlow Castle: Its History and Buildings*, Logaston Press (2006), 150–151

v    British Library, Lansdowne MS 111 fol. 20

vi    British Library, Egerton 2642, fol. 272r–275v

vii    Kent Archives, U1475/A4/5

viii    Kent Archives, U1475/A4/1

ix    Dineley, Thomas, *The account of the official progress of His Grace Henry the first Duke of Beaufort (Lord President of the Council in Wales, and Lord Warden of the Marches) through Wales in 1684.*

x    Cadbury Research Library, University of Birmingham, MYT/3. Transcribed with commentary in Clive R.H., *Documents Connected with the History of Ludlow and the Lords Marcher*, London 1841, 191–306

xi    Todd, H.J., *Comus, a mask presented at Ludlow castle 1634 ... by John Milton*, Canterbury (1798), Shropshire Archives, 552/8/1000–09

xii    Harper G.J., *The Marches of Wales* (1894), 218, Ludlow Library, Q36.8v.f.; Baker, Harry, *An Alphabet of Ludlow Pubs*, 1983 (unpublished)

### 3. Robert Commander, c.1532–1613, Chaplain to Sir Henry Sidney

i    British Library, Egerton MS 2642; 'The Book of Howth', Brewer, J.S. and Bullen, W. (eds), *Calendar of Carew Manuscripts preserved in the archiepiscopal library at Lambeth*, v (London: Public Record Office, 1871), 21

ii    Venn, J., *Alumni Cantabrigienses*; Ormerod, G., *The History of the county Palatine and City of Chester*, II, 128

iii    Gloucester Record Office, Hockaday transcripts, D3439/1/442 iv

iv    Bodleian Library, MS.Eng.hist c.477, fols. 97–8

v    Kent Archives, U1475/A4/1; Morrin, J., *Calendar of the Patent and Close Rolls of Chancery in Ireland*, Dublin (1861–63), ii, 639

vi    Cheshire Record Office, EDB193, 22

### 4. Sir Henry Sidney, 1529–86

i    'The Book of Howth', Brewer, J.S. and Bullen, W. (eds), *Calendar of Carew Manuscripts preserved in the archiepiscopal library at Lambeth*, v (London: Public Record Office, 1871), 205, 207

ii    Brady, Ciaran, *A Viceroy's Vindication? Sir Henry Sidney's Memoir of Service in Ireland*, Cork University Press (2002), 104, 106, 108

iii    Society of Antiquaries, MS 68

iv    *Calendar of State Papers Domestic 1547–1580*, 442

v    Kent Archives, U1475/O14/38, Philip Williams to Sidney, 3 May 1577

vi    Collins, A., *Letters and Memorials of State ...* London (1746) Vol I, 295–6

vii    Shropshire Archives, LB/14/846

viii    The National Archives, SP63/24/29; Andrews, J.H., 'Colonial Cartography in a European Setting: The Case of Tudor Ireland', *The History of Cartography*, Vol 3, 1670

### 5. Governance of Wales, and the Council in the Marches of Wales

i    Kingsford C.L. ed. *Report on the manuscripts of Lord de L'Isle & Dudley, preserved at Penshurst Place*, Vol. 1 Historical Manuscripts Commission; 77 London: H.M.S.O., (1925), 322–332

ii    Gerrard's report to the Privy Council 1575, The National Archives SP12/107/11 fols. 22–25

iii   Croft's Address to Queen Elizabeth on the disorders of the Royal
      Household, British Library Royal MS 18 A XLVI; Walsingham to
      Sidney, 9 Aug 1580, Kent Archives, U1475/C2/29
iv    Brady, Ciaran, *A Viceroy's Vindication? Sir Henry Sidney's Memoir of
      Service in Ireland*, 104


**6. Sir Henry Sidney and the Enhancement of Ludlow Castle**

i     Bodleian Library, Bodley 904, fol. 182
ii    British Library. Lansdowne MS 111 No 20
iii   Shropshire Archives, 20/27/5
iv    St John Hope, W.H., 'The Castle of Ludlow', *Archaeologia*, LXI, 1908
v     Shropshire Archives, 20/27/6
vi    Bodleian Library, Bodley 904 f.44v; Collins, A., *Letters and Memorials
      of State* ... London (1746), Vol I Memoirs, 90
vii   Clive R.H., *Documents Connected with the History of Ludlow and the
      Lords Marcher*, London (1841), 346
viii  Kent Archive U1475/A33/2, A56, A50/13
ix    Hodges, W., *An Historical Account of Ludlow Castle*, 1794 Appendix F;
      Bodleian Library, Bodley 904, fol. 202
x     Bodleian Library, Bodley 904, fol. 90
xi    *Penshurst Place and Gardens*, 2001; Keay, A. and Watkins, J. (eds) *The
      Elizabethan Garden at Kenilworth Castle*, 2013
xii   Weyman, H.T., *Ludlow in Bye-Gone Days*, Ludlow (1913), 57. In 1577
      several people were fined in the town courts for playing illicit games in
      the Castle, tennis and bowls.
xiii  Kent Archive U1475/A4/5; British Library Lansdowne MS 111 No 20
xiv   Bodleian Library Bodley 904, fol. 180; Kent Archives, U1475/A33/2,
      A50/13, A59/1
xv    Manning, Conleth, 'Arms and the Man', *Archaeology Ireland*, Spring
      2010, Vol 24 (1), 8–11


**7. The Sidney Family and Castle and Town Life**

i     Kent Archives, U1475/A4/1, A33/2, A33/3, A50/13, A54
ii    Kent Archives, U1475/A4/1, A33/3, A50/12
iii   Kent Archives, U1475/A4/1, A50/12, A54; *Calendar of Patent Rolls*,
      1566–1569, 2480
iv    Shropshire Archives, LB/2/1/15
v     Shropshire Archives, LB/8/1/48–64 passim, LB8/1/62/C fol7v
vi    Shropshire Archives, LB/2/1/15

## 8. Death and Heraldic Funeral of Sir Henry Sidney

i     Holinshed, Raphael, *Chronicles*, 1587, Vol 2, p 1553, Hereford Cathedral Library, L.1.7

ii     British Library, Commonplace book of Robert Commaundre, Egerton 2642, account of death and funeral fols. 275v–276r

iii     Shropshire Archives, Ludlow Bailiffs' accounts 1585–1586, LB/8/1/64

iv     British Library, 'The charges of bringing the corps of Sir Henry Sidney deceased from Worcester to Penshurst', Lansdowne 50, No 88; College of Arms, William Dethick's Book of Funerals, Vol 1, fols. 2r–4, Funerals Marshalled by William Dethick, A31 fols., 131r–133v

v     Edmonson, Joseph, *A Complete Body of Heraldry*, 1780, 150

vi     *The Gentleman's Magazine*, March 1766, p 152; Will of George Coningsby, The National Archives, PROB 11 1766; *The Gentleman's Magazine*, Sept 1794, p 785

## 9. The Display of Heraldry

i     Lloyd, D. and Klein, P., *Ludlow, An Historical Anthology*, Phillimore 2006, 32

ii     *Journal of the Royal Society of Antiquaries of Ireland*, Fifth Series Vol 4 No 4 Dec 1894 pp 400–425; Bagwell, G., 'Ireland Under the Tudors', (1883), II, 101

iii     Kent Archives, U1475, A4/5,6, A5/7, A50/13, A56,A57, U1500/A9/5

iv     Fletcher A.J., *Drama and the Performing Arts in Pre-Cromwellian Ireland*, Boydell and Brewer (2001), 266; Kent Archives, U1475, A59/4

v     Phillips, T., *Shrewsbury History and Antiquities* (1779), 30; Shropshire Archives, LB/8/1/62/c fol 6r; Bodleian Library – MS Ashmole1112 fols. 65–66

# Bibliography

*Manuscripts*

British Library, Egerton 2642, A Common-place book by Robert Commaundre, Rector of Tarporley, co. Chester., and Chaplain to Sir Henry Sydney

British Library, Lansdowne MS 50, No 88, The charges of bringing the corps of Sir Henry Sidney deceased from Worcester to Penshurst, 1586

British Library, Lansdowne MS 111, fol. 20. Account of Sir Henry Sidney's building works at Ludlow

Cadbury Research Library, Special Collections, University of Birmingham, MYT/3. William Mytton's drawings of arms in Ludlow, c.1735

College of Arms, William Dethick's Book of Funerals, Vol 1

College of Arms, A31, Funerals Marshalled by William Dethick

Kent Archives, De L'Isle MS, U1475, U1500, Papers of the Sidney Family

Kingsford C.L. ed. Report on the manuscripts of Lord de L'Isle & Dudley, preserved at Penshurst Place. Vol 1 Historical Manuscripts Commission; 77 London: H.M.S.O., (1925)

Shropshire Archives, Ludlow Castle Heraldic Roll, 9456

Society of Antiquaries, MS 68 Arms of the President from John Harman 1525/6 to Thomas Lord Gerrard 1617


*Theses*

Stevenson, Sara F., *The Heraldic ideal in England 1560–1610* M. Phil. Thesis, Warburg, 1972


*Sidney Family*

Collins, A., *Letters and memorials of state, in the reigns of Queen Mary, Queen Elizabeth, King James, King Charles the First, part of the reign of King Charles the Second, and Oliver's usurpation.* London, 1746

Brady, Ciaran, *A Viceroy's Vindication? Sir Henry Sidney's Memoir of Service in Ireland*, Cork University Press, 2002

Brennan, M.G., Lamb, M.E., Hannay, M.P. (ed.), *The Ashgate Research Companion to The Sidneys, 1500–1700*, Routledge, 2017

Manning, Con, 'Arms and the Man', *Archaeology Ireland*, Spring 2010 Vol 24 (1), 8–11

### Ludlow and the Council in the Marches of Wales

Churchyard, Thomas, *The worthiness of Wales, a poem. A true note of Auncient Castles, famous monuments, goodly Rivers, fine Townes and courteous people, that I have seen in the noble countrie of Wales and now set forth*, London, 1587

Clive, R.H., *Documents Connected with the History of Ludlow and the Lords Marcher*, London, 1841

Dineley, Thomas, *The account of the official progress of His Grace Henry the first Duke of Beaufort (Lord President of the Council in Wales, and Lord Warden of the Marches) through Wales in 1684*

Faraday, M., *Ludlow 1085–1660*, Phillimore, 1991

Felton, W., *A Description of the Town of Ludlow with an account of the Castle*, 1812

Flenley, R.A., *A Calendar Of The Register Of The Queen's Majesty's Council In The Dominion And Principality Of Wales And The Marches Of The Same, 1569–1591* (from the Bodley MS 904), Cymmrodorion Record Series No 8, 1916

Hodges, W., *An Historical Account of Ludlow Castle*, 1794

Gunn, Steve and Monckton, Linda, *Arthur Tudor Prince of Wales: Life Death and Commemoration*, Woodbridge, 2009

St John Hope, W. H., 'The Castle of Ludlow' *Archaeologia* LXI, 1908

Shoesmith, Ron and Johnson, Andy (eds.) *Ludlow Castle: Its History and Buildings*, Logaston Press, 2018

Skeel, Caroline A.J., *The Council in the Marches of Wales*, Hugh Rees Ltd, London, 1904

Williams, Penry, *The Council in the Marches of Wales*, University of Wales Press, Cardiff, 1958

Wright, Thomas, *History and Antiquities of Ludlow*, Ludlow, 1826

### Biographies

All of the individuals on the Roll except for John Rastall can be found in one or more of the following sources:

History of Parliament Online
Oxford Dictionary of National Biography (available online)
Welsh Dictionary of National Biography (available online)
Williams, W.R., *The History of the Great Sessions in Wales, 1542–1830*, Brecknock, 1899

## Heraldry

Cautley, H. Munro, *Royal Arms and Commandments in our Churches*, Ipswich, Boydell, 1974

Chesshyre, H., Woodcock, T., Grant, J., Graham, I.D.G., and Flower, S., *Dictionary of British Arms*, Vols 1–4, Society of Antiquaries, London, 1992–2014

Burke, Bernard, *The General Armory of England, Scotland, Ireland and Wales*, London, 1884

Murray, H., 'The Great Chamber at Gilling Castle', St Laurence Papers VIII, Ampleforth Abbey, York, 1996

Siddons, M.P., *The Development of Welsh Heraldry*, Vols 1–4, National Library of Wales, 1993

Ramsay, N. (ed.), *Heralds and Heraldry in Shakespeare's England*, Paul Watkins Publishing, 2014

## *Paint Analysis (Appendix 1)*

Anon., *A Very Proper Treatise, Wherein is Briefly Sett Forthe the Arte of limming*, London, 1573 [Anon. 1573]

Ball, P., *Bright Earth: the Invention of Colour*, London, Vintage, 2009 [Ball 2009]

Eastaugh, N. et al., *Pigment Compendium: a Dictionary and Optical Microscopy of Historical Pigments*, Oxford, Elsevier, 2008 [Eastaugh et al. 2008]

Gettens, R.J, Feller R.L., & Chase, W.T., 'Vermilion and Cinnabar', in *Artists' Pigments: a Handbook of Their History and Characteristics*, Volume 2, (Roy, A. ed.) Oxford, OUP, 1993, 159–182 [Gettens, Feller & Chase 1993]

Harley, R.D., *Artists' Pigments c.1600–1835: a Study in English Documentary Sources*, London, Archetype, 1982 [Harley 1982]

Howard, H., *Pigments of English Medieval Wall Painting*, London, Archetype, 2003 [Howard 2003]

Norgate, E., *Miniatura, or the Art of limning*, London?, 1627 [Norgate 1627]

Peacham, H., *Compleat Gentleman* (1661 edition), London, 1622 [Peacham 1622]

Peacham, H., *Gentleman's Exercise*, London, 1612 [Peacham 1612]

# Index

*Index of family names which appear as quarters on the shields can be found in Appendix 2*

Denton, Alexander 172
Denton, Anne (Willison) 168, 172
Denton, Thomas 172
Despenser family 105
Dethick, William (Garter King of Arms) 64, 67
Dethick, Nicholas (Windsor Herald) 64
Devawe, John (Sergeant at Arms of the Council in the Marches in Wales) 64, 66
Dineley, Thomas 8, 13, 16, 48, 52
Dininckhoff, Baernard (glass painter) 76
Dovaston, John 16
Dublin Castle 26, 49, 56, 71
Dublin, Christ Church Cathedral 18, 26, 30, 80
Dudley, Ambrose (Earl of Warwick) 22, 79, 193
Dudley, Edmund 193
Dudley, Guildford 22, 194
Dudley, Henry 22, 153, 194
Dudley, John (Duke of Northumberland) 21–22, 67, 71, 143, 146, 150, 160, 193–197, 200
Dudley, John Jnr (Earl of Warwick) 22, 193
Dudley, Katherine (see Hastings)
Dudley, Mary (see Sidney)
Dudley, Robert (Earl of Leicester) 22, 24–26, 28, 54, 57, 77, 144, 163–164, 166, 176, 194

Edmund of Langley (Duke of York) 109, 114
Edward I 34, 36, 101–102, 141
Edward II 77, 105, 141
Edward III 9, 25, 73, 77, 106–112, 114
Edward IV vi, xii, 2, 10, 36–38, 86–87, 91, 117–121, 179, 180
Edward VI 10, 18, 21–22, 40, 68, 70, 77, 123, 132, 134, 143, 146, 150, 153, 187, 192, 193, 196, 199–201
Edward, Prince of Wales (Edward V) 10, 36–38, 75, 120, 180, 182

Edward, Prince of Wales (the Black Prince) 107, 111–112
Elizabeth I (Elizabethan era) vi, 2, 4, 11–12, 14, 22, 25–28, 40–41, 45, 47, 49, 54, 56–57, 72–77, 82–84, 122–128, 133, 135, 137–138, 141, 143–148, 152–3, 155–6, 158, 164, 166, 168, 170, 196, 200, 202–205, 211, 213
Elizabeth, Queen (Woodville/ wife of Edward IV) 87, 119

Fairfax, Sir William 76
Fermour brasses 79
Fettiplace, George vi, 172–173
fitz Osbern, Roger 96
fitz Osbern, William (Earl of Hereford, d.1071) 95
Fitzwilliams, Sir William 66
Folliet, Agnes (see Commander)
Fox, Catherine (Leighton) 162
Fox, Charles vi, 49, 76, 160–162

Gamage, Barbara 144
Gaunt, John of (Duke of Lancaster) 111–112
Geneva, Maud de (see Geneville)
Geneville, Geoffrey de vi, xi, 99, 101–103, 227
Geneville, Joan de (Mortimer) 102, 104-105, 107, 226, 227
Geneville, Maud de (de Lacy/ Geneva) 99, 101–102, 226–227
Geneville, Peter de 103, 227
Gerald of Wales 30
Gerard, William vi, 25, 41–42, 85, 151, 156–158, 168–169
Gilling Castle (Yorkshire) 76
Glover, Robert (Somerset Herald) 6
Glyn, William (Bishop of Bangor) 135, 141
Goldsbrough, Revd Dr Godfrey 64
Greenwood, Robert (painter) 6–7
Grey, Lady Jane 22, 193, 196, 200
Grindal, Edmund (Archbishop of Canterbury) 132, 138

# Also from Logaston Press (www.logastonpress.co.uk)

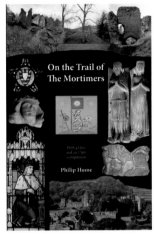

## On the Trail of the Mortimers
Philip Hume
144 pages, 235 × 154 mm
75 colour photographs, maps and family trees
ISBN: 978-1-910839-04-1
**Paperback with flaps, £7.50**

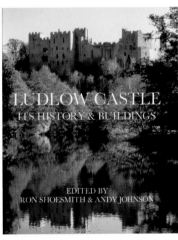

## Ludlow Castle
### Its History & Buildings
Edited by Ron Shoesmith & Andy Johnson
260 pages, 259 × 202 mm
b&w illustrations and colour plate section
ISBN: 978-1-904396-48-8
**Paperback, £14.95**
ISBN: 978-1-904396-49-6
**Hardback, £19.95**

## St Laurence's Church, Ludlow
### The parish church and people, 1199–2009
David Lloyd, Margaret Clark & Chris Potter
272 pages, 242 × 171 mm
70 b&w and 25 colour illustrations
ISBN: 978-1-906663-40-7
**Paperback, £12.95**

more from **Logaston Press** overleaf ...

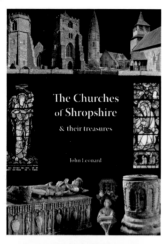

## The Churches of Shropshire & their treasures
John Leonard
384 pages, 242 × 171 mm
500+ colour photographs
ISBN: 978-1-906663-78-0
**Paperback, £10 (sale price)**

## Mistress Blanche
**Queen Elizabeth I's Confidante**
**(revised edition with new findings)**
Ruth Elizabeth Richardson
224 pages, 234 × 157 mm
26 colour and 8 b&w illustrations
ISBN: 978-1-910839-28-7
**Paperback, £12.95**

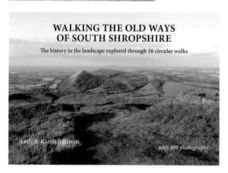

## Walking the Old Ways of South Shropshire
**The history in the landscape explored through 26 circular walks**
Andy and Karen Johnson
272 pages, 148 × 210 mm
400 colour photographs and 27 maps
ISBN: 978-1-910839-34-8
**Paperback with flaps, £12.95**